THE ARYAN MARRIAGE

THE ARYAN MARRIAGE

WITH SPECIAL REFERENCE
TO
THE AGE-QUESTION.

A CRITICAL AND HISTORICAL STUDY

by

R. RAGHUNATHA RAO, B.A.

President,
Chitaldrug Branch of the Theosophical Society.

GYAN

Published by

Gyan Publishing House
5, Ansari Road
Daryaganj, New Delhi-110002
Phone: 011-47034999, 9811692060
E-mail: books@gyanbooks.com

Distribution Network
gyanbooks.com
India, USA, Canada, UK, Australia, France

ISBN : 978-81-212-2319-5 (PB)
First Published, 1908

2nd Impression 2021

Printed at: Gyan Press, Delhi.

The Aryan Marriage
Author: R. Raghunatha Rao

THE
ARYAN MARRIAGE

WITH SPECIAL REFERENCE

TO

THE AGE-QUESTION.

A CRITICAL AND HISTORICAL STUDY

BY

R. RAGHUNATHA RAO, B. A.,

President,

Chitaldrug Branch of the Theosophical Society.

G. A. NATESAN & CO., MADRAS,

TO

MY DEAR NATIVE COUNTRY,

INDIA,

THE LAND OF BRAHMARSHIS AND RAJARSHIS,

I DEDICATE THIS STUDY

OF

THE ARYAN MARRIAGE

IN THE EARNEST HOPE

THAT

HER CHILDREN WILL STRIVE TO REALISE
AND REHABILITATE HER GRAND OLD IDEAL.

R. RAGHUNATHA RAO.

"Read not to contradict and confute, nor to believe and take for granted, nor to find talk and discourse; but to weigh and consider."

LORD BACON.

"There is no Ideal of Marriage like the Indian Ideal. * * * This, then, is the line of thought that I would suggest to you with regard to the Womanhood of India: that you should study and realise the Old Ideal, and that you should then see how it may be re-introduced; that you should educate women everywhere, and choose wisely the kind of education that you give; that you should keep in mind the capacities that they have, that you should evolve those to the utmost of your ability; so that, in the future, as in the past, there may be great, heroic, strong, pure, and devoted women in India; for sooner or later, weakness means degradation; sooner or later, the lack of strength leads to lack of love and lack of fidelity."

MRS. BESANT.

FOREWORD.

This study of Aryan Marriage, critical and historical, suggested itself to me when I was reading Mr. J. Srinivasa Rao's *Vivâha Nisheka Dharma Pradipika*, published in Telugu at Madras last year. The author was so good and generous as to grant me permission to use, in any manner I liked, the materials collected and published by him. As I went on studying his book, I felt convinced that a careful investigation of the Vivâha Mantras was necessary to settle the question of marriageable Age. I accordingly undertook the study of the Vivâha Mantras with the help of the learned scholars, Hosudrug Seshachar and S. M. Anantakrishnamachar, a Pandit of the Mysore Palace. The Vedic Mantras were interpreted as found in the Ekâgni Kânda of the Krishna Yajur Veda with the Commentary of Haradatta Misra, edited by Pandits under the supervision of the learned scholar, Mr. A. Mahadeva Sastriar, B. A., Curator, Mysore Oriental Library, and printed at the Government Branch Press, Mysore.

The study of the Vivâha Mantras revealed to us the grandeur of the Aryan Ideal of Marriage, and I felt increasingly impelled to undertake the writing of the present book. In the course of the study, several difficulties presented themselves for solution, and an attempt has been made to face most of them.

I have endeavoured to depict the Aryan Ideal of Marriage as found in the Sâstras, and I have entered into historical considerations to show how the Modern Hindu Marriage has come to be but a sad travesty of the Grand Old Ideal. "The progress and prosperity of every country," says Mrs. Besant rightly, "depend upon the Ideal of Marriage which dominates the thought of the people, and on the extent to which that Ideal is carried out in conduct." Unless and until the Vedic Ideal of Marriage is carefully studied, intelligently appreciated, and diligently re-adopted in its entirety, I believe there will be no salvation for India, as without proper *Samskâras* no nation can prosper. It is our bounden duty to turn the future of India into the Right Path. "If you will not, then you are digging the grave of India, and She will go down into that grave after you have passed away," says Mrs. Besant, and truly prophetic are her words.

In the translation of the Mantras and other Samskrit passages, I have tried to catch the thought rather than the language, as otherwise it would have been impossible to bring out the grandeur of the Old Vedic Ideal. I have probably been more sanguine than wise in having undertaken the writing of this book without Samskrit scholarship, but I could not keep quiet as I felt it my duty to open the subject *Sâstraically*, and lead the debate in order that others, more talented than myself, may follow.

I am indebted for information to the following publications among others:—

1. The Ekagni Kânda of the Krishna Yajur Veda, Mysore Edition.
2. Yâjusha Prayôga Pârijâta, Bangalore Edition.
3. J. Srinivasa Rao's Vivâha Nisheka Dharma Pradipika.
4. Manu Smriti.
5. Elementary and Advanced Text Books of the Sanâtana Dharma. Central Hindu College Series.
6. Har Bilas Sârda's Hindu Superiority.
7. Mrs. Besant's Pedigree of Man.
8. do Study in Consciousness.
9. do Hindu Ideals.
10. do Ancient Ideals in Modern Life.
11. Srinivasa Sastriar's Marriage after Puberty.
12. Letourneau's Evolution of Marriage.
13. Ethel M. Mallet's First Steps in Theosophy.
14. Frederick Fletcher's The Sixth Sense.

I also avail myself of this opportunity to tender my heart-felt thanks to my friend and co-worker Mr. J. Srinivasa Rao for the generous permission he gave me to use the materials collected by him; to the learned and orthodox Pandits Hosadrug Seshâchar and S. M. Anantakrishnamâchar for the unstinted help rendered by them throughout the writing of the book;

and to all the other kind friends for the ready manner in which they have encouraged me with their thoughts and suggestions. The points, dealt with in the book, are many of them obscure and subtle, and it is likely that in some places mistakes have crept in, and so all well-considered suggestions and criticisms will be welcomed with warm thanks.

BRAHMA VIDYA SADANA.
CHITALDRUG,
August 1908.

R. RAGHUNATHA RAO.

CONTENTS.

——:o:——

THE ARYAN MARRIAGE.

(*With Special Reference to the Age-Question.*)

A CRITICAL AND HISTORICAL STUDY.

I. Introduction

IT is a healthy sign of the times that the exceedingly important question of pre-pubescent marriage is engaging the serious attention of the leaders of the Hindu community in different parts of India. In pre-theosophical days, after a contact of about half-a-century with Europeans, gentlemen in Northern India—men like Raja Ram Mohun Roy, Kesheb Chander Sen, and Dayanand Sarasvati—unable to find their way to true reform through the bewildering intricacies of *Sastraic* speculations, cut the gordian knot of social reform by a rash repudiation of the caste system. Brahma Samaj and Arya Samaj are not, in my humble opinion, true reforms on national lines. In Southern India, our respected countryman, Dewan Bahadur Raghunatha Rao, began to grapple with the problem of the marriage of girl-widows, but has not, to our knowledge, done anything to destroy that seed-bed of girl-widows, viz., pre-pubescent marriage. It is a pity he has not addressed himself to the consideration of this question, qualified as he is by his samskrit learning and his ripe experience. The Madras Hindu Association has made a noble resolve to promote Hindu social and religious advancement on national lines in harmony with the spirit of Aryan civilization. The pamphlet on "Marriage after Puberty," recently issued by this important Association, contains a mass of information, which will materially help students to arrive at a satisfactory solution of the problem of post-pubescent Marriage of Aryan girls. In Mysore also the Arya Dharmojjivini Sabha has commenced to work strenuously in the cause of Reform and Progress. Brahma Sri Mahadeva Sastriar's Lecture on the Vedic Ideal of Marriage is an illuminating one, and it is hoped that our Vedic scholar will soon publish the results of his investigations, which, he says, are in course of elaboration, and will enlighten the lay world with his ideas on the social environments which brought into existence the numerous *Smritis*, some of which deal out their anathemas in a reckless fashion on persons who fail to celebrate pre-pubescent marriages. Why the attention of the intelligent public is thus drawn to the question of marriage, it seems necessary that somebody should make an attempt to depict the holy character of the Aryan marriage ritual, and to show that the ceremonies connected therewith possess a real significance, and are not the mere inventions of crafty priests to enrich their own greedy selves. The subject is a large one, and in a short study like this, it is not possible to go deep into the details. All that I mean to attempt is to invite attention to the important aspects of the holy ritual which, in my judgment, establish beyond dispute the Sastraic character of post-pubescent marriage. With very great diffidence I shall also make an attempt to depict the various environing social conditions which tended to introduce pre-pubescent marriage as doing the least violence to the lofty Vedic Ideal. This attempt I wish to make, not because I pretend to possess any special qualifications for it, but because I consider it my duty to invite the attention of the intelligent public to this portion of the subject. Pre-pubescent marriage has probably been in existence in India for thousands of years past; and unless we can reasonably account for it, it will be next to impossible to persuade our Hindu brethren to give up the custom, petrified as it has become with the lapse of time. The standpoint that is intended to be taken is that of an orthodox *Sàstri*, who is bent upon tracking the way to his goal through the forest of the bewildering teachings of the *Smriti-karas* with the recognised weapons of *Sastraic* investigation. This tangled forest has had few clearings hitherto, and my pioneer attempt may, it is requested, receive all the encouragement of an indulgent public.

2. THE HINDU AND THE EUROPEAN CIVILIZATIONS.

What distinguishes the Hindu or Aryan civilization from the European is the thoroughgoing recognition by the former of the three planes of existence—physical, astral, and mental. All our Aryan institutions are based upon the postulate of the three *lokas* of *Bhuh*, *Bhuvah*, and *Suvah*.* The Aryan

---

* The three great *lokas* with which we are concerned, the *Triloki*, are *Bhurloka*, the physical world, or the earth; *Bhuvarloka* or the world of "becoming"—intermediate between the earth and *svarga*; *Svargaloka*, the heaven-world. Of these three, *Bhurloka* is partly visible and partly invisible to us; *Bhuvarloka* and *Svargaloka* are invisible. In *Bhurloka* the *Prithvi Tattva* is the basis of all forms: it exists in seven modifications—solid, liquid, gaseous, radiant, etheric, super-etheric, and atomic. These latter four are spoken of as the 'ethers'. In *Bhuvarloka* seven similar modifications exist, but the basis is the *Apas Tattva*. In *Svargaloka* there are also seven similar modifications, but the basis is the *Agni Tattva*.

The *Jiva* has three sheaths corresponding to these worlds—the *Annamayakosha*, the *Pranamayakosha*, the *Manomayakosha*. The *Annamayakosha* or food-sheath—so called because it is built up out of the food we eat—corresponds with the visible part of the earth, and is composed of solids, liquids, and gases. The *Prana mayakosha* or Prana-sheath corresponds

marriage is unlike the European, which is a more temporal union than the Aryan, which has a simple ritual with not much of spiritual significance in it. Far otherwise is it with the Aryan ritual, which is based upon the recognition of the various Hierarchies of Intelligences, presiding over the several processes of nature. Beings of three planes or *lokas* are invited to be present at the marriage ritual to bless the union of two beings into one, and to co-operate in the production of an offspring which is to excel the two beings who unite in producing it. Manu says—" Husband and wife are the same"—a puzzle to all Materialists. How can the husband (a male) and the wife (a female) be the

---

with the invisible part of our earth, and is composed of ethers. *Prana* is the life-energy, and includes all the forces that science calls magnetic and electrical, but is much more than these. Both these sheaths are connected with *Bhurloka*. The *Manomayakosha*, mind-sheath, has two parts; the denser part, in which the passions have their seat, is connected with *Bhuvarloka*; the finer part, in which play the emotions and thought, is connected with *Svargaloka*. (Sanatana Dharma Elementary Text-book, pp. 64-65.)

అథ త్రయో వావలోకా—మనుష్యలోకః పితృలోకో దేవలోక ఇతి. (బృహదారణ్యకోపనిషత్తు).

अथत्रयोवावलोकामनुष्यलोकः पितृलोकोदेवलोक इति.

(बृहदारण्यकोपनिषत्).

same ? * The mystery is cleared up when it is understood that man was an androgyne during the early part of the Third Race (*Tririndriya Manava Kula*) before the separation of the sexes took place in the latter part of it. † The distinction of the sexes belongs only to the *Sthula* and *Sukshma Sariras*, not to the *Karana Sarira*. Man and woman, as husband and wife, should be complementary halves of one whole, which was at one

---

* విప్రాఃప్రాహుస్తథాచైతద్యోభర్తాసాస్మృతాంగనా ॥

(మను. అ. ౯. శ్లో 45.)

विप्राः प्राहुस्तथाचैतद्योभर्तासास्मृतांगना ॥

(मनुस्मृ अ - 9 - श्लो 45.)

† In our Puranas, Daksha Prajapati typifies the Early Third Race of Men, holy and pure, as yet devoid of an Individual Ego, and possessing passive capacities only. Brahma ordered him to create; when obeying the command, he made inferior and superior (*Avara* and *vara*) progeny, bipeds and quadrupeds, and by his will gave birth to females, to the gods, the *Daityas* (the giants of the Fourth Race of Men), the snake-gods, animals, cattle, and the *Danavas* and other things. "From that period forward, living creatures were engendered by sexual intercourse. Before the time of Daksha, they were variously propagated—by the will, by sight, by touch, and by the influence of religious austerities practised by devout sages and holy saints". (Vishnu Purana, II. 10.)

time androgynous. The cause of sympathy and perfect compatibility between one particular man and one particular woman is, to European and American investigators, 'a subject of infinite mystery and obscurity.' The *Maharshis* do not despairingly exclaim, as does Philip Gibbert Hammerton:—"Sympathy and incompatibility—these are the two great powers that decide for us whether intercourse is to be possible or not; but the causes of them are dark mysteries that lie undiscovered, far down in the abysmal deeps of personality." They provide means in Astrology to fathom these "mysteries," and find out whether the intended bride will suit the bridegroom or not. An astrological investigation of the *kutas* or affinities of the bride and bridegroom reveals their physical, temperamental, and spiritual compatibility or incompatibility. *Yoni*, *Nadi*, and *Gana kutas* reveal the compatibility or otherwise of their *Sthula* and *Sukshma sariras*, while *Graha Maitri* settles their spiritual agreement or disagreement.

3. THE CHARACTER OF THE HINDU RITUAL.

The Hindu Sastras require that all ceremonies should be performed with *Sraddha* and perfect *Trikarana Suddhi*. *Sraddha* is earnestness, and *Trikarana Suddhi* is purity or sincerity of mind, mouth, and hand; not the slighest discrepancy or conflict should there be between one's thought, word, and deed. The slightest insincerity or untruthfulness spoils the sanctity of the whole ceremony. One has to state his *sankalpa* or resolve with a clear and quieted mind, and to secure this calmness of mind or *Santa chitta*, one has to perform his *Pranayama* at the commencement of each individual ceremony. Such is the exacting character of the Hindu ritual.

4. GANAPATI PUJA.

The performance of the *Ganapati Puja* is essential at the commencement of every important undertaking. Who is *Ganapati?* He is the Lord of *Ganas*—names and forms, *i. e.*—of the *Nama Rupa Prapancha*, the world of names and forms. It is the mind that deals with the world of names and forms; hence *Ganapati Puja* has to do with the mind. Even *Devas*, as they have minds, have to worship him. "What a man thinks, that he becomes," is the verdict of the *Srutis*. Hence to secure the necessary equipoise of mind, *Ganapati Puja* is enjoined. *Ganapati* has also the name of *Vighnesvara*—the Lord of Obstacles. Necessary it is to propitiate the Lord of Obstacles, as a large party gathers for the celebration of marriage, and as there may be a thousand and one obstacles. The Hindu has faith in the old adage that there may be many a slip between the cup and the lip.

5. THE NANDI DEVATAS.

The next ceremony is the invoking of the *Nandi Devatas.* Who are they, and what have they to do with the marriage ceremony? The *Nandi Devatas* are the holy *Pitris*, who live in the *lokas* of *Bhuvah* and *Suvah.* They are the builders of the subtle bodies, *Sukshma deha*, around which physical atoms aggregate to produce the physical body. As the objects of marriage are the maintenance of the *Grihastha Dharma* and the begetting of progeny with spiritual, not carnal, tendencies, the co-operation of the *Pitri Devatas* is essential. These *Pitri Devatas* are not beings to be trifled with, and they are beings who generally avoid the physical plane of the Universe, the *Bhurloka*, and they should be sent away from the physical world as soon as the business for which they are invited is over. Nor are they to be invited frequently.

6. THE GRAHA YAGNA.

Next comes the *Graha Yagna*, or the propitiation of the *Nine Grahas.* The *Nava Grahas* or Planetary Spirits are believed to exercise an important influence on man.

7. THE SNATAKA CEREMONY.

After this, the would-be bridegroom performs the *Snataka* ceremony, which marks the close of his studies under a *guru* with rigid *Brahmacharya.* *

* The *Brahmacharya* (student-life) begins with the

A number of Brahmans are fed, and they wish him good. He then stands forth, and supplicates in this strain :—*

"O Brahman elders that have condescended to respond to our invitation, I pray you to hear attentively what I am going to say :—

Upanayana ceremony, his 'second birth,' and from that time forward certain virtues must be striven for by the boy. He must be hardy and simple in his habits; these virtues make this body strong and healthy; he acquires them by rising early, bathing, eating moderately of plain food, taking plenty of exercise, not allowing himself to lounge luxuriously and idly.....................The student must also strive for the virtues of industry, obedience, humility and serviceableness.................He must be chaste in thought and act, a celibate in mind and body. He must guard his thoughts, for the boy who does not think impurity will not act impurity. He should not think of sex, nor yield to day-dreaming. Only the pure in thought and in body can pass unstained into happy household life. The very name of the student is the *Brahmachari*, which has come now to mean almost exclusively the celibate. Premature age, weakness, disease, race-decay, spring from student-marriage against the Ancient Law. (Elementary Text-book of Sanatana Dharma, pp. 104-105.)

* అశేషేహే పరిషత్ మదీయాం విజ్ఞాపనాం సమ్యగవధార్య మమ ఉపనయనప్రభృతి స్నాతకశులగ్న పర్యంతం మధ్యవర్తన కాలె ఆచార్యోపదిష్టానాం యథోక్త।

अशेषेहेपरिषत् मदीयां विज्ञापनां सम्यगवधार्य. मम उपनयनप्रभृति-स्नातकशुभलग्नपर्यन्तं मध्यवर्तनकाले आचार्योपदिष्टानां यथोक्त.

"Whereas during my *Brahmacharya*, from the time of my *Upanayana* till now, my *gurus* prescribed purity, *Achamana*, *Sandhyavandana* three times a day, *Agni Karya* twice a day, meals begged twice at others' doors, implicit obedience to the commands of the *guru*, study of the *Vedas*, and the constant wearing of the external marks of a *Brahma charin*, viz., *danda*, *ajina*, and *mekhala*;

And whereas they prohibited sleep during the day, the eating of the areca-nut, the chewing of betel-leaves, horse-riding and elephant-riding, attendance at musical performances given by *Natas*, *Vitas*, and *Gayakas*, and association with bad characters such as *Patitas*, *Pashandas* and *Chandalas*;

శౌచాచమనకాలత్రయ సంధ్యావందన ద్విరగ్నికార్య సాయం ప్రాతర్భిక్షాన్న భోజన గురోరభివందన వేదాధ్యయన సదాదండాజిన మేఖలాధారణ దివానిద్రానివర్తనాది నియమోల్లంఘనక్రముకభక్షణతాంబూలచర్వణ అశ్వారోహణ గజారోహణ నటవిటగాయక గీతవాద్యశ్రవణపతితపాషండచండాలసంభాషణాదీనాం సర్వేషాందోషాణాం అపనోదనార్థం పూర్వపూర్వకర్మాతి క్రమకర్మలోపప్రాయశ్చిత్తార్థం.

शौचाचमनकालत्रयसंध्यावंदनद्विरग्निकार्यसायं प्रातर्भिक्षान्नभोजनगुरोरभिवं दनवेदाध्ययनसदादंडाजिनमेखलाधारणदिवानिद्रानिवर्तनादिनियमोल्लंघनक्रमुकभक्षणतांबूल चर्वणाश्वारोहण गजारोहण नटविटगायकगीतवाद्यश्रवण पतितपाषंडचंडालसंभाषणादीनांसर्वेषांदोषाणां अपनोदनार्थं पूर्वपूर्वकर्मातिक्रमकर्मलोपप्रायश्चित्तार्थं

"And inasmuch as it may be that I have been unwittingly guilty of sins of excess, of commission, and of omission;

"And inasmuch as I wish to take up now the *Snataka Vrata* with your permission;

"I stand here in your august presence with a small amount of *Dakshina* (money-offering) which is all that I can afford, and which, though altogether inadequate as a penalty for all the sins possibly committed by me, I do yet beseech ye all to consider as adequate;

"And I do beg of you, my elders, to accept this *Dakshina*, and to absolve me of all the aforesaid sins unwittingly committed, and to declare me as fit and worthy to enter upon the *Snataka*-stage."

Thereupon the Brahman elders receive his *Dakshina*, and declare him to be a *Snataka*.*

ఉత్తరత్రస్నాతక వ్రతాధికారయోగ్యతాసిధ్యర్థం ప్రాయశ్చిత్తం నిశ్చిత్యమయాసమర్పితాం ఇమాం సౌవర్ణీం పరిషద్దక్షిణాంయత్కించిద్దక్షిణామపి యథోక్తదక్షిణామివస్వీకృత్యమామనుగృహ్ణంతుభవంతః ॥

उत्तरत्रस्नातक व्रताधिकारयोग्यतासिध्यर्थं प्रायश्चित्तं निश्चित्यमयासमर्पितां इमां सौवर्णींपरिषत्दक्षिणां यत्किंचिद्दक्षिणामपि यथोक्तदक्षिणामिवस्वीकृत्यमामनुगृह्णंतुभवंतः ।

* A *Snataka* has to choose either the *Grihastha Asrama* or the *Sanyasa Asrama*. The *Snataka* stage is thus a temporary one.

8. THE KASI YATRA.

The *Snataka* now makes up his mind to complete his education by travel, and sets out for holy Kasi or Benares. On the way he meets a company of holy Brahmans, and after conversing with them, he says: "I have finished my *Brahmacharya*, and I have duly performed the four *Vratas*, known as *Prajapatya*, *Saumya*, *Agneya*, and *Vaisvadeva*. I am wending my way to holy Benares. Do you give me leave, therefore, to depart." Says one of the company:—"An unmarried daughter I have who shines in her (natural) decorations. O *Dvija*, her will I give to thee; go thou hand in hand with her together with thy *Grihya* Fire. Do thou, therefore, come unto my house."* The young man, who stands in need of a companion, delays his journey.

Let us examine the ages of the two parties. The bridegroom says he has finished his Vedic (occult)

---

* చరితబ్రహ్మ చర్యోహం కృతవ్రత చతుష్టయః ।
కాశీయాత్రాం గమిష్యామి అనుజ్ఞాందేహిమేశుభాం ॥
ప్రతివాక్యం ॥
సాలంకారాం మమసుతాంకన్యాందాస్యామి తేద్విజ ।
పాణింగృహీత్వాసాగ్నిస్త్వం గచ్ఛస్వ గచ్ఛమద్గృహం ॥

चारितब्रह्मचर्योहंकृतव्रतचतुष्टय: ॥
काशीयात्रां गमिष्यामि अनुज्ञांदेहिमेशुभाम् ॥
प्रतिवाक्यम् । सालंकारां ममसुतांकन्यां दास्यामितेद्विज ।
पाणिंगृहीत्वासाग्निस्त्वं गच्छस्वागच्छमद्गृहम् ॥

studies, and has performed the four *Vratas* of *Prajapatya*, *Saumya*, *Agneya*, and *Vaisvadeva*. He is, besides, travelling by himself. It is plain, therefore, that he has attained at least his majority. But what about the age of the bride? The Samskrit original has సాలంకారాం మమసుతాం కన్యాం (*Salankaram Mamasutam Kanyam*). How are we to interpret this? Let us consider the context. The young man is unmarried. The father says పాణింగృహీత్వా (*panim grihitva*): companionship is evidently implied. సాగ్నిః, *sagnih*, is used. The *Agni* is *Grihya Agni*. Who is to cook the rice for the sacrifice? Evidently the *kanya*. The food cooked by a girl, who has not attained puberty, is not accepted by elderly men and ladies in our households; much less can it be accepted then by the *Devas*. The use of సాగ్నిః, *Sagnih*, therefore, implies that the *Kanya* has attained her age, *i.e.*, is pubescent. Conformably to this సాలంకారాం, *Salamkaram*, must have reference to the natural decorations of youth* as opposed to artificial gold ornaments. A well-developed pelvis, full-grown busts and sprightly

* Compare the following :—

వక్త్రం చంద్రవికాసి పంకజ పరీహాసక్షమే లోచనే,।
వర్ణఃస్వర్ణమపాకరిష్ణునలినీ జిష్ణుఃకచానాం చయః ॥

वक्त्रं चंद्रविकासिपंकजपरीहास क्षमेलोचने
वर्णस्वर्णमपाकरिष्णुनलिनीजिष्णुः कचानांचयः ॥

vivacity are real decorations to a woman. One that is devoid of them is not fit to be a wife. She acquires them during youth and loses them in old age. A young woman alone is serviceable to a youthful Brahman traveller for *dharma*, *artha*, and *kama*.

వక్షోజా విభకుంభ విభ్రమహరాగుర్వీనితంబస్థలీ ।

వాచాంహారిచ మార్దవం యువతిషు స్వాభావికం మండనం ॥

భ్రూచాతుర్యాకుంచితాక్షాః కటాక్షాః ।

స్నిగ్ధావాచోలజ్జితాంతాశ్చహాసాః ॥

లీలామందం ప్రస్థితం చస్థితంచ ।

స్త్రీణామేతద్భూషణం చాయుధంచ ॥

(భర్తృహరి-శృంగారశతకం).

वक्षोजाविभकुंभविभ्रमहरो गुर्वीनितंबस्थली ।

वाचां हारिचमार्दवं युवतिषु स्वाभाविकं मंडनम् ॥

भ्रूचातुर्यातकुं चिताक्षाः कटाक्षाः ।

स्निग्धावाचो लज्जितां ताश्चहासाः ॥

लीलामंदं प्रस्थितं चस्थितं च ।

स्त्रीणामेतद्भूषणं चायुधं च ॥

(भर्तृहरि शृंगारशतकं)

9. VAK NISCHAYA MUHURTA OR THE OCCASION OF THE ORAL PROMISE.

The would-be bridegroom sends two of his intimate and learned friends to go to the bride's house and see and decide about the marriage. They see the father or the guardian of the bride and decide. The father of the bride sends two of his intimate and learned friends to the bridegroom's house to decide the matter. As in the decision of a knotty case the help of disinterested and dispassionate lawyers is considered essential, so in the matter of settling the important question of marriage the help of learned friends is considered essential—and rightly so. The preliminaries are arranged, and the two parties meet in the presence of witnesses. *Shachi Purandara Puja* is performed. Health, wealth, and progeny are prayed for. The bride's father says *:—Receive thou my unmarried

* వాచాదత్తామయాకన్యా పుత్రార్థం స్వీకృతాత్వయా ।
కన్యావలోకనవిధౌనిశ్చితస్త్వం సుఖీభవ ॥
ప్రతివాక్యం ॥
వాచాదత్తాత్వయాకన్యా పుత్రార్థం స్వీకృతామయా ।
వరావలోకన విధౌనిశ్చితస్త్వం సుఖీభవ ॥

वाचादत्तामयाकन्या पुत्रार्थंस्वीकृतात्वया ।
कन्यावलोकनवि धौनिश्चितस्त्वं सुखीभव ॥ प्रातिवाक्यम् ।
वाचादत्तात्वयाकन्या पुत्रार्थंस्वीकृतामया ॥
वरावलोकनविधौ निश्चितस्त्वंसुखीभव ॥

daughter on behalf of thy son to whom she has been already orally given ; see her now, decide, and be thou happy." The father of the bridegroom satisfies himself and replies :—" I do now receive thy unmarried daughter on behalf of my son to whom she has been already orally given ; see my son, decide and be thou happy." The bride's father now sees the bridegroom and becomes happy. *Tâmbula* is given to the Brahmans present, who are all witnesses to the transaction.

The phrase వాచాదత్త, *Vâchâdattâ*, is used. What does it mean ? Aryan Psychology recognises three stages of a gift—మనసాదత్త (*Manasâdatta*), వాచాదత్త (*Vâchâdatta*), and ధారాదత్త (*Dhârâdatta*). These mean, respectively, mentally given, verbally given, and stream given, *i.e.*, actually given. The three constitute a series with the order fixed. The mental precedes the verbal, and the verbal the actual. We shall see how the *Smritikâras* have made use of these stages in the matter of *Kanyâdâna*.

10. THE CONTINUITY OF THE MARRIAGE RITUAL.

The marriage ceremonies form one series. When they are begun, they must be finished or gone through to the end. When the bridegroom accepts the young woman in marriage, the two together state the *Sankalpa* (Resolve) and tie the *Kankana* or *Râksha*. After the *Saptapadi* (the seven steps), even if either of the two die, the remaining ceremonies must be gone through with the corpse as one of the parties; for the Aryan idea is that though life ceases to exist in the *Annamayakosha* or food-sheath—which is what is known as death—it exists in the *Prânamaya* and other *kosas*,* and that the marital

---

* This is what happens at death. First, the *Sukshma Sharira* is separated from the *Sthula Sharira*, the *Jiva* drawing it away by means of the *Pranamayakosha*. This leaves the *Sthula Sharira* a mass of 'lifeless' matter; that is, of matter from which the life that held it together is withdrawn; there is plenty of life left in the cells of the body, and they begin to break away from each other, but the ruling life is gone. The *Jiva* remains in his *Sukshma Sharira*. Very quickly he shakes off his *Pranamayakosha*, and has then the denser part of the *Manomayakosha* as his outermost garment. He is then called a *Preta*, and is an inhabitant of *Pretaloka* (a part of *Bhuvarloka*). If he has been a very good man on earth, he dreams away happily while in this condition; but if he has been a bad man, he suffers while a *Preta*, craving for the earthly pleasures which he is no longer able to obtain. After a shorter or longer time—according to the strength of these cravings and the consequent length of time needed for their exhaustion—the densest part of the *Manomayakosha* falls away, and he goes as a *Pitri* into *Pitriloka* (a part of *Bhuvarloka*). Having spent there sufficient time to purify the *Manomayakosha* from all elements unfit for *Svarga*, the *Jiva* in the purified *Manomayakosha* goes on into *Svarga*, and enjoys there the fruit he

tie is to last through all the lokas. *Garbhâdhâna* (placing the seed) is the culminating ceremony, and the other ceremonies are elaborated towards the main end of taking up the *Grihastha Asrama Dharma* to beget *Sâttvic Praja* or spiritual progeny.

Space does not permit us to go into details; and we shall examine only some of the important *mantras* that are indicative of the bride's age, and understand what their import is. Though the Vedas do not explicitly state in years anywhere the marriageable age, every *mantra* enables us to infer what the Vedic *vidhi* must have been regarding it. We shall take some important *mantras* from the *Yâjusha*

has stored up. When this is exhausted, the time has come for his return to earth, and the purified *Manomayakosha* dissolves away, leaving the *Jiva* in the *Vignânamayakosha*. He quickly puts forth his power to form new vehicles, and create a new *Manomayakosha* for his coming life in the lower worlds. The *Devas* build for him a *Pranamayakosha*, and an *Annamayakosha*, and he is again born into *Bhurloka*. (Elementary Text-book of Sanatana Dharma, pp. 67-68.)

తేతంభుక్త్వాస్వర్గలోకం విశాలం క్షీణేపుణ్యేమర్త్యలోకం
విశంతి ।

ఏవంత్రయీధర్మమనుప్రపన్నాగతాగతంకామకామాలభంతే ॥

तेतं भुक्त्वास्वर्गलोकं विशालंक्षीणेपुण्ये मर्त्यलोकंविशंति

एवंत्रयीधर्ममनुप्रपंन्ना गतागतं कामकामालभंते ।

Prayoga Pârijâta, which is the book used even now by the advocates of pre-pubescent marriages.

11. THE SANKALPA OF THE BRIDEGROOM.

The bridegroom is taken to the house of the bride. He washes his feet, and performs the *Achamana* and *Pranayama*. What is this *Achamana*, which is performed often and often ? What is it intended for ? Before every *Pranayama*(Regulated Respiration), there should be an *Achamana* (sipping of consecrated water) which wets the tongue and helps in the performance of the *Pranayama*. The *Pranayama*, as already stated, steadies the mind *. With his mind thus rendered steady, he says :—ధర్మప్రజాసంపత్త్యర్థం స్త్రియముద్వహే (धर्मप्रजासंपत्यर्थं स्त्रियमुद्वहे), "this woman will I now marry to acquire the wealth of *Dharma* and *Praja*." A *Sankalpa*, as a psychological act, is the determination to direct and control one's energies in such ways as will secure the attainment of

---

. Having enjoyed the spacious *Svarga-world*, their holiness withered, they come back to this mortal world. Following the virtues enjoined by the three (Vedas), desiring sense-objects, they undergo this passage to and fro. (Bhagavad Gita ix. 21).

* *Prânâyâma* consists of three parts—*Puraka* (inhalation), *Kumbhaka* (suspension), and *Rechaka* (exhalation).

the object in view. Let us remember that our bridegroom has studied the Vedas, which are the oldest and best occult books in the world. As an occultist he knows the value of *Sankalpa* ; he knows that he has to conserve, direct and control the *Prânic* currents in his body to be in a position to place his "seed" in the "soil" in a proper way. He knows what orders of High Intelligences he has to propitiate. What is *Praja* born of *Dharma* ? *Praja* is progeny, and progeny is of three kinds—*Tâmasic*, *Râjasic*,and *Sâttvic*. *Tâmasic* progeny is a curse to the world—it is the progeny of dissipation, and is bestial in its character. *Râjasic* progeny is intellectual and energetic, but it lacks godliness. *Sâttvic* progeny is the best, and to obtain it both the husband and the wife should lead a life of continence,and should be spiritual in their thoughts and ways. The husband should take care that his "seed" is of the highest quality; and hence the *Sankalpa* of our bridegroom.

What about the age of the bride ? Why, our bridegroom's *Sankalpa* explains it. She must be fit and ready to receive and nourish his "seed".

12. KANYADANA OR THE GIVING AWAY OF THE BRIDE.

The *Kanyâdâna* ceremony is a highly complex one, and rightly is it so; for marriage makes or mars a life. The bride's parents, glad in their hearts that they have secured a *Vedavit* for their daughter, treat him with due respect. He is to them a *Lakshmi Nârâyana*, for they are believers in the famous dictum of "*Tat tvam asi*—That thou art." They give the bridegroom clothes, ornaments, cows, lands, bedding, &c. The bridegroom assumes a second *Yagnôpavita* to qualify himself for the discharge of the duties of a *Grihastha* or householder. He is fed and is given *Madhuparka*. The eyes (glances) of the bridegroom and of the bride are made to meet, for the eyes are the organs that have the highest powers of attraction or fascination. The bridegroom eyes the bride with అఘోరచక్షుః (*Aghôra Chakshuh*) *i.e.*, with eyes that have not the least trace of fierceness in them, that is, with loving and inviting eyes; for he has his, *Sankalpa* of obtaining *Sâttvic* or spiritual progeny. The bridegroom and the bride now sit facing each other. The bride's father performs his *Prânâyâma*, and states his *Sankalpa*. He invokes the spirit of *Lakshmi-Nârâyana* to dwell in the bodies of the bride and bridegroom. ఆవాహయిష్యే (*Avâhayishye*) is the expression used. His daughter is now a *Lakshmi* to him, and the bridegroom a *Nârâyana*. He describes his daughter as a "*Sâdhvi*," and he gives her away to the bridegroom whom he recognises as a "*Susila*" and "*Sudhimân*" in the presence of "*Sarva Devatas*," all *Devas*. Says he :—"My unmarried daughter who is shining in her youthful decorations and who is also fit to be a devoted wife, to thee of good character and wisdom, do I, a purified soul, give for the attainment of *Dharma*, *Artha*, and *Kâma*.[1]

These are, indeed, noble words! The use of *Sâdhvi* decides the age of the *Kanya* or bride. "*Sâdhvi*" can not be applied to a young girl, whose character is forming and not yet formed, and who is yet unable to be a good housewife.

13. THE BRIDEGROOM'S PROMISE.

The father of the bride knows the condition of his daughter and the imperiousness of the sexual desire. He knows also how difficult it is to resist the temptations of the flesh, and how men often go astray, occultists though they be. Beings of three planes or *lokas* are present, and the occasion is a fit one to exact a solemn promise of fidelity from his son-in-law. Says he solemnly to him :—"In the attainment of *Dharma*, *Artha*, or *Kâma* she is not to be transgressed[2]." The earnestness and the tone of admonition are highly significant and thoroughly appropriate. The son-in-

---

1 కన్యాం సాలంకృతాం సాధ్వీం సుశీలాయ సుధీమతే।
ప్రయతోఽహం ప్రదాస్యామి ధర్మకామార్థసిద్ధయే॥
कन्यां सालंकृतां साध्वीं सुशीलाय सुधीमते ।
प्रयतोऽहं प्रदास्यामि धर्मकामार्थसिद्धये ॥

2 ధర్మార్థకామేషు నాతిచరితవ్యా.
धर्मार्थकामेषु नातिचरितव्या.

law readily and promptly responds. Says he firmly and impressively :—"Transgress her I will not [1]." The father-in-law repeats his admonition a second time, and the son-in-law responds a second time. A third time also the admonition and the response are repeated. The first is intended for beings of the physical plane or *Bhurloka*, the second for those of the *Bhuvarloka*, and the third for those of the *Swargaloka*.

In నాతిచరామి (*Nâticharâmi*), the time indicated is the present, and not a distant future.

14. KANKANA BANDHANA TO SAPTAPADI.

Our bridegroom is fairly progressing in the accomplishment of his *sankalpa*, namely, the securing of *sâttvic* progeny. He has now a young woman, who is certified by her pure-minded father to be a *sâdhvi*. He must now establish a strong link between himself and his spouse. This, however, is not to be done all of a sudden. As a first step in it, he and his spouse perform their *Prânâyâma* together, and they have now the same *sankalpa*. Say they :—" By *us* are sacrifices to be offered, and progeny too obtained."[2]

The *Kankana bandhana* ceremony is of great significance, for from this time forth until the *samâvesana*

---

1 ఆవాభ్యాం కర్మాణి కర్తవ్యాని, ప్రజాశ్చోత్పాదయితవ్యాః ॥
आवाभ्यांकर्माणि कर्तव्यानि प्रजाश्चोत्पादयितव्याः ॥

2 నాతిచరామి. नातिचरामि.

(sexual union) ceremony is performed, the bride and the bridegroom can suffer from no pollution, as they have the *kankana* or *Raksha.*

In the course of the ceremonies that follow, the bridegroom says to the bride :—" After that, hast thou to unite thy body with mine, thy lord's." [1]

Later on he says [2] :—" Go thou to my house ; be thou there its mistress ; control thou the beings that are in it, issuing orders for the sacrificial rites."

Later on still he says :—" First, *Sôma* had thee ; the *Gandharva* had thee next ; *Agni* became thy third lord ; the fourth (lord) is I, born of man. *Sôma* gave thee to the *Gandharva*, the *Gandharva* gave thee to *Agni*; then thee to me has *Agni* given with (the capacity to bring forth) wealth and progeny [3]."

---

1 అథాపత్యాత్తన్వగుం సగుంసృజస్వ ॥
अथापत्यायन्वꣳ सꣳसृजस्व ॥

2 గృహాన్గచ్ఛ గృహపత్నీ యథాసోవశినీత్వం విదథమావదాసి ॥
गृहान्गच्छगृहपत्नी यथासोवशिनीत्वंविदथमावदासि.

3 సోమః ప్రథమోవివిదే గంధర్వోవివిద ఉత్తరః ।
తృతీయోఅగ్నిష్టే పతిస్తురీయస్తే మనుష్యజాః ॥
సోమోదదద్గంధర్వాయ గంధర్వోదదదగ్నయే ।
రయించపుత్రాగుశ్చాదా దగ్నిర్మహ్య మథోఇమాం ॥

सोमःप्रथमोविविदेगंधर्वोविविदउत्तरः ।
तृतीयोअग्निष्टेपतिस्तुरीयस्ते मनुष्यजाः ॥
सोमोददद्गंधर्वाय गंधर्वोदददग्नये ।
रयिंचपुत्रांश्चादादग्निर्मह्यमथोइमाम् ॥

These statements contain profound truths; let us understand them. Three *Devâs* are mentioned—*Sôma*, the *Gandharva*, and *Agni*. Who is *Sôma*, and what are his functions ? *Soma* is *Sasyâdhipati*, the Lord of the Vegetable World, and He presides also over the mind [1]. " First *Sôma* had thee,"—this means that the physical growth of the girl, including that of the hair, was under the care of *Sôma*. The mind of the girl also developed under his guidance. " *Sôma* gave thee to the *Gandharva* "—when ? When the body had grown, and when hair had appeared on all the parts where it could appear, and when intelligence had fairly increased. Why did he give over ? Because to his work something more was to be added, and it was not in his province to do it. Thus the *Gandharva* becomes her second lord. What is the work of the *Gandharva* ? The *Gandharva* is the master of the graces. It is his function to make the woman's body beautiful, and to add richness of tone (*Svarasampattu.*) Under his care the pelvis develops, the busts become round and attractive, the eyes begin to speak the language of love, and the whole body acquires a rich hue. His work is advanced, and he hands her on to *Agni*. Who is *Agni* ? He is the Lord of Fire, the Lord of the *Agni*

---

1 చంద్రమామన సోజాతః ।

चंद्रमामनसोजातः ।

Tattva. Nature is radiant with colour and joy in spring and summer ; animals breed in spring. All know the meaning of an animal being on heat. *Agni* is the Fructifier. It is he who brings about the menstrual flow, and woman then can bear children. *Agni* then gives her to man, her fourth *Pati* or Lord. When is woman fit for marriage ? The *Vedâs* say " after menstruation." At what age does menstruation occur ? At the present time between the fourteenth and the eighteenth year from birth. Why do not the *Vedâs* say so ? Because the *Vedâs* teach *Sanâtana Dharma.* The length of man's life is not, and cannot be, the same at all periods of human history. Men of the Fourth Race (*Daityâs* and *Râkshasâs*) were about 27 feet high, and they lived several hundreds of years. The length of human life has been steadily decreasing, and stands now at 120 years astrologically. The *Vedâs*, therefore, state that woman becomes fit for marriage when *Agni* has been her third lord.[1] To put it in plain words, the *Vedâs* say:—"Marry the maiden after she menstruates."

---

1 వ్యంజనేషుచజాతేషు సోమోభుంక్తేథకన్యకాం ।
పయోధరేషు గంధర్వో రజస్యగ్నిః ప్రతిష్ఠితః ॥ (అత్రి)

व्यंजनेषुच जातेषु सोमो भुङ्क्तेथकन्यकाम् ।
पयोधरेषुगंधर्वो रजस्यग्निःप्रतिष्ठितः ॥ (अत्रि)

"When hair has appeared (on the pubes) *Sôma* enjoys (protects) a maiden ; the *Gandharva* enjoys (protects) her when the breasts are developed, and *Agni* when she has had the menstrual discharge." (Marriage after Peburty, p. 6.)

Taking the bride's hand to lead her to the *Saptapadi* ceremony, the bridegroom says 1:— "Thy hand do I take to get good progeny ! Mayest thou live with me, thy protector, till thou gettest old and feeble !

Bhaga, *Aryama*, *Savita*, (names of the sun at different periods) the all-knowing, have given me thee for *gârhapatya*.[2] After this communication he leads her, and chants more *Riks*. The *Saptapadi* ceremony is gone through. The seven steps are stepped. He then stops and says to her[3] :—" Be-

---

1 గృభ్ణామితేసుప్రజాస్త్వాయ హస్తంమయా పత్యాజరదష్టి ర్యథాసః । భగోఅర్యమాసవి తాపురంధిర్మహ్యం త్వాదుగా ర్హపత్యాయదేవాః ॥

गृभ्णामितेसुप्रजास्त्वायहस्तंमयापत्या जरदष्टिर्यथासः । भगोअर्य मासवितापुरंधिर्मह्यं त्वादुर्गार्हपत्यायदेवाः ।

2 This *mantra* contemplates post-pubescent marriage only. The bride has to live with her husband as a *grihini* from the time of marriage, and beget progeny. Is this possible in the case of a pre-pubescent girl ?

3 సఖాసప్తపదాభవ సఖాయౌ సప్తపదాబభూవ సఖ్యం
తేగమేయగుం సఖ్యాత్తేమాయోషగుం సఖ్యాన్మేమా
యోష్ఠాస్సమయావ సంకల్పావహై సంప్రియౌరోచి
ష్ణూసుమనస్యమానౌ ఇషమూర్జమభిసం వసానౌ సంనౌ
మనాగుంసి సంవ్రతానముచిత్తాన్యాకరం.

सखासप्तपदाभव सखायौसप्तपदाबभूव सख्यंतेगमेयꣳ सख्यात्ते मायोषꣳ सख्यान्मे मायोष्ठास्समयावसंकल्पावहै संप्रियौरोचिष्णू सुमनस्यमानौ इषमूर्जमभिसंवसानौ संनौमनाꣳसि संव्रतासमुचित्तान्याकरम् ।

come thou now my partner, as thou hast paced all the seven steps. Aye! Partners we have become, as we have together paced all the seven steps. Thy partnership have I gained; apart from thee now I cannot live; apart from me do thou not live. We shall live together, and we shall will together; we each shall be an object of love to the other; we each shall be a source of joy unto the other; with mutual good-will shall we live together, sharing equally all foods and powers. Combine I now thy mind, thy actions, thy senses with mine."

"*Rik* thou art, *Sâma* I am; *Sâma* I, *Rik* thou; *Dyaus* I am, Earth thou art; I am *Rethus* (the living seed), thou art the bearer thereof; mind I am, speech thou art; *Sama* I, *Rik* thou. Being what thou art, come thou now unto me, O sweet and pure, for bringing forth sons, wealth and progeny.[1]

How noble and loving this speech is, and how true! Our bridegroom knows, indeed, how to love

---

1 సాత్వమస్యమూహామ మూహామస్మి సాత్వం ద్యౌరహం పృథివీ త్వంరేతో హంరేతో భృత్త్వంమనోహామ స్మి వాక్త్వం సామాహ మస్మ్యృక్త్వం సామామను వ్రతాభవపుంసే పుత్రాయవేత్తవై శ్రియై పుత్రాయవేత్తవ ఏహిసూనృతే ॥

सात्वमस्यमूहममूहमास्मिसात्वं द्यौरहं पृथिवीत्वं रेतोहं रेतोभृत्त्वं मनोऽहमस्मिवाक् त्वं सामाहमस्मि ऋक्त्वं सामामनुव्रता भवपुंसे पुत्रायवेत्तवे श्रियैपुत्रायवेत्तवएहिसूनृते ।

and be loved. Fortunately he has a spouse, who being a *sâdhvi* can reciprocate his love.

Without *Saptapadi*, there cannot be any Aryan marriage. How very glaring the inconsistency is when the marriage is a pre-pubescent one! "Apart from thee *now* I cannot live; apart from me do thou not live," says the mantra. The bridegroom is made to say also—"combine I now thy mind, thy actions, thy senses with mine." We request the advocates of pre-pubescent marriage to act according to these rules. Can they do so?

One more remark has to be made. *Saptapadi* establishes an indissoluble link between the husband and the wife. Each has to care for the spiritual welfare of the other. The surviving party should perform the funeral ceremonies of the other, unless a son is born to relieve the surviving party of this duty.

15. PRADHANA AHUTI OR THE GREAT HOMA.

Our bridegroom is a knowing man. The *Pradhâna Hôma*, which he performs along with his wife, wins for him her high regard and pure devotion. We shall translate some of the mantras :—

(1) This to Soma, [1] (who has nourished my wife so well !)

---

(1) సోమాయజనివిదేస్వాహా

सोमायजनिविदेस्वाहा

(2) This to the Gandharva [2] (who has adorned my wife so well !)

(3) This to Agni [3] (who has given me this *Yuvati* !)

No special praises are appended in these three cases as they have already been praised elsewhere.

(4) This *Kanya*, [4] O Surya, has passed from her father's family to her husband's. Her maidenhood she has resigned ! Do thou be propitious !

There is one important point in this *mantra*. No sexual intercourse has taken place, and yet she is described as having resigned her maidenhood. How is this ? When she, a grown-up woman, allowed him, her husband, to take her hand in his with the determination (*Sankalpa*) of begetting a son by her, she lost her virginity owing to an interblending of positive and negative magnetic currents of the two bodies.

---

(2) గంధర్వాయ జనివిదేస్వాహా

गंधर्वायजनिविदेस्वाहा

(3) అగ్నయే జనివిదేస్వాహా

अग्नयेजनिविदेस्वाहा ।

(4) కన్యలాపితృభ్యో యతీపతి లోకమవ దీక్షామదాస్థస్వాహా॥

कन्यलापितृभ्यो यतीपतिलोकमवदीक्षामदास्थस्वाहा

(5) "O Indra[5] that compellest the clouds to rain on the earth! Do thou release this young woman hence. Bind thou her well in her husband's house, giving her good sons and wealth. Release her not thence. Be thou propitious!

How does the *Sâdhvi*, glowing with youthful vigour, feel when she hears this mantra, which shows the depth of her husband's love and regard for her? This *mantra* also explains the duties of a devoted wife: her duties are to increase wealth and to bring forth spiritual progeny. We have to remember that whenever the marital *mantras* mention wealth, it is not material wealth that is meant but spiritual wealth, which is acquired and patiently *garnered* by a diligent and conscientious performance of all the *Karmas* prescribed for householders. It is "*Tapôdhana*" or wealth of *Tapas*.

(6) "O Indra that bringest rains (prosperity)! Do thou give this bride good progeny and good wealth.

---

(5) ప్రేతో ముంచాతి నాముతస్సుబద్ధామముత స్కరత్ ।
యథేయమింద్ర మీఢ్వస్సు పుత్రాసుభగాసతిస్వాహా ॥

प्रेतोमुञ्चातिनामुतस्सुबद्धाममुतस्करत्
यथेयमिन्द्रमीढ्वस्सुपुत्रासुभगासतिस्वाहा ।

(6) ఇమాంత్వమింద్ర మీఢ్వస్సు పుత్రాం సుభగాంకృణు ।
దశాస్యాం పుత్రానాధేహి పతిమేకాదశం కృధిస్వాహా ॥

इमां त्वमिन्द्र मीढ्वस्सुपुत्राꣳसु भगांकृणु ।
दशास्यां पुत्रानाधेहि पतिमेकादशंकृधि ।

Ten children do thou place in her, making me, her husband, the eleventh (member). Be thou propitious !

Probably the youthful *Sâdhvi* smiles, but her love, we may be sure, increases. Every good child that is born, binds the husband and wife more and more.

(7) May Agni, foremost of the gods, come! May he free and save her offspring from the cords of Death. When Agni makes her know no sorrow for loss of progeny, may Varuna acquiesce ! Be ye, Agni and Varuna, propitious !

(8) May the *Gârha Patya Agni* protect her, grant her progeny long life, make her a mother on whose lap children nestle and play, awake her only to feel the joy of owning sons ! Be thou propitious !

---

(7) అగ్నిరైతు ప్రథమో దేవతానాంసోస్యై ప్రజాం ముంచతు మృత్యు పాశాత్ । తదయగ్ం రాజావరుణో౽నుమన్యతాం యథే యగ్ం స్త్రీపౌత్రమఘంనరోదాత్స్వాహా ॥

अग्निरैतुप्रथमोदेवतानाꣳसोऽस्यै प्रजां मुञ्चतु मृत्युपाशात् ।
तदयꣳराजावरुणोऽनुमन्यतां यथेयꣳस्त्रीपौत्रमघंनरोदात् स्वाहा ।

(8) ఇమామగ్నిస్త్రాయతాం గార్హపత్యః ప్రజామస్యై నయతుదీర్ఘమాయుః । అశూన్యోపస్థాజీవతామస్తు మాతా పౌత్ర మానందమభి ప్రబుధ్యతామియంస్వాహా ॥

इमामग्निस्त्रायतां गार्हपत्यः प्रजामस्यै नयतु दीर्घमायुः । अशून्योपस्थाजीवता मस्तुमातापौत्रमनंदमभिप्रबुध्यतामियꣳस्वाहा ।

(9) In thy house, O bride, be there no cries of sorrow at night! Be the criers other than thee and thine! Be there no dishevelled hair and beating of breast for thee! Shine, O bride, in thy husband's house with thy husband alive and with sane-minded children surrounding thee! To all this, O Surya, the Guardian of brides, do thou look!

(10) May Dyaus nourish thy loins (*Prishtha*), Vayu thy thighs, the Asvins thy breasts! May Surya protect thy child at the breast! May Brihaspati keep thee ever-clothed! May the Visve Devas be Guardian Angels at thy back!

(11) Barrenness, infant-deaths, sins, causes of sins, these all, O bride, do I now throw unto thy

---

(9) మాతేగృహే నిశిఘోష ఉత్థాదన్యత్ర త్వద్రుదత్యస్సంవి శంతు! మాత్వంవికేశ్యుర ఆవధిష్ఠాజీవ పత్నీ పతిలోకే విరాజ పశ్యంతీ ప్రజాగ్ంసు మనస్యమానాగ్ స్వాహా ||

मातेगृहे निशिघोषउत्थादन्यत्र त्वद्रुदत्यस्संविशन्तु । मात्वंविकेश्युर आवधिष्ठाजीवपत्नी पतिलोके विराजपश्यन्तीप्रजाꣳसुमनस्यमानाꣳस्वाहा।

(10) ద్యౌస్తేపృష్ఠగ్ం రక్షతువాయురూరూ అశ్వినాచ స్తనం ధయంతగ్ం సవితాభి రక్షతు । ఆవాససః పరిధానాద్బృహ స్పతి విశ్వేదేవా అభిరక్షంతు పశ్చాత్స్వాహా ||

द्यौस्तेपृष्ठꣳरक्षतुवायुरूरू अश्विनौचस्तनं धयंतꣳसवितामिरक्षतु । आवासस: परिधानाद्बृहस्पतिर्विश्वेदेवा अभिरक्षन्तु पश्चात्स्वाहा ।

enemies like unto the garland of flowers faded through use, which is thrown to the tree-tops by thee. May *Surya*, the Guardian of brides, help in this !

When are the mantras of the *Pradhâna Homa* appropriate ? Only when the bride is fit to bear children, *i. e.*, after puberty. This *Homa* is performed only once : it cannot be repeated at will. Appropriateness of time, therefore, is an all-important consideration. As in the case of other *Samskâras*, the *Karthrus* should have the *Adhikâra* or privilege to perform them. According to Aryan conception, the Universe with its Hierarchies of Intelligences is like a vast factory wherein division of labour is well-nigh infinite. The article of manufacture, which has to undergo multifarious processes at different stages, should reach the hands of the various workers in a definite order or succession. If the order be unheeded, confusion will arise, and the workers will find it impossible to turn out satisfactory work. The article manufactured will be clumsy and worthless. The same law holds good when the article of manufacture is a human being. Suppose a

---

(11) అప్రజస్తాం పౌత్రమృత్యుంపాప్మానముత వాఘం । శీర్ష్ణ స్రజమివోన్ముచ్యద్విషద్భ్యః ప్రతిముంచామిపాశం స్వాహా ॥

अप्रजस्तां पौत्रमृत्युं पाप्मानमुतवाऽघम् । शीर्ष्णस्स्रजमिवोन्मुच्य-द्विषद्भ्यः प्रतिमुंचामिपाशं स्वाहा ।

girl-bride, who is totally ignorant of what sexual union is, and whose figure is like that of a stick, and whose chest is as flat as a flat slate, gives the tenth *âhuti.* The *Devas* invoked—say, the Asvins—come. They look at the girl and feel dissatisfied at being needlessly summoned. They are sure to say :— "This girl has not passed through the hands of Soma as yet; not one hair there is on the pubes; the Gandharva has not yet done his work; Agni has not brought about menstruation;—we are asked to protect her breasts when there are none! Oh, how droll! These degenerate Brahmans know not now their own *Sâstras*!" After a soliloquy of this description they go away in disgust. The girl attains puberty, and as the *Pradhâna Homa* cannot be repeated, she loses the special help of the *Devas*, and generally gives birth to a malformed puny child, when her breast is as dry as an old bean! What is the result? Why, the deterioration of the race,—which needs no proof.

16. THE JOURNEY HOME.

We pass over the *mantras* of *Lâja Homa,* which pray for long life, vigour, and prosperity. One, however, is too important to be left unnoticed. Says the husband :—"From the *Varuna Pâsa* with which the well-knowing *Surya* has tied thee (to the wheel of births and deaths in the three *lokas* of

Bhuh, Bhuvah and *Suvah*), I shall liberate thee ; in *Brahmaloka* [1], that *loka* of good deeds, a place by my side shall I make thee have. ....I shall make thee live with thy husband always."[2] What more can our *Sâdhvi* (devoted wife) desire ? With all her heart and soul, she becomes one with her husband in thought, word, and deed. Our bridegroom's chances of securing *sâttvic* progeny have vastly improved. The couple now think of home, sweet home ! The carriage and pair is ready. Our *Vedavit* has blessings for the horse. He now says to his wife :— " O bride, mount thou to the seat that I occupy, who am of long life. Keep thou in the carriage thy *Streedhana*, which makes thy husband feel happy. Get thou into this superior vehicle, conquer thou thy

---

[1] The seven lokas are :—Bhuh, Bhuvah, Suvah, Mahah, Janah, Tapah, Satyah.—Satya Loka is Brahma Loka.

[2] ప్రత్వాముంచామి వరుణస్య పాశాద్యేనత్వాబధ్నాత్సవి తాసు
కేతః। ధాతుశ్చయో నౌసుకృతస్యలోకే స్యోనంతేసహపత్యాక
రోమి ॥.........................అరిష్టాంత్వాసహ పత్యాకృ
ణోమి॥

प्रत्वामुंचामिवरुणस्यपाशाद्येन त्वाऽबध्नात्सवितासुकेतः। धातुश्चयो-
नौसुकृतस्यलोके स्योनन्तेसहपत्याकरोमि......अरिष्टां त्वासहपत्यां
कृणोमि ॥

enemies, be thou a crown to me, thy husband![1] Shine with progeny; shine thou in the estimation of thy father-in-law; be thou loved by thy mother-in-law; earn thou the affection of thy sisters-in-law; get thou the loving regard of thy brothers-in-law. To thy daughters-in-law, to the brothers of thy father-in-law, to thy progeny, to the wealth in the house, to thy husband, to thy brothers-in-law, to all those born of that same womb, be thou as a loving mistress!"[2]

How useful and appropriate would this exhortation be to a girl of ten or eleven years! What a household that would be which is presided over by a girl-prodigy of ten years of age!

---

[1] A virtuous woman is a crown to her husband.

[2] ఆరోహవధ్వమృతస్య లోకగ్ం స్యోనం పత్యేవహతుం కృణుష్వ। ఉదుత్తరమారోహంతీ వ్యస్యంతీ పృతన్యతః। మూర్ధానంపత్యురారోహ ప్రజయాచ విరాడ్భవ। సమ్రాజ్ఞీశ్వశురే భవసమ్రాజ్ఞీశ్వశ్రువాంభవ। ననాందరిసమ్రాజ్ఞీభవ। సమ్రాజ్ఞీ అధిదేవృషు। స్నుషాణాగ్ శ్వశురాణాం ప్రజాయాశ్చధనస్యచ। పతీనాంచదేవృణాంచసజాతానాం విరాడ్భవ॥

आरोहवध्वमृतस्यलोकं स्योनंपत्येवहतुं कृणुष्व । उदुत्तरमारोहंती व्यस्यंतीपृतन्यतः । मूर्धानंपत्युरारोह प्रजयाचविराड्भव । सम्राज्ञीश्वशुरेभवसम्राज्ञीश्वश्रुवांभव । ननांदरिसम्राज्ञीभव। सम्राज्ञीअधिदेवृषु । स्नुषाणां श्वशुराणां प्रजायाश्च धनस्यच। पतीनां च देवृणां च सजातानां विराड्भव ॥

17. THE GRIHA PRAVESA HOMA.

The happy couple have reached home. *Homas* follow. Our bridegroom works steadily for the realisation of his *Sankalpa* along wiih his wife. [1] Here are some *mantras* :—

(1) "May my dearest wife, that has come into our house with all the cows and horses given her by her father, live long with her long-lived lord! May she attain heaven by her progeny! May she bring forth many a child ! With her wealth ever increasing, may she, O Agni, tend the Holy Fire for a hundred winters." [2]

[1] Says Dr. Lewis :—No man should ever beget a child without weeks, or perhaps months, of preparation for this important office. ....He should cultivate purity of thought, and seek thorough and intelligent sympathy with his wife in all her hopes and aims. (Vivahanisheka Dharma. p. 126.)

(2) ఆగన్ గోష్ఠం మహిషీగోభిరశ్వైరాయుష్మత్పత్నీ ప్రజయాస్వవిత్ । బహ్వీం ప్రజాంజనయంతీ సురత్నేమమగ్నిగ్ం శతహిమాస్సపర్యాత్స్వాహా ॥

आगन्गोष्ठंमहिषीगोभिरश्वैरायुष्मत्पत्नी प्रजयास्वर्वित् । बह्वींप्रजां-जनयंतीसुरत्ने ममाग्निः शतहिमास्सपर्यात्स्वाहा ॥

(2) " May this Agni of my *Upâsana*, who has his shining house, who unceasingly increases my strength, who guards my home, give unto us, husband and wife, wealth, strength, and progeny, as he did to the *Devas*." [3]

(3) O Prajâpati, make thou our progeny happy ! O Indra, O Agni, grant us the happiness of never witnessing the death of our children during the lifetime of us two, husband and wife." [4]

(4) O bride, thee Brihaspati hath given unto me. Protected by me, do thou ever have me in thy

---

(3) అయమగ్నిర్గృహపతిస్సుసగ్ంసత్పుష్టివర్ధనః । యథాభగస్యాభ్యాందదద్రయింపుష్టిమథోప్రజాంస్వాహా ॥

अयमग्निर्गृहपतिस्सुसꣳसत्पुष्टिवर्धनः ।
यथाभगस्याभ्यां ददद्रयिंपुष्टिमथोप्रजाꣳस्वाहा ॥

(4) ప్రజాయా ఆభ్యాంప్రజాపత ఇంద్రాగ్నీ శర్మయచ్ఛతం । యథైనయోర్న ప్రమీయాతా ఉభయోర్జీవతోః ప్రజాస్స్వాహా ॥

प्रजायाआभ्यां प्रजापतइन्द्राग्नी शर्मयच्छतम् ।
यथैनयोर्नप्रमीयाता उभयोर्जीवतोःप्रजास्स्वाहा ॥

mind. [5] Do thou unite with me, and begetting sons, live thou long."

This mantra shows that our *Vedavit* knows what he has to do to obtain a son who is to be an exact image of himself.

(5) " O Antarâtma ! Tvashtri Prajapati created this wife, the same Tvashtri created thee her husband. May that same Tvashtri give you both a long, long life and prosperity. "[6]

It is Tvashtri that shapes the forms in the womb when the seminal and the germinal fluids combine. His help is necessary for the growth of the fœtus in the womb.

(5) Goethe in his "Elective Affinities" says :— A husband and wife, each loving another, and each thinking of that other at the instant of sexual intercourse, found evidence of their mutual unfaithfulness when their child was born, for it presented in its face the double likeness of the lovers whom the parents had had in mind. (J. S.'s Vivaha Nisheka Dharma, p. 232.)

ధ్రువైధిపోష్యమయిమహ్యం త్వాదాద్బృహస్పతిః మయా పత్యాప్రజావతీ సంజీవశరదశ్శతం స్వాహా ॥

ध्रुवैधिपोष्यामयिमह्यंत्वादाद्बृहस्पतिः ॥
मयापत्याप्रजावती संजीवशरदश्शतं स्वाहा ॥

(6) త్వష్టాజాయామజనయత్త్వష్టాస్యైత్వాంపతిం । త్వష్టా సహస్రమాయూంగ్ం షిదీర్ఘమాయుః కృణోతువాగ్ స్వాహా ॥

त्वष्टाजायामजनयं त्वष्टाऽस्यै त्वांपतिम् ।
त्वष्टासहस्रमायूंषि दीर्घमायुः कृणोतुवाम् ।

(6) "May love grow in this house with progeny Be thou ever ready here for the discharge of thy duties as *Grihini*. Unite thy body with mine thy lord's, Grow thou old here, and teach sacrificial law to thy sons and grandsons with a gladdened heart." [7]

The *Pravesa Homa Mantras* all imply that the bride is a grown-up woman. This *Homa* also is performed only once, and cannot be repeated at will.

18. THE THREE NIGHTS' BRAHMACHARYA.

We omit, for want of space, the consideration of the *Agneya Sthâli Pâka* and the *Aupâsana* ceremonies. After this the so-called *Tri Râtra Brahmacharya* commences. What is this *Brahmacharya* for three nights? *Brahmacharya* does not here mean celibacy, for that term is evidently inadmissible as there has been marriage. It does not mean abstinence from sexual intercourse, for the first sexual intercourse has not taken place. The best term to use is continence. Let us consider the circumstances. Our bridegroom is a fine robust young man, whose

---

(7) ఇహప్రియం ప్రజయాతే సమృధ్యతామ స్మిన్గృహే గా ర్హపత్యాయజాగృహి । ఏనాపత్యాతన్వగ్ంసగ్ంసృజస్వాథాజీవ్రీ విదథమావదాసి ॥

इहप्रियंप्रजयाते समृध्यतामास्मिन्गृहेगार्हपत्यायचागृहि ।
एनापत्यातन्व ॅस ॅ सृजस्वाथाजीवीविदथमावदासि ।

Sankalpa (determination) is to discharge the duties of a householder and beget spiritual progeny. He has married a full-grown young woman, who has been certified to be a *Sâdhvi*. The couple have jointly offered several sacrifices praying for progeny. Each loves and appreciates the other. There is nothing whatever to prevent them from performing the *Sesha Homa*, and indulging in sexual intercourse. Still they undertake to observe *Brahmacharya* for some time. Is it meant that this life of continence should last only for three days? Not at all. Three days is the minimum period. Baudhayana advises three days' continence or self-restraint when the object is to beget a *Srotriya*; twelve days to beget an *Anuchana*; one month to beget a *Rishikalpa*; four months to beget a *Bhruna*; six months to beget a *Rishi*; and one year to beget a Deva.* So three days is the minimum period. This *Brahmacharya* is to be observed under really trying circumstances. Both the parties have to eat food without salt, they have to sleep on the floor, and they have to wear

* See Baudhayana. *Prasna* I, *Adhyaya* 7, *Khanda* 11. A *Shrotriya* is a Brahman that has studied one *Shakha*; an *Anuchana* is one that has studied the *Angas*; a *Rishikalpa* is one that has studied the *Sutras* and the *Pravachanas*; a *Rishi* is one that has studied the four *Vedas*; and a *Deva* is one that has passed beyond that stage. (Marriage after Puberty, page 9.)

ornaments. They have to lie on the same bed with the *Visvâvasu Ghandharva* occupying the middle position. If there be any seminal or germinal discharge, the *Vrata* is gone, and there will be no really spiritual progeny. The life of continence * which is to last throughout life begins now. All dissipation or waste of the seminal fluid is entirely prohibited by our *Sâstras*.

---

* Dr. Sylvester Graham, author of the Lectures on the Science of Human Life, says :—The genital secretion, or the semen, may be called the essential oil of animal liquors, the rectified spirit, the most subtle and spirituous part of the animal frame, which contributes to the support of the nerves. The greatest part of this refined fluid is, in a healthy state and conduct of the system, reabsorbed and mixed with the blood, of which it constitutes the most rarified and volatile part, and imparts to the body peculiar sprightliness, vivacity, muscular strength, and general vigour and energy to the animal machine. It causes the beard, hair and nails to grow, gives depth of tone, and masculine scope and power to the voice, and manliness and dignity to the countenance and person, energy and ardour and noble daring to the mind. The loss of semen enfeebles the body more than the loss of twenty times the same quantity of blood, more than violent cathartics and emetics. Hence the frequent and excessive loss of it cannot fail to produce the most extreme debility and disorder and wretchedness of both body and mind. (J. S.'s Vivaha Nisheka Dharma Pradipika, page 222.)

Our bridegroom, however, is a *Vedavit*, and the bride a *Sûdhvi.* They both acquit themselves most creditably. On the fourth night, after the *Pakva Homa*, they request in these terms the *Gandharva* to depart :—" Rise, O Visvâvasu, from this our bed; rise, we pray. Seek thou a girl that is tender in years, and that needs thy assistance. Leave thou this bride, my wife, unto me, and let her unite herself to me. O *Gandharva*, this bride, now united to me, her husband, prostrates to thee, and begs this favour of thee. Depart and find thou an immature girl that still dwells in her father's house. Such a one is verily thy portion. nay, thy birthright." *

Needless it is to say that the *Tri Râtra Bramhacharya* is a most ludicrous farce in the case of a pre-pubescent girl. It is a mere form without any spirit in it.

---

* ఉదీర్ష్వాతో విశ్వావసో నమసేడామహే త్వా । అన్యామిచ్ఛ ప్రఫర్వ్యగ్ం సంజాయాం పత్యాసృజ । ఉదీర్ష్వాతః పతివతీ హ్యేషా విశ్వావసుం నమసాగీర్భిరీట్టే । అన్యామిచ్ఛ పితృషదం వ్యక్తాగ్ం సతే భాగో జనుషా తస్య విద్ధి ॥

(స్తనోద్గమాది రాహిత్యేనా ప్రౌఢాం. సాయన)

उदीर्ष्वातोविश्वावसो नमसेडामहेत्वा । अन्यामिच्छप्रफर्व्यं॑ सं जायांपत्यासृज । उदीर्ष्वातःपतिवतिह्येषाविश्वावसुंनमसागीर्भिरीट्टे, अन्यामिच्छपितृषदं व्यक्ता॑ सतेभागोजनुषातस्यविद्धि । (स्तनोद्गमादि राहित्येनाप्रौढाम् । सायनः ।)

19. THE SESHA HOMA.

Our couple, happy in the consciousness of having duly performed the necessary ceremonies, and feeling assured that they have secured the goodwill of the Higher Intelligences, commence the *Sesha Hôma*, preparatory to *Samâvesana* or Sexual union. Both the husband and wife are bent upon securing spiritual progeny, and so they again propitiate the Higher Powers. *Ahuties* or oblations are devoutly offered to Agni, Vayu, Aditya, Prajapati' *Prasavâdi Devatâs*, *Madhvâdi Devatas*, *Chittâdi Devatâs*, *Bhuh*, *Bhuvah*, *Suvah*. The *Sesha Hôma* is intended to put the parties in the proper frame of mind for the sexual act. The two parties must be steady in their minds, and their powers must be at their highest point. There must be no lascivious thoughts, and the idea of animal gratification must be thrown entirely into the back-ground. Both must consciously and deliberately will with all their might that the progeny shall be spiritual. Our bridegroom is a *Vedavit* and our bride a *Sâdhvi*. They know that the act of procreation is a holy act, and they are both mentally ready. The *Sâstrâs* say that man should co-habit with woman only when she desires it, and not at other times. *

* Says Dr. Trall :—In the animal Kingdom, the female does exercise her supremacy in this respect. No male animal offers violence to the female; but

Says the bride now :—" Know I what thou hast in thy mind, lovingly do I view thee as one knowing my mind, thee that hast had thy birth in *tapas* and that art enriched with *tapas*. Here in my house, do thou enrich me with progeny and wealth, being born in thy son, thou that hast a desire for sons." * Responds the bridegroom † :—" Know I what thou hast in thy mind ; lovingly do I view thee as one seeking impregnation in thy body during the *Ritu* period, thee

---

when she is in proper condition for his embrace and desires it, she solicits it ; and he invariably responds. So it should be ; so it is in the order of nature with man and woman ; and when her supremacy is fully recognised, there will soon be an end of still births, and of frail and malformed offspring who can seldom be reared to adult age, or if they can, are only curses to themselves and to the world. (Vivaha Nisheka Dharma p. 196).

* అపశ్యం త్వామనసా చేకితానం తపసోజాతం తపసోవిభూతం । ఇహప్రజామిహ రయిగ్ంరరాణః ప్రజాయస్వ ప్రజయా పుత్రకామ ॥

अपस्यंत्वामनसाचेकितानं तपसो जातं तपसो विभूतम् । इहप्रजामिहरयिं रराणः प्रजायस्वप्रजयापुत्रकाम ।

† అపశ్యం త్వామనసాదీధ్యానాగ్ స్వాయాం తనూగ్ం ఋత్వియే నాథమానాం । ఉపమాముచ్చాయువతిర్బభూయాః ప్రజాయస్వ ప్రజయా పుత్రకామే ॥

अपश्यंत्वामनसादीध्यानां स्वायांतनूं ऋत्वियेनाथमानाम् । उपमामुच्चायुवतिर्बभूयाः प्रजायस्वप्रजयापुत्रकामे ॥

that hast had me in thy mind. A youthful woman, *Yuvati*, thou art; lie thou below, and with me above, enjoy thou me, and be thou born in thy son, desirous as thou art of a son." These *Riks* contain profound truths connected with *Tat Tvam asi*, which, however, we cannot stop to discuss. The verbal stage of the action is passed, and the ideas in their minds are now to be translated into deeds. The bridegroom lovingly throws his right arm round the right shoulder of the bride, and touching the region of her heart, and putting himself in communication with her, (1) he fervently prays in this strain :—(2) "May the Visve-devas unite our hearts! May the Udaka Devatas, Vayu and Dhâta unite our hearts! May Sarasvati vouchsafe to us appropriate speech." (3) O Prajapati, enter thou

---

(1) When sympathy is well established between two individuals, we say they are in communication.

(2) సమంజంతు విశ్వేదేవాస్సమాపో హృదయానినౌ । సం మాతరిశ్వా సంధాతాసముదేష్ట్రీదిదేష్టునౌ ॥

समञ्जन्तुविश्वेदेवा स्समापोहृदयानि नौ । संमातरिश्वासंधातासमुदेष्ट्री दिदेष्टुनौ ।

(3) ప్రజాపతే తన్వంమే జుషస్వత్వష్టదేవేభిస్సహసామఇంద్ర । విశ్వైర్దేవై రాతిభిస్సగ్ం రరాణః పుగ్ంసాంబహూనాంమాత రస్స్యామ॥

प्रजापते तन्वंमेजुषस्वत्वष्टर्देवेभिस्सहसामइन्द्र । विश्वैर्देवैरातिभिस्स ॰ रराणः पुं॰ सांबहूनांमातरस्स्याम ॥

my body ! O Tvashta, Fashioner of Forms, enter thou my body with Vishnu and other Devas ! O Indra, come thou with thy friends, the Visve Devas, and enter thou our bodies with them to grant us our wish. Parents of a numerous progeny are we to be ! ([4]).

" May Prajapati give us progeny till we grow old. May Surya make us each love the other ! O bride ! live thou long in the house of thy husband ; and enjoy thou the companionship of thy husband ever more ! May we be happy in the wealth of two-legged and four-legged beings ! " *

These appropriate prayers are offered, but they alone are not enough. Men and women have physical bodies with bone, flesh, blood, and nerves ; and the spiritual progeny that our couple have made up their minds to have, must also have sound bone, sound flesh, sound blood, and sound nerves ; and to secure these, the physical bodies of the husband and the wife

---

([4]) This is intended to exclude temporary marriages which prevail in some countries.

* ఆనః ప్రజాంజనయతు ప్రజాపతి రాజరసాయ సమనక్త్వర్య మా । అదుర్మంగలీః పతిలోక మావిశ శంనోభ వద్విపదే శంచతు ష్పదే ॥

आनः प्रजांजनयतु प्रजापति राजरसायसमनक्त्वर्यमा । अदुर्मंगलीः पतिलोकमाविश । शंनोभवद्विपदे शंचतुष्पदे ॥

must have strength and must be duly excited. Surya or the sun is the source of all terrestrial energy, and so our *Vedavit* inwardly prays :—" O Surya Deva, her whom men deem fit to receive the human seed, her who wide apart opens her thighs to me through sexual desire, her whose *linga* mine strikes with lusty strokes, her do thou, O Surya Deva, help and encourage to heartily co-operate." *

The diseased humanity of modern days may be disposed to find fault with the Vedas, and more especially with our *Vedavit*; but our *Vedavit* knows what the conditions of the realisation of his *Sankalpa* are, and so he prays in this strain; for the slightest cry, the slightest shyness, the slightest repugnance, during the holy and responsible act, spoils the spiritual character of the progeny.†

---

* తాంపూషన్ఛివతమా మేరయస్వ యస్యాంబీజం మను ష్యావపంతి । యానఊరూ ఉశతీవిశ్రయాతై యస్యాముశంతః ప్రహారేమ శేఫం ॥

तांपूषन् छिवतमामेरयस्वयस्यांबीजं मनुष्यावपन्ति। यानऊरूउशती विश्रयाते यस्यामुशन्तः प्रहरेमशेफम् ॥

†Dr. Trall says in Sexual Physiology :—There must be mental harmony and congeniality. Each must be able to respond to the whole nature of the other bodily, morally and intellectually to the extent that there shall be no sense of discord, no feeling of repugnance, but, on the other hand, an utter abnegation of self-hood. (J.S's Vivaha Nisheka Dharma Pradipika page 110.)

Night arrives. The joyous couple prepare themselves for the holy function. Our *Vedavit* inwardly prays:—"O *Sarira Atma*, mount thou her thighs, stretch thine arms affectionately; embrace thou her with thy whole mind. O *Sarira Atma* and O bride, be lusty both, unite *lingas* together. Conserve your powers, produce numerous progeny, and grow (spiritually). *

"Like unto the manner in which man produces fire by friction with a ghee-besmeared rod, like unto the manner in which Indra and others produced children in woman by the use of the human *linga*, ye both unite your *lingâs*, and live ye eternally through offspring, remaining in householdership."†

"By means of my *Srauta* and *Smârta Karma* do I place seeds in the vegetable kingdom. I, forming, as I do, a part of Paramâtma, dwell in all the

---

* ఆరోహోరుముపబర్హస్వ బాహుంపరిష్వజస్వజాయాగ్ం సుమనస్యమానః । తస్యాం పుష్యతం మిథునౌసయోనీబహ్వీం ప్రజాంజనయంతౌసరేతసా ॥

आरोहोरुमुपबर्हस्वबाहुं परिष्वजस्वजायाᳩ सुमनस्यमानः । तस्यां पुष्यतं मिथुनौसयोनी बह्वींप्रजांजनयंतौसरेतसा ॥

† ఆర్ద్రయారణ్యా యత్రామంథత్పురుషం పురుషేణ శక్రః । తదేతౌ మిథునౌసయోనీ ప్రజయామృతేనేహ గచ్ఛతం॥

आर्द्रयारण्यायत्रामंथत्पुरुषं पुरुषेणशक्रः । तदेतौमिथुनौ सयोनी प्रजयाऽमृतेनेहगच्छतम् ॥

Lôkas. Being thus that that I am, do I beget for the *Pitri Devâs*. And thus in the daughters-in-law, that are to come hereafter, let grandsons be born through my sons." *

"O husband and wife, have ye progeny, both male and female, and live ye long. Be your *Varnas* pure, sacrifice ye to Agni, earn ye thus your wealth."†

"To obtain *Devahood*, welcome ye guests and gladden ye their hearts. Unite ye *lingas* that are covered with hair. Cultivate ye friendship with the *Devâs*! ‡.

Such are the lofty and appropriate thoughts of our

---

* అహంగర్భమదధామోషధీష్వహం విశ్వేషు భువనేష్వంతః। అహంప్రజా అజనయం పితౄణామహం జనిభ్యో అవరీషు పుత్రాన్॥

अहंगर्भमदधामोषधीष्वहं विश्वेषु भुवनेष्वंतः।
अहंप्रजाअजनयं पितॄणामहं जनिभ्योअवरीषु पुत्रान्।

† పుత్రిణేమాకుమారిణా విశ్వమాయుర్వ్యశ్నుతం। ఉభాహిరణ్య పేశసావీతిహోత్రా కృతద్వసూ॥

पुत्रिणेमाकुमारिणाविश्वमायुर्व्यश्नुतम्।
उभाहिरण्यपेशसावीतिहोत्राकृतद्वसू॥

‡ దశస్యంత్వా మృతాయకగ్ం। శమూధో రోమశగ్ం హథో దేవేషుకృణుతోదువః॥

दशस्यंत्वाऽमृतायकं शमूधोरोमशं हथोदेवेषुकृणुतोदुवः।

Vedavit before sexual intercourse. * No marriage is legally complete without the *Samâvesana Mantra*, and the *Samâvesana Mantra* plainly and explicitly indicates the age when it enjoins—" Unite ye *lingâs* that are covered with hair." Pre-pubescent marriage is a mock-marriage and is unquestionably unvedic.

At this point the *Yâjusha Pryoga Pârijâta*, the Book of Ritual, which now is in use, stops and proceeds to the *Nâka Bali* ceremony. But the *Sankalpa* of our *Vedavit* is not accomplished; nor the wifehood of the bride secured. † He has patiently and intelli-

---

* Fowler in his "Hereditary Laws" says:—" Let parents learn and remember, then, that their prospective children will be the images of themselves, reflecting all their shades of feeling and phases of character; inheriting similar tastes, swayed by similar passions, governed by kindred sentiments, debased by kindred vices; ennobled by kindred virtues, adorned by kindred graces, and endowed with similar powers, great, good, or bad, happy or miserable, as they themselves may be." (Vivaha Nisheka Dharma Pradipika p. 29.)

† Harihara in his Commentary on *Pâraskara* says:— " Even when, through inability to abstain for the longer period, the three nights' period is chosen, after the completion of the fourth nights' ceremony, intercourse may happen on the fifth and succeeding nights; the wifehood of the bride is not secured until the fourth night's ceremony is over, as it is a part of the marriage ritual." (Marriage after Puberty, page. 16.)

సంవత్సరాది పక్షాశక్తౌ ।

త్రిరాత్రపక్షాశ్రయణేపి చతుర్థీకర్మానంతరం పంచమ్యా

gently prepared the "soil," but "the living seed" has not been planted. To stop at this point is evidently a case of much Ado about Nothing. To prepare elaborately the soil and the seed, and not to plant the seed in the soil is clearly unwise and even foolish. The ludicrous nature of pre-pubescent marriage is most apparent here, and the needless trouble given to the *Devâs* most glaring. What have the *Prasavâdi Devatas* and *Prajâpati* to do if the *Garbhâdhâna* (placing the "seed") is not to take place? Therefore it is that the *Sutrakârâs* * insist upon the *Garbhâdhâna* ceremony being performed on the fourth night. The *Samâvesana* ceremony is the prelude to the *Garbhâdhâna* ceremony, and the separation of the two by any long interval of time is unnatural and *unsâstraic.*

20. THE GARBHADHANA.

The *Garbhâdhâna Mantrâs* are chanted by the husband immediately before sexual intercourse. The contents are intended to furnish the parties with information as to how they should behave during the

---

దిరాత్రావభిగమనం । చతుర్థీకర్మణః ప్రాక్తస్యాభార్యాత్వమే వనసంవృత్తం వివాహైకదేశత్వాచ్చతుర్థీకర్మణః ॥

संवत्सरादिपक्षाशक्तौत्रिरात्रपक्षाश्रयणेपिचतुर्थीकर्मानंतरं पंचम्यादिरात्रावभिगमनम् ।

चतुर्थीकर्मणः प्राक्तस्याभार्यात्वमेवनसंवृत्तम् । विवाहैक देशत्वाच्चतुर्थीकर्मणः ।

* Jaimini, Baudhayana, Hiranyakesin, and Apastamba, for instance.

performance of the holy act. The act of procreation should be a conscious and deliberate act with clearly defined objects in view, not an act of revelry and dissipation, the consequences of which are, indeed, most serious. George Combe in his Constitution of Man gives the following case in point:—"In the summer of 1827, the practitioner alluded to was called upon to visit professionally a young woman in the immediate neighbourhood, who was safely delivered of a male child. As the parties appeared to be respectable, he made some enquiries regarding the absence of the child's father; when the old woman told him that her daughter was still unmarried; that the child's father belonged to a regiment in Ireland; that last autumn he obtained leave of absence to visit his relations in this part of the country, and that on the eve of his departure to join his regiment an entertainment was given at which her daughter attended. During the whole evening she and the soldier danced and sang together; when heated by the toddy and the dance, they left the cottage, and after the lapse of an hour were found together in a glen, in a state of utter insensibility from the effects of their former festivity; and the consequence of this interview was the birth of an idiot. He is now nearly six years of age, and his mother does not believe that he is able to recognise either herself or any other individual. He is quite incapable of making signs whereby his wants can be made known—with this exception that, when hungry, he gives a wild shriek. This is a case upon which it would be painful to dwell; and I shall only remark that the parents are both intelligent, and that the fatal result cannot be otherwise accounted for than by the total prostration or eclipse in the intellect of both parties from intoxication." The *Maharshis* recognised clearly the importance of the holy act of procreation, and so there is one whole *Sukta* for it. The *Mantrâs* are somewhat as follow :—

(1) May *Vishnu* make thy *Yôni* (*linga*) fit to bear the *garbha* (foetus)! May *Prajâpati* enter my body and eject the *rethus* (seed) duly and well! May *Dhâtri* make the *rethus* develop into a foetus in thy *Yôni*! May *Tvashta* (the Fashioner of Forms), develop the forms thereof! *

(2). O bride, shadowed thou art now by *Sinivâli* and *Sarasvati*; bear now the *garbha* then! May the *Asvins*, whose garlands are of lotuses, preserve the *garbha* in thee! †

---

* విష్ణుర్యోనింకల్పయతు త్వష్టారూపాణి పింశతు ।
ఆసించతు ప్రజాపతిర్ధాతా గర్భందధాతు తే ॥

विष्णुर्योनिंकल्पयतुत्वष्टारूपाणिपिंशतु ।
आसिंचतुप्रजापतिर्धाता गर्भंदधातुते ।

† గర్భంధేహి సినీవాలి గర్భంధేహి సరస్వతి ।
గర్భంతే అశ్వినౌదేవావాధత్తాం పుష్కరస్రజా ॥

गर्भंधेहिसिनीवालि गर्भंधेहिसरस्वति ।
गर्भंते अश्विनौदेवा वाधत्तांपुष्करस्रजा ।

(3). May the *Asvins* protect the receptacle which is like unto a golden *Arani* in which thy *garbha* is developed! May thy *garbha*, developed unto the tenth month, become fit for delivery, containing progeny beautiful like the *Asvins* themselves! *

(4). Like unto the great earth, who, lying motionless, doth receive the seed, do thou now receive the seed; do thou now receive the *garbha* that becomes fit for delivery in the tenth month.†

(5) Like unto the Earth that bears Agni, like unto Dyaus that bears Indra, like unto the *Diks* that bear Vâyu, do thou bear the *garbha* that I do place in thee.‡

---

* హిరణ్యయీ అరణీయంనిర్మంథతో అశ్వినా ।
తంతేగర్భంహవామహేదశమేమాసిసూతవే ॥

हिरण्ययी अरणीयंनिर्मंथतो अश्विना ।
तंतेगर्भं हवामहेदशमेमासिसूतवे ॥

† యథేయంపృథివీ మహీంతిష్ఠంతీగర్భమాదధే ।
ఏవంత్వం గర్భమాధత్స్వ దశమేమాసిసూతవే ॥

यथेयं पृथिवीमहीतिष्ठंतीगर्भमादधे ।
एवंत्वंगर्भमाधत्स्व दशमेमासिसूतवे ।

‡ యథాపృథివ్యగ్నిగర్భా ద్యౌర్యథేంద్రేణ గర్భిణీ ।
వాయుర్యథాదిశాంగర్భ ఏవంగర్భం దధామితే ॥

यथापृथिव्यग्निगर्भाद्यौर्यथेन्द्रेणगर्भिणी ।
वायुर्यथादिशांगर्भ एवंगर्भं दधामिते ॥

(6) O Vishnu, do thou in this pleasing woman, develop a *garbha* that emerges as a beautiful male in the tenth month! *

(7) O Nejamesha! be thou far away! If approach thou must, approach thou with progeny! Preserve thou the *garbha* in her that is my half and that is desirous of progeny! Let that progeny be male.†

(8) O bride, do thou receive my *rethus* distending thy *Yôni*. Be that *rethas* male! Bear thou him for ten months. May he be born as the boldest of the bold among his kin! ‡

---

* విష్ణోశ్రేష్ఠేనరూపేణా స్యాంనార్యాంగవీన్యాం। పుమాగ్ం సంగర్భమాధేహి దశమేమాసి సూతవే ॥

विष्णोश्रेष्ठेनरूपेणास्यांनार्यांगवीन्यां । पुमाꣳ संगर्भमाधे हि दशमे-मासिसूतवे ।

† నేజమేషపరాపత సపుత్రః పునరాపత। అస్యైమే పుత్రకామాయైగర్భమాధేహి యః పుమాన్ ॥

नेजमेषपरापतसपुत्तः पुनरापत, अस्यैमेपुत्रकामायै गर्भमाधे हि यः पुमान् ।

‡ వ్యస్యయోనింప్రతిరేతో గృహాణ పుమాన్పుత్రోధీయతాం గర్భో అంతః। తంమాతాదశమాసోబిభర్తుసజాయతాం వీరతమస్వానాం ॥

व्यस्ययोनिंप्रतिरेतोगृहाण । पुमान् पुत्रोधीयतांगर्भो अंतः ।
तंमातादशमासो बिभर्तुसजायतांवीरतमस्स्वानाम् ॥

(9) May the *garbha* make its way well into thy *Yôni*! May that *garbha*, making its way well into thy *Yôni*, lodge therein as doth the arrow in the quiver! May the male progeny, borne for ten months, be born as the boldest of the bold! * .

(10) "With thee do I now perform the act of procreation! Let the seed lodge well in thee. May he be born endowed with all perfections—without the thoughts of *Pishâchâs*, without lameness, without defects!" †

(11) Well, my woman! May thy first-born be a son! May other sons follow him! May the Rishabha Devatas generate in us both such prosperous seeds only! ‡

---

* ఆతే గర్భో యోనిమేతు పుమాన్బాణ ఇవేషుధిం ।
ఆవీరో జాయతాం పుత్రస్తే దశమాస్యః ॥

आतेगर्भो योनिमेतु पुमान्बाणइवेषुधिम् आवीरोजायतांपुत्रस्तेदश
मास्यः ।

† కరోమి తే ప్రాజాపత్యమా గర్భో యోనిమేతు తే ।
అనూనః పూర్ణో జాయతామ శ్లోణో పిశాచధీతః ॥

करोमितेप्राजापत्यमागर्भोयोनिमेतु ते ।
अनूनःपूर्णोजायतामश्लोणोऽपिशाचधीतः ।

‡ పుమాగ్ంస్తే పుత్రో నారితం పుమానను జాయతాం ।
తానిభద్రాణి బీజాన్యృషభా జనయంతు నౌ ॥

पुमांँस्तेपुत्रोनारितं पुमाननुजायतां ।
तानिभद्राणिबीजान्यृषभाजनयंतुनौ ॥

(12) May the Rishabha Devatas bless us with such prosperous seeds only! Bring thou forth progeny! Shine thou like unto the *Dhenu* (milch-cow)! *

(13) "May my act, which is brimful of such desires, progress unhindered! May my act be unfrustrated! O Vâyu, help thou me in the attainment of this my desire." †

Such are the prayers devoutly offered by our *Vedavit* before commencing the holy act of procreation. He then sprinkles consecrated water on his spouse, and commences the sexual act. Comment is needless. How unnatural the separation of the *Samâvesana mantrâs* is from those of the *garbhâdhâna mantrâs* by a long period of time, is self-evident. How the institution of pre-pubescent marriage has marred and mauled the lofty and noble Vedic Ideal needs now no pointing out.

---

* యానిభద్రాణి బీజాన్యృషభా జనయంతినః ।
తైస్త్వంపుత్రాన్విందస్వసా ప్రసూర్ధేనుకాభవ ॥

यानिभद्राणिबीजान्यृषभाजनयंतिनः ।
तैस्त्वं पुत्रान् विन्दस्वसाप्रसूर्धेनुकाभव ।

† కామప్రమృధ్యతాం మహ్యామ పరాజితమేవమే ।
యంకామంకామయేదేవతం మేవాయోసమర్ధయ ॥

कामप्रमृध्यतांमह्यमपराजितमेव मे ।
यंकामंकामयेदेवतं मेवायोसमर्धय ॥

S. R. Wells exclaims :—"Than a happy union of two ripe, rich, congenial, and loving human hearts, satisfied and cemented in a thorough understanding of each other, and a perfect adaptation to each other in the well-adjusted bonds of holy wedlock, what can be more pleasing to contemplate!" *

What is even now a speculative dream with the advanced American investigators was an accomplished fact, for a time at least, with the Aryans thousands of years ago!

The position assigned to woman by the Hindu Sâstras is the highest and best in the world. Mr. Har Bilas Sarda Says :—

"The high ethical teachings of the *Hindu Sâstras* prepared the men to assign to women a peculiarly privileged position, keeping them safe from the rough and degrading work that now often falls to their lot in the West in consequence of the severe struggle for existence raging there. While providing the freest possible scope for the exercise of their peculiar gifts, which enabled them to achieve in the superlative degree, the high and noble work which it is the privilege of women to perform for the well-being and advancement of a people, the ancient Hindu constitution not only accorded to them the position which the mothers, the sisters, the wives, and the daughters of

* See Vivaha Nisheka Dharma Pradipika. p. 6.

the highest and the lowest in the nation are justly entitled to, but (also that) which enabled their true feminine nature and character to receive full development so as to fulfil their high destiny of giving to the world a race of men yet unequalled in intellect, character and energy.

"In Europe, as well as in India, the woman is styled 'the half of the man'—in Europe as 'the *better* half', in India, simply as *Ardhângini*(lit. half-self). In Europe (and America), however, it is a meaningless phrase, rather pointing to the desirability of assigning woman a position which is hers by nature than signifying the position actually occupied by her—showing the desirable but yet unattained ideality rather than, as amongst the Hindus, an actual reality. No doubt there are women in Europe, who, as wives, are treated by their husbands with the same respect and generous consideration as Hindu ladies command in all truly Hindu families. True, in every grade of European Society, women are to be met with, whose position, domestic as well as social, is not only perfectly happy and satisfactory, but, to all outward appearance, looks higher than that enjoyed by their Hindu sisters: true also, that European women enjoy in some respects, and in certain directions, privileges neither enjoyed by any Asiatic women nor desired by them. They enjoy a freedom of action in certain matters which is not only one of the distinguishing features of the European civilization, but emphasizes the negation of all that is meant by *Ardhângini* or the half. In Europe, woman has a distinct individuality of her own, which flourishes independently of man, though by his side and connected with him. Both men and women there lead separate, distinct, independent lives, albeit nature and necessity compel them to live together. Not so in India. Woman has no distinctive, independent individuality in Hindu social polity. From her birth to her death she is a part of man, and cannot be separated from him. With marriage, she merges her individuality into her husband's, and both together form a single entity in society. The one without the other is only a part and not a whole.

"It must not, however, be supposed that the woman loses herself in the man, and is, therefore, inferior to him. The man, too, after his union with woman is, like her, only a part of the social entity. All important religious, social, and domestic concerns of life recognise the entity only when it is complete, *i.e.*, formed of a man and a woman.

"In Europe, the power and position enjoyed by woman are not recognised by the authority which sanctions all social law, and on which the entire fabric of society is ultimately based. What position and privilege she enjoys, she evidently cannot claim as of right—a right inherent in and inseparable from womanhood. In some of the most important concerns of life she is utterly ignored. Not so amongst the Hindus. In India she is in possession of her rights, which no power on Earth can take away from her. The Hindu woman is not indebted, like her European sister, for her position to a man's love or affectionate regard, or to the exigencies of social life. It is her birth-right, inalienable, and recognised by all ; it lives with her and dies with her. Man is as much subject to it as the woman is to a man's. Take, for instance, the most important concern of life, the *marriage*. In Europe, the father gives away the daughter ; in his absence, the brother, or the uncle or some other male relation, as the case may be. He by himself performs this sacred and most important function in life. Where comes in the *better half* of the father, the brother, the uncle, or other relation ? She has no place in the rite, no *locus standi*, no indispensable, inalienable position in the function. She is not a necessary party. She may be happy in the event and join the festivities, but she is an utter outsider so far as the rite itself—the right of giving away—is concerned. But what do we find in India ? Amongst the Hindus, in order that the ceremony of giving away (called *Kanyâdâna*) may be complete, the *Ardhângini*, or the wife of the father, the brother, the uncle or other male relative must take part in it. The "giving away" is not complete till the husband and the wife both do it. Nay, there is something more to mark the unalterable position of the wife as the "other half" of the husband. If, owing to any cause—death, illness or unavoidable absence—the better half of the father, brother or the other relative cannot be present at the sacrament, a piece of cloth or something else is placed by his side, as a substitute for her, to show that he, by himself, is only an incomplete individual, and cannot perform the most important functions of life unless and until joined by his wife. And it is so not with marriage only. From the marriage down to a dip in the sacred Ganges; the worship of the sacred *bar tree* (the Ficus Indica) in the *Bar Tirat* ceremony (when the wife keeps a fast for three days); the worship of the household gods, and other simple, ordinary duties, ordained by religion or sanctioned by social usage, no ceremony is complete unless the wife joins the husband in its performance. What a difference here between the respective positions of the European and the Hindu woman! How inferior is the position of a European woman to that of her Hindu sister! With all the love and devotion she receives and the freedom of action she enjoys, she in Europe is even now as far away from the position of the *other half* of a man as she was two thousand years ago. But society in Europe is still in its making. Important and far-reaching changes will yet have to be made before it arrives at a stage of evolution, when it will come into line with its sister organization, the Hindu Society, as it is found in the *Sâstras.*

"In the west, woman's sphere is yet limited; woman's position yet precarious, owing to the selfish and hypocritical conduct of man, the product of a material civilization divorced from spiritual ideals. Their principal interest in public affairs, however, is directed to secure for themselves rights which they regard as essential to assure their position in the cold, pitiless struggle for existence, which respects neither age nor sex. In ancient India people never thought of usurping from women their rights and privileges. They were safe from the turmoil of life; they were secure against the attacks which all have to meet who are governed by the complicated machinery of a civilization based on the worship of Mammon, with its horizon bounded by the desires, aspirations and capabilities of the physical man." (Hindu Superiority, pp. 96—100.)

21. NAKABALI AND THE KANKANA VISARJANA.

Our object is not to describe all the ceremonies of marriage, but only such of them as reveal important truths relating to the question of marriageable age. In the *Nâkabali* ceremony, the *Devas* are sent away first, and then the *Nândi Devatas*. Then the bridegroom and the bride remove their *Kankana* or *Raksha*, as they have finished the ceremony for which they had tied it. The *Sankalpa* of the bridegroom was to marry a young woman for taking up the *Grihastha Asrama Dharma* and begetting *sâttvic* progeny by her. At the *Garbhâdhâna* ceremony he did it, and so he removes the *Kankana* as does his wife also.

22. THE PROBLEM OF PRE-PUBESCENT MARRIAGE.

We have explained the leading *mantras* of the marriage ceremony. We find that they are all intended for post-pubescent marriages only. There cannot be the least doubt of this. The advocates of pre-pubescent marriages use the *mantras* clearly composed for post-pubescent marriages,—what an anomaly this is! We have found pre-pubescent marriage to be a mock marriage and to be unquestionably unvedic, and still no less than eight *Smritikâras* insist on it, and pronounce anathemas recklessly. Going to the *Sutrakâras*, we find some of them wavering in their pronouncements. The Vedas are clearly against it. Examining the actual practice in different parts of India, we find the *Kânya kubjas* of Northern India, the *Nambudiri* Brahmans of Malabar, and *Kshatriyas* in nearly all parts of India still celebrating post-pubescent marriages in spite of the anathemas of eight or more *Smritikâras*. * Were these eight or more *Smritikâras* ignorant of the *Vivâha Mantras*? It is hard to say they were. Then why do they denounce post-pubescent marriages? The confusion into which Hindu Society has fallen is really deplorable. Some want to ascribe the introduction of pre-pubescent marriage to the ravages, depredations, and oppressions of the Mussalmans; but there are reasons to believe that pre-pubescent marriage existed in India long before the time of the Mussalman Invasions. † What shall we do in these circumstances? How are

---

* In some families of *Mandyam Brahmans*, the couple are made on the fourth night to lie together for a couple of minutes or so with a blanket covering them. In the Telugu country, to this day, after the *Nâgavalli* ceremony is over, the couple sit together on a cot for sometime with a baby-doll on the brides' lap. Clearer indications of the ancient custom (of post-pubescent marriage) exist in Bengal. Though child-marriage is as prevalent there as elsewhere, the practice seems to be kept up of allowing the couple to come together at night whenever they happen to be under the same roof. (Marriage after Puberty, page. 23.)

† The *Chândogya Upanishat*, which is much older than the time of the Mahomedan Invasions, has :—" When owing to thunder and hail there was famine in the *Kuru* country, *Ushasti Châkrâyana* with his *immature* wife went in distress to the village of the lord of Elephants." (Marriage after Puberty, p. 28.)

we to account for the existing state of things? Will History help us?

23. Manu's Prophecy.

There is a passage in the second chapter of *Manu Smriti*, which states that it is the mission of India to teach all the nations of the world. This is, indeed, a remarkable statement. Says Manu * :—" The region between the sacred rivers Sarasvati and Drishadvati is formed by the *Devas*, and Brahmâvarta it is called. The *Achâras* established in this country, and adhered to by the four *Varnas* with their subdivisions, have become famous as *Sadâchâras*. Kurukshetra, Matsya, Pânchâla and Sûrasena form what has been called Brahmarshi Desa, and they are very near to Brahmâvarta. From the First-born of these countries all the men in the world are to have their schooling."

The wonderful researches of two great men Count Bjornstjerna and Mr. Pococke—have shown Manu's

---

సరస్వతీ దృషద్వత్యోః దేవనద్యోర్యదంతరం। తందేవనిర్మితందేశం బ్రహ్మావర్తం ప్రచక్షతే॥ తస్మిన్దేశేయ ఆచారః పారంపర్యక్రమాగతః। వర్ణానాం సాంతరాళానాం ససదాచారఉచ్యతే॥ కురుక్షేత్రంచమత్స్యాశ్చపాంచాలాశ్శూరసేనకాః । ఏషబ్రహ్మర్షిదేశోవై బ్రహ్మావర్తాదనంతరః॥ ఏతద్దేశప్రసూతస్య సకాశాదగ్రజన్మనః। స్వంస్వంచరిత్రం శిక్షేరన్ పృథివ్యాంసర్వమానవాః॥

सरस्वतीदृषद्वत्योर्देवनद्योर्यदंतरम् ॥ तंदेवनिर्मितंदेशंब्रह्मावर्तं प्रचक्षते ॥ तस्मिन् देशेयआचारःपारंपर्यक्रमागतः ॥ वर्णानांसान्तरालानांस सदाचारउच्यते ॥ कुरुक्षेत्रंचमत्स्याश्च पांचालाश्शूरसेनकाः । एषब्रह्मर्षिदेशो वैब्रह्मावर्तादनन्तरः ॥ एतद्देशप्रसूतस्य सकाशादग्रजन्मनः । स्वंस्वंचरित्रंशिक्षेरन् पृथिव्यांसर्वमानवाः ।

statement to·be true. Count Bjornstjerna in his Theogony of the Hindus says :—"It is there (Aryâvarta) we seek not only for the cradle of the Brahmin religion, but the cradle of the High Civilization of the Hindus; which gradually extended itself in the West to Ethiopia, to Egypt, to Phoenicia; in the East, to Siam, to China, and to Japan; in the South, to Ceylon, to Java, and to Sumatra; in the North, to Persia, to Chaldea, and to Colchis, whence it came to Greece and to Rome, and at length to the remote abode of the Hyperboreans". There is now a large mass of evidence to show that the remarkable civilization of Ancient Egypt was Indian in its origin. Those who feel interested in this interesting question may refer to the *Indian Review* of January, 1908, where the Hon. Alex. Del Mar, of New York, states the evidence in a very able article entitled "Indian Marks upon Early Egypt." Mr. Pococke in his "India in Greece" brings to light a large mass of evidence, which goes to show that the talented Greeks were but Hindu tribes. "If the evidences of Saxon Colonization in this Island (Great Britain)," says Mr. Pococke, "are strong both from language and political institutions, the evidences are still more decisive in the parallel case of an Indian Colonization of Greece—not only her language but her philosophy, her religion, her rivers, her mountains and her tribes; her subtle turn of intellect, her political institutes, and above all, the mysteries of that noble land, irresistibly prove her colonization from India." We know that Buddhism had its birth in India. "As regards the propagation of Buddhist doctrines, it is probable that at one time they spread over the whole world. In Burmah, Siam, in most of the islands of the Indian Archipelago and Ceylon, in Thibet, Mongolia, Japan, Nepal, Bhutan and the Lesser Thibet, it is still the prevailing religion; but that at one time it spread to Turkistan, Persia, Egypt, and Rome, and even Scandinavia and the British Islands, is most probable." *

It is hardly an exaggeration to say that knowledge and civilization went forth to the world from India. The Mathematical Sciences were first cultivated and elaborated in India. The Medical Science of the Greeks and the Arabs is Hindu. In recent times, Europe has had her Philology, and America her Yoga Philosophy from India. Theosophy has made India its home, and India has presented to the world that Priceless Book, that Bible of Humanity—the Bhagavad Gita. But India has one very peculiar institution, which she has reserved to herself, and which is unknown in other parts of the world, *viz.*, a

* Mr. Har Bilas Sarda in his "Hindu Superiority" has devoted one whole part, consisting of 12 chapters, to the elucidation of the question of Hindu Colonization. All lovers of India will do well to make a regular study of his book.

rigid caste system. Where was the necessity for this institution, and what important purpose has it served? These questions are important, but it is very difficult to answer them satisfactorily. We shall, however, try; but to do so we have first to know some important things about the several races of mankind and their manner of development.

24. THE ROOT RACES.

The evolution of the elements is stated in our *Sâstras* as follows:—ఆకాశాద్వాయుః, వాయోరగ్నిః, అగ్నేరాపః, అద్భ్యః పృథివీ (आकाशाद्वायुः, वायोरग्निः । अग्नेरापः —— ——) From *Akâs* comes forth *Vâyu*; from *Vâyu*, *Agni*; from *Agni*, *Apah*; from *Apah*, earth. The characteristics of the elements are respectively sound (శబ్ద शब्द), Touch (స్పర్శ स्पर्श), Form (రూప रूप), Taste, (రస रस), and smell (గంధ गन्ध.)The law of development is what is called ఏకోత్తరవృద్ధి एकोत्तरवृद्धिः (*Ekôttara Vriddhi*), that is, each element, as it evolves, adds to its own characteristic those of its predecessor. Thus *Akâs* has the characteristic of Sound; *Vâyu* or air has the characteristics of Sound and Touch; *Agni* those of Sound, Touch, and Form or colour; *Apah* those of Sound, Touch, Form and Taste; *earth* those of Sound, Touch, Form, Taste and Smell. In the development of animals including man, a similar Law prevails; that is, each Root-Race adds the characteristic sense of the preceding Race, as each element adds its own characteristic to those of its predecessor. Aryan Philosophy speaks of animals with one sense (ఏకేంద్రియప్రాణి एकेन्द्रियप्राणि), animals with two senses (ద్విరింద్రియప్రాణి द्विरिन्द्रियप्राणि), animals with three senses త్రిరింద్రియప్రాణి (त्रिरिन्द्रियप्राणि.), animals with four senses (చతురింద్రియప్రాణి चतुरिन्द्रियप्राणि) and animals with five senses (పంచేంద్రియప్రాణి पञ्चेन्द्रियप्राणि). Human evolution also proceeds on the same lines. The First Root-Race (ఏకేంద్రియమానవమహాకుల एकेन्द्रियमानवमहाकुल) was ethereal and was dimly conscious of sounds only. The Second Root Race (ద్విరింద్రియమానవమహాకుల द्विरिन्द्रियमानवमहाकुल) was boneless, had two senses—Hearing and Touch, and could hear sounds and touch objects. The Third Root-Race (త్రిరింద్రియ మానవమహాకుల त्रिरिन्द्रियमानवमहाकुल) had three senses,—Hearing, Touch, and Sight—and could hear, touch, and see. The Fourth Root-Race (చతురింద్రియమానవమహాకుల चतुरिन्द्रियमानवमहाकुल), which was the first physical race in the proper sense of the term, had four senses—Hearing, Touch, Sight, and Taste—and so could hear, touch, see, and taste. The Fifth Root-Race (పంచేంద్రియ మానవమహాకుల पञ्चेन्द्रियमानवमहाकुल) has five senses—Hearing, Touch, Sight, Taste, and Smell—and can hear, touch, see, taste, and smell. Thus has Humanity developed.

Each Root-Race has seven sub-races (*Sâkhâkula*). The first two Root-Races were boneless, and so we may leave them out of consideration as not wanted for our purpose. The Third and the Fourth Root-Races have each had seven sub-races; and of the Fifth or Aryan Race five sub-races,—the Aryans of India, the Aryan-Semetic peoples, the Parsis or Iranians, the Celts and the Teutons—have already appeared.

The Third Root-Race flourished on the continent of Lemuria or *Sâlmali*, which was destroyed by volcanic eruptions. The Early Third Race was born under *Sukra*, Venus; and under this influence, the hermaphrodites were evolved; the later sub-races separated into sexes under Lohitanga, Mars, who is the embodiment of *Kâma*, the passion-nature. Like all the forms then on Earth, Man was gigantic in bulk, compared with his present size. The Third Race men were, according to modern ideas of beauty, ugly in appearance. "The head with retreating forehead, the dully lurid eye, glowing redly over the flattened nose, the projecting heavy jaws," offered a repulsive picture. A few remnants of the Third Race men are now found here and there. The *Dânavas* were the sixth and seventh sub-races of the Third Root Race.

The early sub-races of the Fourth Root-Race flourished on the continent of Atlantis or *Kusa*, which contained two groups of countries inhabited by two races

—a fighting warrior race (*Asuras*) and a pious meditative race (*Suras*). The pious group of countries was continually visited by the gods or *Devas*. The belligerent group was inhabited by various beings, invulnerable by iron, who could be mortally wounded only by stone and wood. The later sub-races of the Fourth Race were non-spiritual.

25. THE ORIGIN OF THE FIFTH OR ARYAN RACE.

Mrs. Besant says :—" The Dragons of wisdom (the *Maharshis*) bade one of their number, *Vaivasvata*, choose out of the turbulent fifth sub-race (of the Fourth), the Semetic, the seeds of the Fifth Root-Race, and lead them to the Imperishable Sacred Land (around the North Pole), the cradle, as before said, of every Root-Race. One million years have rolled away since the seeds of the Fifth Race were thus separated out from the Fourth. To that impregnable fortress were led successive emigrations of the elect Race to be guarded in safety through the coming tumults (the sinking of Atlantis or *Kusa*), far away from the scenes of strife. In that peaceful sunny land we may see *Vaivasvata* presiding over his disciples and the infant, nay, embryonic Race. There is the future Zarathustra, the future Hermes, the future Orpheus, the future *Gautama*, the future *Maitreya*, with many another watching over the growing seed." (Pedigree of Man, page 138.)

"Meanwhile the surface of the globe is undergoing manifold changes of land and sea. The new continent *Krauncha*—the Europe, Asia, Africa, America, Australia—of our own age is not yet born; with many throes one portion after another is upheaved and others are submerged, until the great convulsion of 200,000 years ago left Poseidonis alone in Mid Atlantic, and the outlines of the great continents much as they are to-day. (Pedigree of Man, p. 145.)

"Under *Budha*, Mercury, was the Fifth or Aryan Race evolved, for the development of the mind was its chief work, and the Planet of Knowledge shed its beneficent rays upon its birth-hour. Hence in Puranic story, *Budha* is said to be the son of *Indu*—*Indu*, the moon, being the Lord of the Fourth Race, the Progenitor, and *Budha* of the Fifth Race, the progeny.

When the Manu had established the type of His Race, He led them southwards to Central Asia, and there another age-long halt was made; and the home of the Race, whence its several streams should issue, was established.

Then came the First Emigration perhaps some 850,000 years ago; the first sub-race—often specifically called the Aryan, though the name applies to the whole Fifth Race—was led southwards, across the mighty belt of the Himalayas, and settled in Northern

India, in Aryavarta.* At its head were the seven *Rishis*—Marichi, Atri, Pulastya, Pulaha (Kavi), Angiras (? Kratu), Kardama and Daksha—the names vary in different lists—who had long been guiding their evolution. In *Manu Smriti* we find them given as above, save that Daksha is called Prachetas. With them were three others, making up the "ten *Rishis*," Vasishtha, Bhrigu and Nârada. These led the sub-race into India, already built into the fourfold order by Manu, the *Bârhishad Pitris* having lent their aid in the shaping of the type of subtle body for each caste. ... ... It must suffice us to recall that these Aryans received the Zodiac directly from the *Sons of Will and Yoga*, who came among them as Teachers, ... that they had brought with them from Central Asia the Senzar language, "the secret sacerdotal tongue," the true language of the gods, from which Samskrit † was derived, still "the mystery tongue of the Initiates," that among them arose the twenty-four

* In the days of the Mahabharata and for long after, Afghanistan was a part of Aryavarta.

† Samskrit means perfect, finished. The Samskrit language is, according to Prof. Bopp, more perfect and copious than the Greek and the Latin, and more exquisite and eloquent than either. Prof. MaxMüller remarks that Samskrit is to the science of Language what Mathematics is to Astronomy.

Buddhas,still reverenced among the Jains as the twenty-four *Tirthankaras*." (Pedigree of Man, pp. 146-7.)

"Nations have characteristics, just as have individuals, and among the characteristics, of the Hindu (Aryan) Nation in old days were *order* and *balance*. The *Sanâtana Dharma* stamped these characteristics on the people, and thus shaped a very-dignified type of man, evenly developed and well-balanced. So much are these the characteristics of the true follower of the *Sanâtana Dharma*, that Sri Krishna said: "Equilibrium is called Yoga." (Elementary Text Book of the Sanatana Dharma, page 101.)

These are the Aryans, the first sub-race, "*the Agra Janmas*" mentioned by Manu; and from these may the other races of the world rightly have their civilizations *—at all events the noble ideal of the Aryan marriage which we have examined. Let us now see by what nations or sub-races these were surrounded.

26. THE SURROUNDING NATIONS.

The surrounding nations were mostly men of the

---

* Says Mousieur Delbos :—"The influence of that civilization worked out thousands of years ago in India is around and about us every day of our lives. It pervades every corner of the civilized world. Go to America, and you find there, as in Europe, the influence of that civilization which came originally from the banks of the Ganges." Hindu Superiority, p. 200.

Fourth Root Race; some were remnants of the Third Root Race; some others, mixed races:—

(1). **Lemurian Remnants**:—Where a really black race is found, such as the Negro, Lemurian descent is strongly marked. (Pedigree of Man, p. 114.)

(2). **The Dravidians**:—These are a mixture of the Seventh Lemurian sub-race with the second Atlantean sub-race. (Pedigree of Man, p. 123.)

(3). **The Turanians or Turashkas**:—These were the fourth sub-race of the Fourth Race. They were pre-eminently the *Râkshasas*, giants of a brutal and ferocious type, and their conflicts with the young fifth Race (Aryan) find much place in Indian story.

(4). **The Semetic Races**:—These were the fifth sub-race of the Fourth Race. These were a turbulent fighting people, and a branch of one of their families, selected by *Vaivasvata Manu* as the seed of the Fifth Race (Aryan) and rejected again because of its lack of plasticity is the far-off ancestor of the Jewish people. (Pedigree of Man, page 143.)

(5) **The Akkadians**:—These were the sixth sub-race of the Fourth Race. One-third of these went North, and later on mixed with the fifth evolving Race.

(6) **The Mongolians**:—These were the seventh sub-race of the Fourth Race. They sprang from the

Turanian stock, and from these have descended the inland Chinese—the Malays, Tibetans, Hungarians (*Hunas*), Finns, and Esquimaux; some of their offshoots mixed with the *Toltecs* in North America, and thus the Red Indians have in them some Mongolian blood. The Japanese are one of their latest offshoots. Many of this sub-race travelled westwards, settling down in Asia Minor, Greece, and adjoining countries; there improved by the intermixture of Fifth Race (Aryan) blood, from the second sub-race of the Fifth, they gave rise to the old Greeks and the Phoenicians. (Pedegree of Man, p. 144.)

(7). **The Aryan-Semetic Nation**:—This was the second sub-race of the Fifth Race. They migrated westwards from Central Asia, peopling Afghanistan, passing along the Oxus, and crossing the Euphrates into Arabia and Syria; these aryanised many of the Turanian and Akkadian tribes, dwelling along this route, and the great Empires of Assyria and Babylonia arose as the result of their impulse. The Phoenicians and the later Egyptians and the old Greeks arose from their intermixture with the seventh Atlantean sub-race. "The last seven dynasties referred to in the Egyptian and Chaldean records," says H.P.B., "belonged to the Fifth Race." Some offshoots of this Race travelled eastwards, and mingling with the Mongolian sub-race along the coasts of China, gave rise to the Chinese of the coasts, and also to the family which now sits on the Dragon throne of China. * (Pedigree of Man, page. 148.)

(8). **The Iranians**:—The Iranians are the third sub-race of the Fifth Race. They, led by Zarathustra, went forth northwards and eastwards, following in the track of the second, but settling down for the most part in Afghanistan and Persia, the great Prophet dwelling in this latter country. Some wandered as far as Arabia, and thence into Egypt, inter-marrying there with the Egyptian Atlanteans." (Pedigree of Man, p. 148.) These Iranians were given Fire as the sole permissible symbol of Deity.

Our Samskrit Literature teems with the names of *Dasyus* (a black race), *Dânavas* (the sixth and seventh sub-races of the Third Race), *Daityas* (the third sub-race of the Fourth Race), *Râkshasas* (the fourth sub-race of the Fourth Race), *Hunas* (a branch of the seventh sub-race of the Fourth Race), *Sakas*, *Yavanas* (Ionians, a mixed race), *Chinas* (the seventh sub-race of the Fourth Race), and *Dravidas* (a mixed

---

* According to the traditions noted in the *Schuking*, the ancestors of the Chinese conducted by Fohi came to the plains of China 2,900 years before Christ, from the High Mountainland which lies to the west of that country. This shows that the settlers into China were originally inhabitants of Kashmir, Ladakh, Little Thibet, and Panjab, which were parts of Ancient India. (Hindu Superiority, page 181.)

race). The Aryans were prohibited from intermarrying with these peoples. Why ? Let us know the characteristics of the Fourth Race Men.

27. THE FOURTH RACE PEOPLES.

"The great Toltec sub-race (the third sub-race of the Fourth Root Race, known in our Puranas as *Daityas*) was a race handsome and well-cut in feature, gigantic still, some twenty-seven feet in height, but well-modelled in figure, red to red-brown in colour. Their bodies and those of the fourth (Turanian) and fifth (Semetic) sub-races were denser in material than any before or since; of a hardness sufficient to bend a bar of the iron of the present day, were it launched against them; or to break a bar of our steel, were they heavily struck by it; one of our knives would not cut their flesh, any more than it would cut a piece of the present-day rock. Needless to add that the minerals of their day were so much harder than our own, that their relative hardness to these human bodies was much as that of our minerals to our bodies now. Another peculiarity was the extraordinary recuperative power they possessed; they recovered from the most ghastly and extensive wounds, received in battle or accident, the flesh joining and healing with the most astonishing rapidity; nor did they at all suffer from nervous shock, consequent on serious lacerations, nor suffer very keenly from physical torture or even that inflicted by deliberate human cruelty. The nervous organisation was strong but not fine, nor was it delicately balanced in its internal co-ordinations; hence it could stand without injury shocks which would prostrate a man of the Fifth Race, and could endure strains and convulsions that would leave him a nervous wreck. Flesh like rock, nerves like wires of steel, would best describe the bodies of these sub-races. The developing sense of taste answered only to very powerful stimulants, and could not distinguish any delicate flavours; putrid meat, strongly smelling fish, garlic and all herbs of pungent flavour, the sharpest and most fiery solids and liquids, were to them the only delicious foods. All else was tasteless and vapid. As they possessed no sense of smell, they could dwell undisturbed amid the most appalling stenches; and although the higher classes were most scrupulously clean in their persons and dwellings, the neighbourhood of malodorous filth—provided it did not offend the eye—troubled them not at all. Traces of these physical peculiarities still remain in many of their descendants. The North American Indians recover from wounds which would kill the Fifth Race man, whether from injury to tissue or from nervous shock; he can bear, unblenching, tortures under which the Fifth Race man would incontinently faint away. The Burman will bury fish and meat, and find them, in their putrid condition, a toothsome delicacy. And all can live amid smells that would turn the Fifth Race man sick. ... ... In the days of Toltec (*Daitya*) degradation, processes of black magic were resorted to by the upper classes, in order to deprive of this quality those whom they oppressed and enslaved. They not only ceased to train it, as was done in the earlier days, but sought actively to stunt and even to destroy it. Despite all, however, it still remains, to some extent, in many Fourth Race nations and tribes." (Pedigree of Man, pp. 124—26.)

Here then we have the characteristics of the sub-races of the Fourth Race. They had not well developed the sense of taste, and they ate putrid things. They had hardly any sense of smell. The sixth and the seventh sub-races (the Akkadians and the Mongolians), however, had something of it, but still they were distinctly inferior beings. Their character was bad: they were far from being *Sâttvic.* Let us know something of the superior organisation of the Fifth or Aryan Race.

28. THE CHARACTERISTICS OF THE FIFTH OR ARYAN RACE.

(1) "There is, in the Fifth Root-Race, a fuller stream of life pouring down, causing the greater internal development of the permanent atom (Prâtisvika Bhûta Sûkshma) and increasing as that development proceeds. As evolution goes on, there is an increasing

complexity of vibratory powers in the physical permanent atom, a similar increase in the astral atom, and again in the mental unit. As birth follows birth, and these permanent nuclei are put out on each plane to gather round them the new mental, astral and physical encasements, the more highly developed permanent atoms draw round them the more highly developed atoms on the planes to which they belong, and thus build up a better nervous apparatus through which the ever-increasing stream of consciousness can flow."

(2) In the Fifth Race man the internal differentiation of the nervous cells is much increased, and the intercommunications are much more numerous. Speaking generally, the consciousness of the Fifth Race man is working on the astral plane, and is withdrawn from the physical body except so far as the cerebro-spinal nervous system is concerned. The control of the vital organs of the body is left to the sympathetic system, trained through long ages to perform this work, and now kept going by impulses from the astral centres other than the ten, without deliberate attention from the otherwise occupied consciousness, although of course sustained by it.

(3) "The sense organs of the Fifth Race body are less active and acute than those of the highest fourth Race in responding to purely physical impacts. The eye, the ear, the touch do not respond to vibrations which would affect the fourth Race sense-organs.

It is significant also that these organs are at their keenest in early childhood, and diminish in sensitiveness from about the sixth year onward. On the other hand, while less acute in receiving pure sense impacts, they become more sensitive to sensations intermingled with emotions, and delicacies of colour and of sound, whether of nature or of art, appeal to them more effectively. The higher and more intricate organisation of the sense centres in the brain and in the astral body seems to bring about increased sensitiveness to beauty of colour, form, and sound, but diminished response to the sensations in which the emotions play no part."

(4) The Fifth Race body is also far more sensitive to shock than are the bodies of the fourth and third Races, being more dependent upon consciousness for its upkeep. A nervous shock is far more keenly felt, and entails far greater prostration."

(5) "In the highly evolved fifth Race body, mental conditions largely rule the physical, and intense anxiety, mental suffering, and worry, producing nervous tension, readily disturb organic processes and bring about weakness or disease. Hence mental strength and serenity directly promote physical health, and when the consciousness is definitely established on the astral or the mental plane, emotional and mental disturbances are far more productive of ill-health than any privations inflicted on the physical

body." (Extracted from Mrs. Besant's Study in Consciousness, pp. 175-180.)

29. THE CASTE SYSTEM.

When we compare the characteristics of the fourth and the fifth Root Races, we see plainly that a rigid system of caste as regards marriage was absolutely essential if the superior organisation of the Aryan Race was to be maintained untainted; and since India was intended to be a sort of University for the nation-pupils of the world, the *Rishis* organised the four castes or *varnas*, and prescribed appropriate *Samskâras* and duties.

The *varnas* are not the colours of the physical bodies, but the colours of the *Sukshma* or subtle bodies, visible to *Yogic* or clairvoyant vision. As *Varna* and *Varna Sankara* are frequently mentioned in our sacred books, it is necessary that we should have clear and definite ideas on these points.

"All things exist for the sake of the Atma, the Self, and by his will. They exist merely to give him the experiences he desires to pass through. He wills to unfold his powers in the lower worlds, and to become the self-conscious Ruler of the outer realms of denser matter, as he is ever the Inner Ruler, Immortal. He is not in haste, being eternal, and knows it best to take each experience in order, and thus to unfold symmetrically and harmoniously. This order is imposed by Ishvara, the supreme Self on the lower Kingdoms of our world; the seed, the root, the stem, the leaves, the flower, the fruit, succeed each other in due order, and each has its place and its beauty in its season; so also He imposes the stages of human life—infancy, childhood, youth, maturity, old age; this sequence man cannot escape from nor change; but the unfolding *Jivâtma* in man, clouded by the matter he has not yet mastered, pushes irregularly in various directions, led by *Manas* dominated by *Kâma*, grasping at the things of one stage while yet in another, and so hindering his due evolution in each. The child would be a youth, the youth a man; the old man grasps backward at the joys of youth; thus life is robbed of its serenity and thereby of half of its usefulness.

"In order to counteract this mistaken eagerness and lack of balanced order, the great *Rishis* marked out for the eldest-born family of the Aryan race the definite stages in the life of the individual from birth to death, and the definite stages in the life of the *Jivâtma* in his long evolution through myriads of births and deaths. In each case these stages are four: in the life between one birth and one death they are called *Asramas*, resting places, dwellings; in the life passing through countless births and deaths, they are called *Varnâs*, colours, or castes." (Elementary Text Book of Sanatana Dharma, pp. 101-2.)

In the life of the *Jivâtma* there are four stages. "The first is that which includes the infancy, childhood and youth of the *Jivâtma*; he is unfolding youthful virtues, developing obedience, serviceableness, patience; he has few responsibilities; his duties may be summed up in the word, service. Where there is no caste confusion (*Varna Sankara*), such young *Jivâtmas* are born only into the lower social stratum; they are labourers, artisans, servants, manual workers of every kind. In the social polity of the Sanâtana Dharma, such *Jivâtmas* were born into the caste of *Sûdras*. In these days of caste confusion, such young *Jivâtmas* whether born into the *Sûdra* caste in India, or into the corresponding class elsewhere, are happy, contented and useful; but where, as often happens now-a-days, they are born into higher castes, or classes, they do much harm to their surroundings by their incapacity to discharge higher duties, and to bear the weight of higher responsibilities. So also difficulties arise when older *Jivâtmas* are born into the lower bodies, and fret against their environment, are discontented and rebellious. Of course, a really advanced *Jivâtma* is content in any body, but the mediocre *Jivâtmas* quite naturally and inevitably fight against uncongenial surroundings, and their restlessness is used by Isvara to help on Evolution and to bring out necessary changes.

"The second stage covers the first half of the *Jivâtma's* manhood, when he is fit to gain wealth, to enjoy it and use it, to organize labour and direct it, to undertake great responsibilities, and administer well accumulated possessions. This includes the commercial class, the great traders, and the organisers of industry, the capitalists, bankers, the managers of large industrial concerns. In the social polity of the Sanâtana Dharma, such *Jivâtmas* were born into the caste of *Vaisyâs*, and were trained in it gradually to see as aim the common good and the general prosperity, instead of mere personal aggrandisement.

"The third stage makes the second half of the *Jivâtma's* manhood, when his responsibilities and powers widen out to include the nation, and he is called to legislate, to rule, to work unselfishly for the State, and to use his power to protect and to regulate, not to aggrandise himself. This includes kings, judges, legislators, warriors, all who rule and keep order in the State. In the social polity of the Sanâtana Dharma, such mature *Jivâtmas* were born into the *Kshatriya* caste, and bore the burden of Kingship and of fighting for the national defence.

"The fourth stage embraces the serene age of the *Jivâtma*, when earthly things have lost their charm, and he becomes the counsellor and friend and helper of all his youngers. This includes the priests, the counsellors, the teachers of every kind—authors, scientists, poets, philosophers. In the social polity of the Sanâtana Dharma, such *Jivâtmas* were born into the caste of the *Brâhmanas*, the advanced and unselfish ones who gave much and needed little. Caste confusion in India has struck this caste most hardly, as the degradation of the higher is always worse than that of the lower. The *Sûdra Jivâtma* in the *Brâhmana* body is the greatest danger to the Sanatana Dharma." (Elementary Text Book of Sanatana Dharma, pp. 112—114.) *

"In the first two races there was nothing of the nature of caste; 'they made men of one element,' it is said; men were very much alike, there were no sharp and decided differences, but only hints and indications, and the forms were not distinctly human. These *Pitris* are all called by the name of one of the sons of Brahma, the sons of Atri.. In the Third Race, the Lemurians, also known as the *Dânavas*, the forms became denser; and in the Fourth, the Atlanteans or *Daityas*, they were better formed and became distinct-

* "Much of the (present) evil has grown from men of each caste grasping at the work of the other castes, and from each thinking more of the rights his caste gives him than of the duties it imposes. The *Brâhmana* and the *Kshatriya* have claimed their privileges ardently, and have shrunk from the heavy burdens belonging to their castes. Naturally this attitude has provoked opposition, antagonisms have replaced mutual service and goodwill. Hence caste has become a source of social bitterness, instead of a frame work, maintaining all in happy order. (Elementary Text Book of Sanatana Dharma. p. 114.)

ly human. When the Fifth Race was born, they were ready to receive a finer polity; in the First Family the model was given for the whole race (the Fifth), and from it the sub-races went out into the various parts of the world. The Manu came from Tibet, crossed the Himalayas into India, and there established the Aryan polity. The second great family founded the Chaldean Empire, which spread and gave birth to the Arabs and the earlier Greeks; but the best type was the Chaldean. Then the Iranian people separated off and settled in Persia, and later on came the later Greeks, the Romans, Spanish and Italians, a very well marked sub-race; last came the Teutonic, the Germans, Danes, Saxons, &c. The Celts and Teutons intermarried and made a mixed race.

All these great families carried with them the same type of civilization, its most perfect form being the First Family, in which the Manu himself incarnated. He called to his aid the *Pitris*, who helped in establishing the polity that seemed the most promising for the new race; and he decided to divide the people into four great classes, called in India castes or *varnas*. In Hindu books these are called by the names of the sons of the four great *Rishis*, who gave their names to the four classes of the *Pitris*, Bhrigu, Angiras, Pulastya, and Vasishtha. In the first class, the Sons of Bhrigu, the causal body was the most highly developed; they used it as their body of action; they gave the *Sukshma Sarira* for the Brahman Caste, in whom intellect was to be developed; philosophy and science were their great employment in life, and for that this special type of *Sukshma Sarira* was needed. It was the function of the *Pitris* to provide the *Sukshma Sarira.* The next class, the Sons of Angiras, in whom the mental body was the most highly developed, gave the *Sukshma Sarira* for the *Kshatriyas,* who were to be the warriors, the law-givers, the guides and protectors of the people, and who needed a very active mental body. Then came the Sons of Pulastya, who had to do with the production of wealth and organisation; in them the astral body was developed, for objects of desire were what they specially turned to, not for their own sakes, but for the sake of the people whom they were to guide; they gave the type of body for the *Vaisya* caste, who were to be the stewards of the nation. The fourth class were the Sons of Vasishthà, who gave the *Sukshma Sarira* for the *Sudra* caste; they possessed the etheric double, on which was moulded a very strong aud active physical body, fit for manual employment. In India these four classes are called *Varnas*: they are really distinguished by colours; the colour of the *Sukshma Sarira* of the Brahman is dark blue, that of a *Kshatriya* is electric green, that of the *Vaisya* scarlet or rose, according to their coarser or finer development, aud of the *Sudra* violet tinged with grey. These were the four colours of the castes, which are therefore quite properly called *Varnas.* (Mrs. Besant's Lecture on the Caste System. Theosophy in India, April 1908.)

The *Varnas* of the earlier races with their defective and inferior senses were coarse and highly discoloured, and marriage with them was sure to produce highly disastrous results. Says S. R. Wells in his Holy Wedlock or the Right Relations between the Sexes :—

" A person with a highly developed moral nature would be rendered miserable by a union with a partner in whom the animal propensities predominate in development and activity, and give their tone to the character and the life. So delicacy, refinement, and love of the beautiful can not associate happily with coarseness, vulgarity, and a hard repulsive insensibility to the finer feelings of the soul." (Vivaha Nisheka Dharma Pradipika, p. 125.)

The histories of the hybrid races of America and India confirm our statement. Dr. Bryce is of opinion that " such admixture in the long run tends to diminish the wealth of character and the potency for civilization which human communities possess. Although the weaker community may gain a little in quality and in vigour by the admixture with a comparatively stronger one, the stronger community loses a great deal more by its correlated admixture with the weaker one. The loss of the stronger community being more on the whole than the gain of the weaker community, such admixture is clearly not desirable in the interest of the progress of humanity as a whole."*

To maintain the Aryan superiority, and to ensure its further evolution, means had to be found. The means prescribed by the *Rishis* are the *Samskâras*.

30. SAMSKARAS AND THEIR IMPORTANCE.

Brâhmanya or spiritual superiority cannot be maintained without appropriate *Samskâras*.† "By birth a man is but a *Sûdra*; *Samskâras* make him a *Dvija* (twice-born) by inducing in him spiritual vision. By the study of the Vedas, he grows to be a *Vipra*, and a *Brâhmana* he becomes when he attains to the knowledge of the Brahman." Many *Kshatriya* tribes, who went forth and colonized the other parts of the world, neglected the *Samskâras*, and deteriorated into the condition of the *Sûdras*; and this circumstance Manu mentions in the Tenth Chapter of his

* All the attempts that have been hitherto made to ignore the Caste System in India have failed. Mrs. Besant in her Hindu Ideals, p. 155, says:—"Chaitanya ignored caste, but his followers are caste-people. Guru Nanak overrode caste, but it has reappeared among the Sikhs. The Lord Buddha was careless of it, but his religion did not succeed in living permanently in India. Modern movements have repudiated it, but cast out at the front door, it creeps in again at the back. It is as though the lesson were ever being repeated, that the divisions are natural ones, and therefore can not be destroyed."

Smriti. Says he:—"By ignoring the *Kriyas* or sacred rites, and by ceasing to have intercourse with the *Brahmans*, the following tribes of *Kshatriyas* have gradually sunk into the state of *Vrishalas* or outcastes, *viz.*, Poundrakas, Odhras, Dravidâs, Kâmbojas, Yavanas, Sakas, Pâradâs, Pahlavas, Chinas, Kirâtas, Daradâs, and Khasâs."† When there are no *Samskâras*, deterioration there must be. This law is universal, and no escape from it is possible. "As the outline of a picture is lighted up slowly with the careful filling in of many colours, even so is *Brâhmanya* with *Samskâras*

---

† శనకైస్తు క్రియాలోపాదిమాః క్షత్రియజాతయః ।
వృషలత్వంగతాలోకే బ్రాహ్మణాదర్శనేనచ ॥
పౌండ్రకాశ్చౌఢ్రద్రమిడాః కాంభోజాఃయవనాః శకాః ।
పారదాః పహ్లవాశ్చీనాః కిరాతాఃదరదాః ఖశాః ॥
(మనుస్మృతి. అ. 10).

शनकैस्तुक्रियालोपादिमाः क्षत्रियजातयः ॥
वृषलत्वंगतालोके ब्राह्मणादर्शनेनच ॥
पौड्रकाश्चौड्रद्रमिडाः कांभोजायवनाश्शकाः ॥
पारदाः पह्लवाश्चीनाः किरातादरदाः खशाः ॥
(मनुस्मृति. अ. 10.)

"The Sakas were the ancient Sacae. The Pahlavs were the Medes speaking Pahlavi or the ancient Persian. The Câmbojas were the inhabitants of Kamboja or Cambodia; the Yavanas, as is well known, were the Greeks. The Dravids may be the Druids of Great Britain. Kirâtas were the inhabitants of Baluchistan, Daradas of Dârdastan in the Chinese territory. The Khasas were probably some people of Eastern Europe." (Hindu Superiority, page 195.)

conducted with appropriate *Mantras*."* *Samskâra* is a training, discipline, or *Siksha*, physical, mental, moral, and spiritual : its importance cannot be over-estimated. "It affects all the *Kôshas* or Sheaths. Its uses are:—(1) to help the *Jiva* to conquer and purify his Sheaths; (2) to bring to his aid Superior Intelligences, such as the *Devas* and the *Rishis*; (3) to improve the atmosphere about him, and so make it easier for him to steady and concentrate his mind. To these ends there are used material objects, gestures, postures, and *mantras*, all carefully arranged to bring about the results aimed at. The material objects used are chosen for their magnetic properties, and they help in establishing a link between the object of meditation and the worshipper. Gestures and postures, for the most part, affect the *Prânas*—the sub-divisions of the life-breath that circulate in the body; some prevent the magnetism of the body from escaping into the surrounding atmosphere, and force its currents to move in a way suitable for calm and quiet

---

* చిత్రకర్మయథానేకై రంగైరున్మీల్యతేశనైః ।

బ్రాహ్మణ్యమపితద్వద్ధి సంస్కారైర్మంత్రపూర్వకైః ॥

चित्रकर्मयथानेकैरंगैरुन्मील्यतेशनैः ॥

ब्राह्मण्यमपितद्वाद्धिसंस्कारैर्मन्त्रपूर्वकैः ॥

thought. *Mantras** are used for all the three purposes mentioned above. They give rise to vibrations, and as these vibrations are regular and even, they make the vibrations of the *Sukshma Sarira*—which are very sensitive and easily affected—regular and even also. When these vibrations of the *Sukshma Sarira* are made regular, the *Jiva* is much helped in steadiness of thought and devotion. Sounds of a suitable kind attract the attention of the *Rishis* and *Devas* to the person uttering the sounds, and they help him. Further, suitable sounds drive away hostile Intelligences and bad magnetic influences, and so improve the surroundings of the speaker."

"There is another thing to remember about *Mantras*; if the man who utters a mantra is not trying to lead a good life, the vibrations of the *Mantra* will do him harm, not good. For, as they work on his *Sukshma Sarira*, they bring to bear on it a force antagonistic to evil desires and evil thoughts, and shake it very violently, and may even wound and tear it, as his evil resolves make it vibrate in one way and the vibrations

---

* "A *mantra* is a succession of sounds, a definite sequence. the sounds being arranged in a certain order; if the sounds are changed, the vibrations are changed, and the results are changed. That is why a mantra cannot be translated. A translated *mantra* is like a sentence in which all the letters of the words are jumbled up, and so convey no meaning." (Elementary Text Book of Sanâtana Dharma, page 74.)

of the *Mantra* force it into another. If his resolves are good, then they work with the *Mantra*, and cause no conflict; however weak they may be, they aid and do not hinder.

"*Mantras* need not be spoken aloud, and their silent repetition is, indeed, more powerful than audible recitation. They affect the subtler kinds of matter more than the denser." (Elementary Text Book of Sanatana Dharma, pp. 73-75.)

Mrs. Besant describes the effects of Mantras in these words:—" The sounds of the *Mantra* produce vibrations, which assume a definite form, and according to the sounds will the form be. You learn in Physics about the formation of sound-figures, geometrical shapes produced on a disk vibrating under a note; and further experiments have shown that elaborate forms are produced by musical phrases. These vibrating forms cause vibrations in the medium around them, first here on Earth, and then in Bhuvarloka and beyond; these in turn throw into corresponding vibrations bodies against which they strike, when those bodies are capable of responding to them. As these vibrations come up against the *Sukshma Sarira*, they throw it into corresponding vibrations, and the result is the purification of the *Sukshma Sarira*, for the vibrations shake out the coarser matter which cannot vibrate with them, and it is this coarser matter which corresponds to unclean and coarse and wrong thoughts. Now when an Evil thought is in a person's mind, it sets up vibrations, and these vibrations affect any *Sukshma Sarira* in which suitable coarse matter is found ; but the *Sukshma Sarira* which has been purified by *Mantras* does not contain such coarse matter, and hence there is no response to the vibrations of the evil thought, and it cannot reach the mind within that pure *Sukshma Sarira*. (Hindu Ideals, pp. 159-60.)

It is imperatively necessary that the *Sukshma Sarira* should be kept pure; and "its purity depends on the purity of its owner's thoughts and desires, and herein lies the most fertile source of impurity in the physical *Kosas*. No physical *Kosas* can be pure and healthy if the thoughts and desires are impure. A man may observe the rules of *Saucha* to the last point of strictness, but if he be proud, passionate, harsh, vain, suspicious, he is pouring impurity into his lower *Kosas* faster than any rules can wash it out. In the eyes of the *Rishis* and the *Devas*, such a one is ever *Asuchi*." (Elementary Text Book of Sanatana Dharma, page 87.)

Of the sixteen *Samskâras*, the *Upanayana* and the *Vivâha* are the most important, and each of them is a long and strict discipline extending over years and years. It is true that there is no *Upanayana* for girls as there is for boys, for the girl does not learn the Vedas, and has no *gurukulavâsa* or residence in the *Guru's* house. The mere absence of these two items does not mean that there is no student's stage or *Brahmacharya* for the girl. The parents are the *Gurus* or Teachers, and she ought to have the *Samskâra*, like boys, but without the study of the Vedas. The girl, like the boy, has to be trained for the duties and responsibilities of adult life. At marriage both the youth and the maiden enter upon the householder's stage, and both should be ready to take up immediately the duties and responsibilities of household life. "Of all the *Asramas*, this is the most important, for it supports all the others. The welfare alike of the family and of the nation depends on the householder, and their happiness and prosperity are in his hands. A good husband, a good father, a good master, a good citizen, is the noblest of men. The home is the school of unselfishness, compassion, tenderness, temperance, purity, helpfulness, prudence, industry, right judgment, charity. The qualities that make the good householder, when shown to his own circle in house and state, are the qualities that make the Sage and the Saint." (Elementary Text Book of Sanâtana Dharma, pp. 105-6.)

Vivâha being a *Samskâra* or discipline, appropriateness of time is and must be an all-important consideration. A child can not have the *Samskâra* of an adult. The Marriage Ritual teaches both the bridegroom and the bride what they have to do immediately as husband and wife. It teaches them that marriage is not for sensual pleasure, but for the acquisition of *Dharma* and *praja.* The *Mantras* of the *Sapta padi* ceremony explain the relations that should subsist between husband and wife. They teach that the husband and the wife should be one in thought, word, and deed. The several *Homas* show what orders of Intelligences uphold the world, and how they ought to be propitiated. The *Tri Râtra Brahmacharya* shows that for increase of spirituality and for begetting *Sâttvic* progeny a life of continence is absolutely necessary. The *Samâvesana* and *Garbhâdhâna Mantras* reveal what the conditions of begetting *Sâttvic* progeny are. The husband and wife should both live the life that is revealed to them at the marriage ritual, and then only the good effects of the *Samskâra* are clearly seen.

What is the difference between a man that has the *Samskâra* and another that has it not ? The difference is great. The man that has the *Samskâra* and practises it with diligence, grows spiritually, begets increasingly *Sâttvic* progeny, and becomes an ornament to the world, while the man that has it not declines spiritually, begets increasingly *râjasic* or *tâmasic* progeny, and becomes a curse to the world. The process is a gradual one, and *Karma* never ceases to act. It is not the lip-repetition nor the intellectual appreciation, but the actual living of the life indicated by the *mantras*, that constitutes the core of the *Samskâra*. A man may repeat every day for years without *Sraddha* and *trikarana suddhi*, the *mantrâs* of the *Sandhyâvandana*, and may understand the meanings too, but he will not be profited, if he will not live the life indicated by the *Mantrás*. The test of the proper performance of the *Sandhyâvandana* is the increase of *ôjas* and *tejas*, and the uniform maintenance of vigorous health and strength. The test of the *Vivâha Samskâra* is the excellence of the physical, mental, moral, and spiritual development of the husband and the wife, and the corresponding character of the progeny they bring forth. When the life indicated is actually lived, the birth of malformed, *tâmasic* progeny becomes an utter impossibility.

There may be, and there are, *Samskâras* without *Mantras*. Physical exercise, deep breathing, etc , are instances in point, and they produce their own good effects on the body. *Mantrâs* affect the inner bodies. *Samskâras* with appropriate *Mantrâs* are more efficacious, and produce results more rapidly than those without them. The advance of the European and the American nations illustrates the effects of *Samskâras* without appropriate *Mantras*.

31. THE EARLY ARYANS.

Non-Aryans surrounded the Aryans in India, and the Aryans had to wage long wars to subjugate them. The *Kshatriyas*, Aryans as they were, became oppressive, and *Parasu Rama* well-nigh exterminated the race. Divine dynasties followed, and *Râma Râjya* or Rama's rule became proverbial for probity. The Aryans under their Divine Rulers and Teachers perfected their sciences and institutions. The work of organisation and systematization being over, the Divine Rulers and Teachers withdrew, leaving the Aryan Race to work out its destiny. The troubles of India now commenced, and owing to the vicissitudes of incessant wars with Non-Aryans and the consequent neglect of the several *Samskâras* deterioration set in.

32. THE VEDIC AGE.

By the Vedic Age we mean the age when woman was the helpmeet of man in the real sense of the word, when she was free, and was as well educated as man himself was.* The rules of the four *Asramas* apply to woman as they do to man. As man has his *Bramacharya* period, so woman must have hers. Without education, which is itself a *Samskâra*, man or woman is no better than a beast. That women were well educated at one time, our marriage *mantras* themselves do reveal. In *Pradhâna Hôma*, *Pravesa Hôma*, and *Sesha Hôma*, the priest was only an

---

* Visvâvare, Lopâmudre, Maitreyi, and Gârgi are instances. Visvâvare and Lopâmudre composed Sûktas of the Rig Veda. Maitreyi was the wife of Yâgnavulkya, and her account may be read in the Brihadâranyaka Upanishat. Gârgi held a disputation with Yâgnavalkya in a large assembly.

onlooker. The husband and wife both performed the *Prânâyâma*, and both stated the *Sankalpa*, and both offered the *âhuties* chanting the *Riks*. We find the bride herself chanting the *Rik* అపశ్యంత్వాచేకితానం, (अपश्यंत्वाचेकितानम्), and intimate delicately and philosophically to her husband that on her part she is ready to receive and nourish the human "seed." The study of the Vedas, however, requires a well-regulated life and accurate knowledge of sounds, as otherwise it does irreparable harm.† "The *Mantra* defective in *svara* or *Varna*, is uttered falsely, and declareth not the true meaning. That lightning-word injureth the performer himself as *Indra-Satru* for fault of *svara*." After the departure of the Divine Rulers and Teachers, men ceased to be spiritual and began to be worldly. The existence of priests as a separate class among Brahmans is a proof of this degeneracy. Women ceased to learn the Vedas, and then ceased to learn Samskrit well, beginning to converse in Prâkrit dialects with their defective sounds, as is amply proved by our Dramatic Literature. With the degradation of woman the degrad-

---

मंत्रोहीनस्स्वरतोवर्णतोवामिथ्याप्रयुक्तोनतमर्थमाह ।
सवाक्वज्रोयजमानंहिनस्तियथेन्द्रशत्रुस्स्वरतो पराधात् ।

† మంత్రోహీనస్స్వరతో వర్ణతోవామిథ్యా ప్రయుక్తోనత మర్థమాహ । సవాగ్వజ్రోయజమానంహి నస్తియథేంద్ర శత్రుః స్వరతో పరాధాత్ ॥

ation of man also commenced and proceeded apace.* In short, the Vedas became the special property of a few families, and the majority of the *Dvija* community became ignorant and carnal; and as the important truths of the Vedas could not be ignored, some sort of a "made-easy" series became necessary, and we pass on to the *Sûtra* Period. Marriage, however, was universally post-pubescent during the Vedic Period, as the *Vedic Mantras* of marriage clearly prove.

33. THE SUTRA PERIOD.

During the *Sûtra* Period things went from bad to worse. The Aryan sciences and the Aryan institutions were excellent; † and India, as Manu says, was intended to be a University for the nation-students of the world. The University was ready to receive students,

* Says a great writer:—"No nation can ever be great unless women rise to a high plane of thought and life, and kindle and foster similar ideas in the minds of the young."

† Mr. W. C. Taylor thus speaks of Samskrit Literature:—

"It was an astounding discovery that Hindustan possessed, in spite of the changes of realms and chances of time, a language of unrivalled richness and variety; a language, the parent of all those dialects that Europe has fondly called classical—the source alike of Greek flexibility and Roman strength; a philosophy, compared with which, in point of age, the lessons of Pythagoras are of yesterday, and in point of daring speculation Plato's boldest efforts were tame and common-

and the first-born, "*Agra Janmas,*" of *Brahmâvarta* and *Brahmarshi Desa* were the Instructors.* The nation-students came one after another, and were benefited. But how was all this to happen? It happened in this wise. India has ever been known as a Land of Gold and Diamonds, and the cupidity and greed of the surrounding non-Aryan nations were insatiable, and wars were waged incessantly. The masterpieces of Aryan Science and Literature benefited the nations that came to India, but the incessant wars themselves produced disastrous results upon the people. The social polity of the Aryans was rudely disturbed. The Brahmans could not lead the Vedic Life, and the diligent study of the Vedas had to be neglected. The utmost that could be done was to learn the chanting of the Vedas without studying the inner meaning; for the Vedas speak for the most part

place; a poetry more purely intellectual than any of those of which we had before any conception; and systems of science whose antiquity baffled all power of astronomical calculation. This literature with all its colossal proportions, which can scarcely be described without the semblance of bombast and exaggeration, claimed, of course, a place for itself—it stood alone, and it was able to stand alone." (Hindu Superiority, pp. 201-2.)

* Mrs. Manning exclaims:—" The Hindu had the widest range of mind of which man is capable." (Hindu Superiority, p. 348.)

enigmatically, and require a deep study to unravel the sense. A number of *Sûtras* that could be committed to memory became necessary, and these were also useful for purposes of instruction. The rules of the Vedic *Svara* and *Varna* are not required in the *Sutras*. Besides, the *Sutras* were also suited to the inferior intellectual capacities of the Fourth Race nation-students, and the Unseen Helpers helped in these efforts as they were beneficial to Humanity at large. The late Right Honourable Prof. Max Muller saw in the *Sutras* profound wisdom, while, with all his great learning, he pronounced the Vedic Hymns to be mere "babblings of an Infant Humanity." Deterioration proceeded concomitantly with the incessant wars, and another result was produced.

The beauty of Aryan maidens is well-known. The Aryan beauties were straight-eyed, while the Fourth Race beauties were oblique-eyed.* The non-Aryans were and are a sensual race and hardly spiritual. It became more and more difficult to protect Aryan beauties from non-Aryan violence. The *Kshatriya* Race had deteriorated, and monogamy amongst them had become an exception to the rule instead of being the rule itself. The Brahmans themselves had deteriorated along with the others, and were less spiritual and more

* The great majority of the Mongolians and the Japanese have still oblique eyes.

worldly. The Vedic spirit of uncompromising truthfulness and *trikarana Suddhi* was fast disappearing. The education of women had been neglected, and women were looked upon more as toys for sensual pleasures than as beings through whose co-operation and chaste life spiritual progeny was to be produced. All the surrounding circumstances conspired to make post-pubescent marriages more and more difficult, and some of the *Sutrakâras* began to think that owing to altered circumstances marriage should be celebrated immediately after puberty or about the time of puberty.

In the meantime another practice seems to have become common. We have already distingnished the three stages of a gift—viz., మనసాదత్తా, వాచాదత్తా, ధారాదత్తా मनसादत्ता, वाचादत्ता, धारादत्ता. In these times of turmoil and turbulence, parents often promised by word of mouth to give a girl in marriage to a particular man, and waited till the girl attained her age. If anything very serious happened in the interval, she was given in marriage to another man. Later on, the serious things were defined to be "loss, death, renunciation of the world, impotence, and loss of caste."*

---

* నష్టేమృతే ప్రవ్రజితే క్లీబేచపతితే పతౌ ।
పంచస్వాపత్సు నారీణాంపతిరన్యో విధీయతే ॥

नष्टेमृतेप्रव्रजितेक्लीबेचपतितेपतौ ॥
पंचस्वापत्सुनारीणांपतिरन्योविधीयते ॥

This practice was possible only so long as men were honest and were true to their word; but soon a time came when it became inexpedient to allow a long interval between the promise and the performance.

Occurrences of a curious nature unsettled men's minds. Imagine a man to be seriously ill—say, his father dies when he is in that condition. He, the son, *must* perform the funeral ceremonies of his father, but he is not in a condition to bathe often, and—we shall suppose that the doctor prohibits his bathing. Our *Sâstras* allow that in such cases a *Mantra Snâna* (a mere sprinkling of water) may suffice. In his name the funeral ceremonies are performed by some other man. We shall suppose our patient recovers somewhat by the eleventh day. The question arises whether he should or should not perform all the *Mâsika* ceremonies in advance. It is distinctly known that the man is not likely to live for a year longer. What should he do? Considering all the circumstances, our *Sâstras* decide that such a man may be allowed to perform all the *Mâsika* ceremonies in advance on the understanding that, in the case of the patient continuing to live, he should go on performing the *Mâsikams* again as they fall due.

Take another case. Say that a man is performing the funeral ceremonies of his father or mother, and that he is ordered to proceed to a battle. The chances of his surviving the battle are uncertain. Should he or should he not perform the *Mâsika* ceremonies in advance? Our *Sâstras* decided that he should.

Take a third case. Imagine a father having a daughter who is about to attain puberty, and whom he has verbally promised to give in marriage to a young man. He is going to war, and it is uncertain whether he will survive the fight. What should he do? Here was a ticklish question, which the *Sûtrakâras* could not easily decide. In the meantime *Kanyâdâna* was included among the well-known sixteen *dânas* or gifts. Selfishness was increasing, and considerations of policy and convenience came to have weight. The study of the Vedas had declined, and the *Virâha Samskâra* had lost its importance *as a Samskâra*. Some were for the marriage and some against.

Take a fourth case. Say a marriage is going on between a young man and a young woman. During the performance of the *Tri Râtra Brahmacharya*, the bridegroom falls suddenly ill. The *Garbhâdhâna* night comes, but he is too ill to have sexual intercourse. What should be done? The ceremony must not be stopped, as the *Devas*, and the *Nândi Devatas* should not be made to wait on the physical plane. The decision was that the *Mantras* might be repeated, and the physical act postponed.

Take a fifth case. Say that a marriage is arranged between a young man and a young woman, and that all the relatives are invited. The marriage day arrives, but both the bride and bridegroom feel indisposed. Is the marriage to be stopped? How can it be stopped, when the bride and the bridegroom feel only indisposed and are not seriously ill? The bride and the bridegroom sit like dumb animals, and the *Purôhitas* (priests) voice forth the *Mantras*, and the ceremonies are gone through. What about the *Samâ vêsana*? The *Mantras* are repeated and the marriage is *mantraically* over.

Thousands of such cases as have been mentioned above had occurred, and there were many precedents to quote. Times had changed, but caste had to be preserved. Strong and beneficent Government had come to an end. Selfishness had increased in all classes of the society. It is no wonder that the *Sutrakâras* accommodated themselves to circumstances. From the writings of the *Sutrakâras* we may infer that pre-pubescent marriages were in existence about that time, some *Sutrakâras* merely tolerating them. But worse times came.

The caste system now exerted its influence. The *Varnas* of old are the *Varnas* of the subtle bodies and not of the gross physical body. But the *Varnas* of the subtle body not being visible to the physical eye, physical descent alone was taken into consideration. In spite of all the care that had been exercised, the several castes had inter-connections, and several subcastes came into existence. The circles within which brides and bridegrooms of the original purity could be selected became narrower and narrower. The convenience of the parties had to be taken into consideration. At the same time the competition for brides and bridegrooms increased. Considering the unsettled condition of the times and the uncertainty of the future, it became more and more expedient to marry when there was a suitable bride or bridegroom available. The performance of the *Mâsika* ceremonies in advance was held up as an analogy.

Astrology also lent its aid in making pre-pubescent marriages common. As it was difficult to secure suitable bridegrooms within limited circles, parents were, as in modern days, in search of bridegrooms from the time a daughter was born to them. When the total number of *Kûtas* was very fair, it was considered a sign that the *Devas* had intended the two beings to be husband and wife; and as they were so intended by the Heavenly Powers, what mattered the time? The sooner the union was effected, the better it was for all concerned. The fact of marriage being a *Samskâra* was ignored.

The so-called *Vaidikas* shared the general degeneracy, and as the writings of the later *Smritikâras* amply prove, they were even ignorant. Thus we pass on to the Metrical Smriti period, which may be styled the period of the second "made-easy" series.

34. THE PERIOD OF THE METRICAL SMRITIS.

This period marks a further decline of the old Aryan intellect. The framers of the *Sûtras* were intellectual giants as compared with the Metrical *Smritikâras*. The comprehensive mental grasp, the remarkable powers of analysis, the unrivalled powers of compression, which the *Sutrakâras* have exhibited excite the admiration of the whole world. The unceasing wars, which mark the history of *Bharatakhanda* from the very commencement of the Aryan settlement in India, have affected the Brahmans most; and considering all the circumstances, we may be thankful that the metrical *Smritis* have been vouchsafed to us. Brevity may be the soul of wit, but it is often not the soul of perspicuity. The trouble of interpreting a particular *Sûtra* lies in referring to the previous *Sûtras* for light and guidance, and strong powers of memory are needed. As ordinary persons have neither the ability nor the time required to master the *Sûtras*, the metrical *Smritis* serve as ready books of reference, and are really a "made-easy" series. They are intended to put one in mind of what the *Srutis* say, and serve as minor courts, from which there is an appeal to a higher court, the *Sûtras*; from which again there lies an appeal to a still higher court, namely, the Vedas. The metrical *Smritis* being the books most commonly consulted in these degenerate days by the great majority of persons, unauthorised additions or interpolations, intended to sanctify un-sâstraic deviations, should be expected more there than in the *Sûtras* or in the Vedas. To interpolate cleverly in the *Sûtras* one has to be an intellectual giant himself, but to insert *slokas* in the metrical *Smritis* is an easy thing even for ordinary scholars; and we find that interpolations have been made on a large scale. The very existence of no less than six and thirty *Smritis* is an indication of their doubtful value, as truth can hardly have so many as six and thirty different aspects. Regarding disputed questions, their statements are not of much consequence, unless they are supported by the Vedas. Of all these *Smritis* Manu's has the highest authority. Brihaspati says :—" The *Smriti* of Manu stands high as embodying the teachings of the Vedas: that *Smriti* which is at variance with the statement of Manu deserves little regard."* The metrical *Smritikâras* seem to have recorded the practices in vogue in their times, and they are all apparently in favour of pre-pubescent marriage, some allowing post-pubescent marriages in exceptional cases under specified penalties, and others denouncing them in unmeasured terms. It is not necessary to

---

* వేదార్థోపనిబంధృత్వాత్ ప్రాధాన్యం హి మనోః స్మృతం ।
మన్వర్థవిపరీతా యా సా స్మృతిర్న ప్రశస్యతే ॥

वेदार्थोपनिबन्धृत्वात्प्राधान्यं हि मनोः स्मृतम् ।
मन्वर्थविपरीता या सा स्मृति र्नप्रशस्यते ॥

count the numbers for and against pre-pubescent marriage as no number of votes can make a black dog white, and as the Vedic *Mantras* are not in favour of it.

35. THE DEGENERACY OF THE METRICAL SMRITI PERIOD.

We shall now give some remarkable illustrations of the degeneracy of the age of the second "made-easy" series:—

I. Gobhila's son justifies his father's preference for a *Nagnika* in the following terms*:—"A girl is known as *Nagnika* till puberty; after that she is an *Anagnika*. One ought to give a *Nagnika* in marriage. She in whom the menstrual flow has not begun is a *Gauri*, she in whom it has is a *Rohini*. While yet there is no sprouting of hair (on the pubes) she is called a

* నగ్నికాంతువదేత్కన్యాం యావన్నర్తుమతీభవేత్ । ఋతుమతీత్వనగ్నికాంతాం ప్రయచ్ఛేత్తునగ్నికాం ॥ అప్రాప్తరజసోగౌరీ ప్రాప్తేరజసిరోహిణీ। అవ్యంజితాభవేత్కన్యా కుచహీనాచనగ్నికా॥ వ్యంజనైస్తుసముత్పన్నై స్సోమోభుంజీతకన్యకాం । పయోధరైస్తుగంధర్వః రజసాగ్నిః ప్రకీర్తితాః ॥ తస్మాదవ్యంజనోపేతా మరజామపయోధరాం । అభుక్తాంచైవసోమాద్యైః కన్యకాతుప్రశస్యతే ॥

नग्निकांतुवदेत्कन्यां यावन्नर्तुमतीभवेत् । ऋतुमतीत्वनग्निकातां प्रयच्छेत्तुनग्निकाम्॥ अप्राप्तरजसोगौरी प्राप्तेरजसिरोहिणी । अव्यंजिताभवेत्कन्याकुचहीना चनग्निका ॥ व्यंजनैस्तुसमुत्पन्नै स्सोमोभुंजीतकन्यकाम् । पयोधरैस्तुगंधर्वः रजसाग्निः प्रकीर्तिताः ॥ तस्माद्व्यंजनोपेता मरजामपयोधराम् । अभुक्तांचैवसोमाद्यैः कन्यकातुप्रशस्यते ॥

Kanya; while yet the breasts are not developed, she is called a *Nagnika*. When hair begins to appear, *Sôma* enjoys a maiden; when the breasts begin to grow, the *Gandharva* enjoys her; and when menstruation has set in, *Agni* is said to enjoy her. Therefore before any of these things begins to show itself—hair, breasts, or menstruation—it is best to marry a girl, for then she would not have been enjoyed by *Sôma* and others." (Marriage after Puberty, page 33.)

Marriage before puberty is recommended, and the reason assigned is that it should take place before any gods, *Sôma* and others, can "enjoy" her! The implication evidently is that the gods, *Sôma*, the *Gandharva*, and *Agni*, are libertines, and that they should not be given any chance of defiling the girl! It is to be doubted whether the author is really serious for, if he is, he betrays a really culpable ignorance of the Vedantic Religion. In the early part of this study we have explained the Vedic Rik embodying this idea; and we have found it to contain profound truths. These gods "protect" the girl, and look to her development; they do not "enjoy" her, in the vulgar sense of the word. Suppose the girl is married when she is a *Nagnika*, has she not to pass through the hands of these gods afterwards? Is it possible for anybody to elude the gods, who preside over the processes of Nature? The Sun is the source of all terrestrial energy,—can anybody escape his influence, and still live? The theory of this author deserves only to be dismissed with contempt. The truth seems to be that the author, unable to find cogent arguments for pre-pubescent marriage, hits upon the mean expedient of utilising the second meaning of the root of *Bhunjita* (భుజపరిపాలనాభ్యవహారయోః भुजपरिपालनाम्यवहारयोः) ignoring the meaning of "to protect."

II. *Atri* is made to say:—No paramour can defile her; not even though she conceives by him; for on being delivered of the child, she becomes pure like refined gold!" * (Marriage after Puberty, p. 33.)

Oh, what a scandalous statement this is! Aryan philosophy cannot tolerate it. Re-marriage of women is disallowed mainly on the ground of the sexual intercourse with the first husband leaving a permanent taint in the body of the woman.† Such being the case,

---

* అసవర్ణేనయోగర్భః స్త్రీణాంయోనౌనిషిచ్యతే । అశుద్ధాతు భవేన్నారీ యావచ్ఛల్యంనముంచతి ॥ నిస్సృతేతుతతశ్శల్యే రజసోపి హదర్శనాత్ । తతస్సాశుధ్యతేనారీ విమలాకాంచనోపమా ॥ (అత్రి)

असवर्णेनयोगर्भः स्त्रीणांयोनौनिषिच्यते । अशुद्धातुभवेन्नारी यावत्शल्यंनमुंचति ॥ निस्सृतेतुततश्शल्येरजसो पीहदर्शनात् । ततस्सा शुध्यते नारीविमलाकांचनोपमा ॥ (अत्रि).

† Professor Austin Fleet in his Text Book of Human Physiology writes:—"A peculiar and inexplicable fact is that previous pregnancies have an influence upon offspring. This is well known to breeders of animals. If pure blooded mares or bitches have been once covered by an inferior male, in subse-

to say that adultery is of no consequence, and that the woman after the delivery of the child becomes pure like refined gold, is simply awful. *Atri* is one of the seven *Maharshis* of the Fifth or Aryan Race, and also one of the organisers of the caste system. To attribute this statement to him is simply blasphemous. Some wretched interpolator out of interested motives has composed these Slokas and fathered them upon *Atri*!

III. *Marichi* is made to say: *—"The gift of a *Gauri* in marriage procures *Nâka Loka*; that of a

---

quent fecundations the young are likely to partake of the character of the first male, even if they be afterwards bred with males of unimpeachable pedigree. What the mechanism of the influence of the first conception is, it is impossible to say; but the fact is incontestable. The same influence is observed in the human subject. A white woman, who has had children by a Negro, may subsequently bear children to a white man, but these children present unmistakable peculiarities of the Negro Race." (Vivaha Nisheka Dharma Pradipika, p. 73.) Randolph in his "Eulis" says that the taint produced in a woman's constitution is such that, for instance, no Negro woman can produce a perfectly Negro child after once bringing forth a child by a white man.

* గౌరీందదన్నాకపృష్ఠం వైకుంఠంరోహిణీందదత్ ।
కన్యాందదద్బ్రహ్మలోకం రౌరవంతురజస్వలాం ॥

गौरींददन्नाकपृष्ठं वैकुंठंरोहिणींददत् ॥ कन्यांददद्ब्रह्मलोकं रौरवंतुरजस्वलां ॥

Rohini, *Vaikuntha* ; that of a *Kanya*, *Brahmaloka* ; that of a post-pubescent girl, the *Raurava Hell*."

Marichi, let us remember, is one of the seven *Maharshis* of the Fifth or Aryan Race. The terms *Gauri*, *Rohini*, *Kanya*, and *Rajasvala* were defined differently by different *Smritikâras* or rather by the interpolators. "In her eighth year a girl is a *Gauri* ; in her ninth a *Rohini* ; in her tenth a *Kanya* ; and after that a *Rajasvala* " * is the version attributed to Yama. "In her eighth year a girl is a *Gauri* ; in her ninth a *Nagnika* ; in her tenth a *Kanya* ; and in her twelfth a Sudra woman," † is the version attributed to Samvarta. "In her eighth year a girl is a *Kanya* ; in her ninth a *Rohini* ; in her tenth a *Gauri*; and after that a *Rajasvala* "‡ is another version.

---

* అష్టవర్షాభ వేద్గౌరీ నవవర్షాతురోహిణీ । దశవర్షాభ వేత్క-
న్యా అతఊర్ధ్వంరజస్వలా ॥

अष्टवर्षाभवेत्गौरी नववर्षातुरोहिणी । दशवर्षाभवेत्कन्या अत
ऊर्ध्वंरजस्वला ॥

† అష్టమేతుభ వేద్గౌరీ నవమేనగ్నికాభ వేత్ । దశమేకన్యకా
ప్రోక్తా ద్వాదశేవృషలీస్మృతా ॥

अष्टमेतुभवेत्गौरी नवमेनग्निकाभवेत् । दशमेकन्यकाप्रोक्ता द्वादशे
वृषलीस्मृता ॥

‡ అష్టవర్షాభ వేత్కన్యా నవవర్షాతురోహిణీ । దశవర్షాభ వే
ద్గౌరీ అతఊర్ధ్వంరజస్వలా ॥

अष्टवर्षाभवेत्कन्या नववर्षातुरौहिणी । दशवर्षाभवेत्गौरी अत
ऊर्ध्वंरजस्वला ॥

The Vedantic Religion is a most complex one, dealing with seven *Lokas*, five *Kosas*, the Law of *Karma* and a series of Re-incarnations. The several Hierarchies of Intelligences simply administer the Law entrusted to them. The Vedantic Religion gives no room for partiality. It prescribes *Samskâras* at definite intervals for the harmonious development of the *Kôsas*. As we see clearly and plainly in the *Mantras* of the marriage ceremony, the *Vivâha Samskâra* should be performed only after the bride and bridegroom have attained age.* To perform that important *Samskâra* before *adhikâra* is acquired is not only a waste of time and energy, but also an offence against the *Devas*. *Surya* says to *Kunti*: "Inviting us needlessly, O maiden, is, no doubt, a sin."† A father is bound to give away his daughter in marriage to a suitable bridegroom, when she is willing to become a *grihini*, and by doing so he maintains his *dharma*. The performance of it brings no great merit, while the non-performance of it brings great sin. To say that by giving

---

* I am told that according to the Ayur Veda the bride and the bridegroom, at the time of marriage, should be sixteen and eighteen years old, respectively.

† వృథాహ్వానేపితేభీరు దోషస్స్యాన్నాత్ర సంశయః॥ (మ. భా. ఆది అ. ౧౧. శ్లో. ౧౪.

वृथाह्वानेपितेभीरु दोषस्स्यान्नात्र संशयः ॥ (म. भा. आ. प. अ. ११. श्लो. १४.

away a girl in marriage before she is fit for it, the father goes to heaven is an unpardonable perversion of Hindu Philosophy.* *Smritis* are intended to put one in mind of what the *Srutis* say.† Here the teaching is entirely inconsistent with that of the Vedic *Mantras*; and the *Sloka* in question is evidently a later addition or interpolation to justify parents in celebrating pre-pubescent marriages. The attempt to give technical meanings to *Gauri*, *Rohini*, *Kanya*, and *Nagnika* and not make any real use of them is, to say the least, ridiculous.‡

36. THE COMMUNITIES WHICH HAVE NOT GIVEN UP POST-PUBESCENT OR VEDIC MARRIAGE.

Unfortunately for the advocates of pre-pubescent marriages, there are three communities which stand forth conspicuously as champions of Vedic or post-pubescent marriage :—

---

* This is an odious way of looking at the marriage of one's daughter. *Vivâha* is, and must be, a *Samskâra*. The idea of "*dâna*" or gift is intended merely to prohibit the selling or *Vikraya* of a girl.

† స్మృతింపశ్యంతిమునయః స్మరంతిచతథాశ్రుతిం ॥

स्मृतिपश्यंतिमुनयः स्मरन्तिचतथास्मृतिम् ॥

‡ *Gauri* means "white," *Rohini* means "red," *Kanya* means "not used by man," *Rajasvala* means "having the menstrual flow." The technical meanings given to these words are not made use of by the *Smritikâras*.

(1) The *Kânya Kubjas* of Northern India, who live in the sacred lands mentioned by Manu, have become famous in Indian History as champions of Vedic practices. They are a race of intellectual giants, and they are also pious in their way. It has furnished from among its ranks several great men. How they strove in times of old for their religion and their gods may be inferred from the manner in which they strove for the preservation of their religion when the Mussalmans established kingdoms in Hindustan in the 13th century A. D. The Mussulmans of the present day are of mixed blood, as they have received with full privileges into their community converts from all races. The African Negro (a remnant of the Third or Lemurian Race) is a Mussulman; the Arab (the descendant of a mixed race with Aryan blood) is a Mussulman; the Persian (belonging to the third sub-race of the Aryan race) is a Mussulman; several Hindus (belonging to the first sub-race of the Fifth Race) are Mussulmans. One thousand years ago they were mostly men of the Fourth Race. The Mussulmans that established dynasties in Northern India were sensual, cruel, and vindictive, as Indian History amply proves.* The author of the high-

* Col. Tod says:—"If we consider the political changes and convulsions which have happened in Hindustan since Mahmud's invasion, and the intolerant bigotry of many of his successors, we shall be

ly popular work *Visvagunâdarsa* has praised the Kânya Kubjas in very high terms, and has extolled them as having greatly assisted in the preservation of the Hindu Religion in Northern India.* The *Kânya-Kubja* assumed the sword and cut down the vile

---

able to account for the paucity of its national works on history, without being driven to the improbable conclusion, that the Hindus were ignorant of an art which was cultivated in other countries from almost the earliest ages." (Hindu Superiority. p. 140.)

* యేకాయస్థజనాశ్రయే నృపసుతాయేచద్విజాశ్శస్త్రిణః । తేయత్నాదనుసృత్య నిర్దయతయాశుష్కాంస్తురుష్కాధిపాన్ ॥ దేవాన్ భూమిసురాంశ్చపాంతి కృతినస్తేచేత్స్వగేహాస్సతే । బ్రాహ్మణ్యాయజలాంజలిః కలభువిప్రాజ్ఞైః ప్రదేయోభవేత్ ॥ ఆక్రాంతాసువసుంధరాసు యవనైరాసేతు హైమాచలం । విద్రాణేక్షితిభృద్గణే వికరుణే నిద్రాతినారాయణే ॥ నిర్విఘ్నప్రసరేకలావపి బలాన్నిష్కంటకంవైదికం । పంథానంకలత్రతత్ర పరిపాత్యేకోపిలోకోత్తరః ॥ త్యజతువిహితమే తద్దేశవాసీనిషిద్ధం । భజతుతదపిలోకే నాస్తిధన్యస్తదన్యః ॥ శ్రియుగళదనఘ శ్రీదత్తశుద్ధిర్యదంగే । లగతిదురితభంగే లగ్నకోగాంగపూరః ॥ ప్రౌఢేషుగౌడేషు చకాన్యకుబ్జే । స్వగాధమేదేషు చమైథిలేషు ॥ అన్యేషుసత్స్వేషు బుధేషుధన్యే । షట్స్వప్యపి జీవంత్యధి భూమివిద్వాన్ ॥ ప్రాతశ్శీతజలేనిమజ్య విబుధానభ్యర్చ్యయత్యుచ్చకై । రార్యఃపర్యుషితంతు నాభ్యవహరత్యంధః క్షుదంధోప్యసౌ ॥ భాగేగోమయలిప్తఏవ పచతేభుంక్తేతతో న్యత్రయ । నిష్ఠతంతద్విజహోతి భుక్తనియమోదృష్టః క్వభూయానియాన్ ॥ (విశ్వగుణాదర్శ-కాశీవర్ణనె).

येकायस्थजनाश्रये नृपसुतायेचाद्विजाश्शास्त्रिणः । तेयत्नादनुसृत्य-निर्दयतयाशुष्कांस्तुतुरुष्काधिपान् ॥ देवान्भूमिसुरांश्चपांति कृति-

Mussulman that dared to violate the virginity of his grown up but unmarried daughter, and the Mussulman feared and respected him. He was denounced by the other Brahmans as having violated the rules of his caste by taking up military service, but the *Kânya-kubja* retorted that that Brahman that did not take up the sword in defence of his home did not deserve to be called a man. With him his Vedic injunctions were worth fighting for, and he disdained to cover his retreat from his faith with the vile expedient of interpolations. Some interpolations were apparently inserted in the *Smritis* about this time to justify pre-pubescent marriages.

(2) The *Kshatriyas* of Rajaputana come next. During the Mahomedan Period they carried on a brave struggle against the Mussulmans. Todd's

---

नस्तेचेत्गृहेष्वासते । ब्राह्मण्यायजलांजालि: किलभुविप्राज्ञै: प्रदेयोभवेत्॥ आक्रान्तासुवसुंधरासु यवनैरासेतुहैमाचलं । त्रिद्राणक्षितिभृद्गणे त्रिकरुणे-निद्रातिनारायणे ॥ निर्विघ्नप्रसरेकलावपि बलान्निष्कंटकंवैदिकं । पंथानं-किलतत्रतत्र परिपात्यंकोहिलोकोत्तर: ॥ त्यजतुविहितमे तद्देशवासी-निषिद्धं । भजतुतदपिलोकेनास्ति धन्यस्तदन्य: ॥ त्रियुगपदनखश्रीदत्त-शुद्धिर्यदंगे । लगतिदुरितभंगे लभ्नकोगांगपूर: ॥ प्रौढेषुगौडेषु चकान्य-कुब्जे । ष्वगाधमेधेषुचमैथिलेषु ॥ अन्येषुसत्स्वेषु बुधेषुधन्ये । ष्वद्यापिजी-वन्त्यधि भूमिविद्या: ॥ प्रातश्शीतजलेनिमज्य विबुधानभ्यर्चयत्युश्चकै । गार्य: पर्युषितंतु नाभ्यवहरत्यंध: क्षुदंधोप्यसौ ॥ भागेगोमयालिप्तएवपचते-भुक्तेततोन्यत्रयन्नीतंतद्धिजहातिभुक्ति नियमोदृष्ट: कभूयानियान् ॥

Annals of Rajastan and Mr. Rajani Kânta Gupta's *Aryakirti* relate their exploits. The *Kshatriyas*, being a warrior race, considered it a disgrace to resort to the base expedient of pre-pubescent marriage, supported by false texts, for fear of non-Aryan foreigners. Not in Rajaputana only but also in the other parts of India do the *Kshatriyas* continue to celebrate post-pubescent marriages. In the State of Mysore, the learned *purohits* and *pandits* still assist at the celebration of *Kshatriya* post-pubescent marriages. Vedic *Riks*, which are appropriate, are recited, and so far as the *Mantras* go, there is hardly any difference between the *Kshatriya* marriage and the *Brahman* marriage. There is one and the same *Dharma Sâstra* for all *Dvijas* in the matter of marriage. No advocate of pre-pubescent marriage dares to say that there is a separate principle for the *Kshatriya* community. The *Kshatriya* may well say to the Brahman Pandit :—" Venerable Sir, one and the same *Dharma Sâstra* there is for you and me. If post-pubescent marriage takes you to the *Raurava* Hell, it should take me also there. How is it you still enthusiastically assist at our post-pubescent marriage, while you yourself do not adopt it in the case of your own daughter ? Is not pre-pubescent marriage an empty form without a soul ? Are you willing to be guilty of *Anrita*, untruthfulness ? " We shall leave the *Pandit* to think over the answer.

(3) In Malabar, the South Western corner of India, the land which gave brith to the great Sankarâchariar, we have the *Nambudiri* community, a chip evidently of the old Aryan block, living in undisturbed seclusion. They went over to Malabar long, long ago, and they are living there still in the old Aryan way. At one time they found fault with the great Sankarâchariar himself. They are a very pious, learned, and conservative people.

We beg to assure the advocates of pre-pubescent marriage that the three communities we have mentioned above are not insignificant communities whom they can afford to despise. In the scale of caste the *Kshatriyas* stand second only to the Brahmans. The *Nambudiris* of Malabar are the living examples of the old Aryan ways. The *Upanayana Samskâra* is much more strict with them than it is with the Brahmans of the Tableland. The old Aryan learning in its pristine purity is found more in Malabar than in the other parts. It is worthy of note that not a single *Nambudiri* Brahman has yet been demoralized by western modes of thinking and living. The long extract from *Visvagunâdarsa* explains clearly what sort of people the *Kânyakubjas* are. The use of the epithet (అగాధమేధః, अगाधमेधेषु, of unfathomably profound intellect) is sufficiently expressive. In these days of rapid communication, the art of snubbing and reviling is not likely to succeed as it did more than five hundred years ago.

Post-pubescent marriage is a real *Samskâra*, and is supported by the highest of authorities, *viz.*, the Vedas, while pre-pubescent marrage is not, and can not be, a *Samskâra*, and is not supported by any authority worthy of mention, as we shall show. The test of *Samskâra* is *Gunântarâdhâna* or the inducing of qualities or properties which otherwise do not well develop. As we have already explained what *Samskâra* is, we now content ourselves with pointing out that the proper *Samskâra* for a pre-pubescent girl is education, physical, mental, moral, and spiritual, and not the *Vivâha Samskâra* which deals with the proper mode of acquiring and rearing Dharma and Praja. Is it not foolish and even sinful to preach to a pre-pubescent girl the secrets of begetting progeny ?

37. THE MUSSULMANS IN SOUTHERN INDIA.

Let us now turn to the history of Southern India. It was in the fourteenth century A. D. that the Mussulmans established Kingdoms in Southern India. Of these the Bahmini Kingdom * was important.

---

* This Kingdom was bounded on the East by Telingana, on the South by the Krishna and the Tungabhadra, on the West by the Konkan and the Sahyâdri Range, and on the North by Mâlva. It was founded in 1347. It had for some time a Brahman Minister. (Hara Prasad Shastri's History of India, page 90.)

The majority of the Mussulmans in the Deccan belonged to the Fourth Race, and were sensual and unscrupulous. The great majority of them, being soldiers, were without wives, and naturally they became a terror in the Deccan; and unmarried young women were extremely unsafe, the Mahomedan Law only forbidding the laying of violent hands on married females. "You are forbidden to take to wife free women who are married, except those women whom your right hand shall possess as slaves! Such is the law of God", says the Koran (Sourate IV. 28). If the Brahmans of Southern India had taken up the sword, determined to shed their blood in defence of their religion, the Brahman physique of Southern India would have been different from what it now is. Probably circumstances prompted them to consider that prudence is the better part of valour, and they humoured the new rulers and got on well in their service. The Mussulmans did not molest Malabar, the physical features of the country rendering foreign invasion very difficult, if not impracticable; and the pious *Nambudiris* went on with their post-pubescent marriages. The Brahmans of the Tableland of the Deccan were celebrating pre-pubescent marriages, and naturally the *Nambudiris* found fault with them for giving up the Vedic customs. The Mussulman Rulers were aware of the customs of the *Nambudiris* and of the *Kânyakubjas*. The Brahmans of the Tableland had to account for their custom. The *Nambudiris* were comparatively few in number, and lived secludedly in a corner. The Brahmans of the Tableland were more numerous, and as the Mussulmans lived in their midst with their Fourth Race tendencies, it became evidently necessary to show that their *Sâstras* entirely prohibited post-pubescent marriages, and that the sin of not celebrating pre-pubescent marriage was something very heinous. The honour and caste of their own girls was at stake, and the cunning Brahmans were equal to the occasion; and the absence of printing and of newspapers materially helped them. To introduce interpolations into one or two *Smritis* was not doing business thoroughly. There was a community in the north also which had to be snubbed. And considering the degeneracy of the age, it is not surprising that the extravagant and unvedic denunciations of post-pubescent marriages were introduced into many *Smritis* about this time.* The reason was dire necessity, which knows no law. ఆపత్కాలే నాస్తిమర్యాదా आपत्काले नास्ति मर्यादा.

38. THE UNSASTRAIC CHARACTER OF PRE-PUBESCENT MARRIAGE.

We shall now state some objections to pre-pubescent marriage, and call upon its advocates to refute them *Sastraically.*

---

* This subject is of great importance from the practical standpoint, and so it is dealt with in an elaborate manner in the Appendix.

I. The first objection is that the Vedic *Mantras* do not sanction pre-pubescent marriage. All the *Mantras*, as we have seen, contemplate post-pubescent marriage, and none is in favour of pre-pubescent marriage. As the Vedas are the highest authority, pre-pubescent marriage has no Vedic or authoritative basis.

II. Though the *Smritikâras* advocate pre-pubescent marriage, they do not prescribe appropriate *Mantras* for them. If it is true that the punishment for post-pubescent marriage is the *Raurava* Hell, and sundry other unmentionable things, clearly it was their bounden duty to prohibit the use of post-pubescent marriage *Mantras*; and this they have not done, and the *Slokas* which are paraded as authorities for pre-pubescent marriage, but which are in conflict with the ritual, cannot be considered genuine.

III. Performing pre-pubescent marriages with post-pubescent marriage *Mantras* is inconsistent with truthfulness. The *Srutis* say that there is no religion higher than Truth.* As Truth is Brahman, those who seek Brahman must be truthful.† "Truth is

---

* సత్యాన్నాస్తి పరోధర్మః ।

सत्यान्नास्ति परोधर्मः ।

† సత్యంసత్సుసదాధర్మః సత్యంధర్మస్సనాతనః ।
సత్యమేవనమస్యేత సత్యంహిపరమాగతిః ।
సత్యంధర్మస్తపోయోగః సత్యంబ్రహ్మసనాతనం ।
సత్యంయజ్ఞః పరఃప్రోక్తః సర్వంసత్యేప్రతిష్ఠితం ॥

ever the *Dharma* of the good. Truth is the *Sanâtana Dharma.* Bow only to the Truth. Truth is the final way. Truth is *Dharma,* Truth is *Tapas,* Truth is the eternal *Brahman.* Truth is the highest sacrifice, for all is founded on, and supported by, Truth."

IV. The analogy of the *Mâsika* ceremonies being performed in advance or before they fall due, is no analogy at all; for, firstly, the *Kartru* in the *Mâsika* ceremony has acquired the *Adhikâra,* while the pre-pubescent bride has not acquired it, if she is to use the present marriage-mantras; and, secondly, while the *Mâsika* ceremonies are repeated by the *Kartru,* if alive, as they fall due, the marriage ceremonies cannot be so repeated without stultification.

V. *Vivâha* is an important *Samskâra,* and it ought not to be performed before the girl attains age, and acquires the *Adhikâra* or privilege of offering sacrifices to certain *Devatas,* and of living the life indicated by the *Mantras.*

This is a most important point, and, as already pointed out, it vitally affects Hindu society. And we request the advocates of pre-pubescent marriage to examine their position calmly and dispassionately.

सत्यंसत्सुसदाधर्मः सत्यंधर्मस्सनातनः ।
सत्यमेवनमस्येत संत्यंहिपरमागतिः ।
सत्यंधर्मस्तपोयोगः सत्यंब्रह्मसनातनम् ।
सत्यंयज्ञः परः प्रोक्तः सर्वंसत्येप्रतिष्ठितम् ॥

39. IS PRE-PUBESCENT MARRIAGE FOR GIRLS THE COUNTERPART OF THE UPANAYANA FOR BOYS?

An idea still prevails in many "learned" quarters that the marriage ceremony in the case of pre-pubescent girls stands as the counterpart of the *Upanayana* ceremony for boys. Plainly stated, the idea is that what *Upanayana* is to a boy as a *Samskâra*, that marriage is to a pre-pubescent girl. Let us examine if this statement can be true.

What is *Upanayana*, and what is its real object? *Upanayana*, strictly speaking, is the commencement of an occult training. *Sandhyâvandana* is no ordinary affair, no mere lip-repetition of *Mantras* in a hurry-burry fashion. The core of the *Sandhyâvandana* is the *Gayatri Japa*; and to prepare oneself for this important *Japa*, a number of preliminary ceremonies are necessary, in which the *Prânâyâma* plays a leading part. If the *Prânâyâma* is not properly performed, there can be no real or efficacious *Gayatri Japa*. *Prânâyâma* occupies the fourth position in *Ashtânga Yoga*, and pre-supposes *Yama* (self-control), *Niyama* (strict observance of certain rules of conduct), and *Asana* (bodily postures). What is *Yama* or self-control? What is it that controls, and what is it that is controlled? "Know the Self the chariot-owner, the body the chariot; know Reason (Buddhi) the charioteer, and the mind as the reins; they call the Senses the horses, the sense-objects their province," says the

Kathopanishat. * Reason or Buddhi has to control the senses by means of the mind. Yoga is Chitta Vritti Nirôdha, and the first requisite of Yoga is Yama, which implies the rule of Buddhi or Reason over the Mind and the Senses. Boys ought to be able to reason pretty well before they can be declared fit for Prânâyâma. Yama implies *Ahimsa* or doing no injury to living beings, *Satyavachana* or veracity, *Asteya* or avoidance of thieving, *Bramacharya* or chastity, and *Aparigraha* or non-acceptance of gifts. *Niyama* is the diligent observance of certain rules of conduct: it implies *Saucha* or purity, *Tripti* or contentment, *Tapas* or austerity, *Adhyayana* or Vedic study and *Ijya* or devotion. Thus *Prânâyâma* pre-supposes a decent mental equipment, and a high moral discipline. *Prânâyâma* is regulated Respiration, and if properly practised along with âsanas (bodily postures), it keeps the body and the mind in a steady, healthy, vigorous condition. *Sandhyâvandana*, regularly and yogically continued for years, purifies and invigourates all the three *kosas*—*Annamaya*, *Prânamaya*, and *Manomaya*;

---

* ఆత్మానం రథినం విద్ధి శరీరం రథమేవతు ।
బుద్ధింతు సారథిం విద్ధి మనః ప్రగ్రహమేవచ ॥
ఇన్ద్రియాణి హయానాహుః విషయాంస్తేషు గోచరాన్ ॥

आत्मानं रथिनंविद्धि शरीरं रथमेवतु ।
बुद्धिंतु सारथिं विद्धि मनः प्रग्रहमेवच ॥
इन्द्रियाणि हयानाहुः विषयांस्तेषु गोचरान् ॥

and when all these three are kept in a healthy and vigorous condition, the way is certainly paved for the advanced stages of Yogic practice—*Pratyâhâra* or the control of the various organs, *Dhârana* or abstraction of the mind, *Dhyâna* or contemplation, and *Samâdhi* or Super-consciousness. * The ideal training of the three *kosas*—*Annamaya*, *Prânamaya*

---

* Patanjali, in the First Chapter of his Yoga Philosophy, enumerates eight angâs or stages of Yoga. They are:—

1. *Yama* (Self-control).
   (a) *Ahimsa* or doing no injury.
   (b) *Satyavachana* or truthfulness.
   (c) *Asteya* or thieving nothing.
   (d) *Brahmacharya* or chastity.
   (e) *Aparigraha* or accepting no gifts.
2. *Niyama* (Diligent Observance).
   (a) *Saucha* or purity.
   (b) *Tripti* or contentment.
   (c) *Tapas* or austerity.
   (d) *Adhyayana* or Vedic study.
   (e) *Ijya* or devotion.
3. *Asanas* (Bodily Postures).
4. *Prânâyâma* (Regulated Respiration).
   (a) *Puraka* or inhalation.
   (b) *Kumbhaka* or suspension.
   (c) *Rechaka* or exhalation.
5. *Pratyâhâra* (Restraint of the Organs).
6. *Dhârana* (Abstraction of the Mind).
7. *Dhyâna* (Contemplation).
8. *Samâdhi* (Super-consciousness).

In Ashtânga Yoga the relation of the *angas* or constituents is one of *Ekôttara Vriddhi*, that is, each succeeding constituent adds to its own characteristics

and *Manomaya*—is the real object of *Sandhyâvandana* in its rigorous sense. It is for this lofty training according to the varying capacities of individuals that *Sandhyâvandana* is intended. In order that the acquired capacities may not deteriorate, and that the development of the *kosas* may go on continuously, *Sandhyâvandana* is rigorously enjoined till the close of the *Vânaprasthâsrama*. When the householder has continued the training till his old age, when he has succeeded in detaching himself from worldly attachments, when he is fit to become a *Sannyâsi*, *Sandhyâvandana* in its ordinary form ceases to help him, and it is given up. Such, I believe, is the real import of *Sandhyâvandana*.

---

those of its predecessor. The eight *angas* are in reality the eight stages of development.

"After giving the above-mentioned sub-divisions the author describes the nature of *Samâdhi* and its two divisions. The second chapter describes in detail the ways and means to perform *Samâdhi*. The third chapter describes the powers developed in a Yogi, when he has reached the last stage of Yoga. *Samâdhi* on different objects imparts different powers to the Yogi. *Samâdhi* on the Moon gives one particular power, on Jupiter another, and so on. The fourth chapter treats of *Môksha*. Patanjali declares that when a man becomes an adept at *Samâdhi*, he gains a knowledge of the past and the future, a knowledge of the sounds of animals, of the thoughts of others, of the time of his own death, &c." (Hindu Superiority, pp. 291-2.)

Now let us consider the age at which the occult training indicated by the Sandhyâvandana may commence. "From the eighth year to the sixteenth year" is the period recommended. We see clearly here that the extreme limits are indicated. The Upanayana Samskâra should not take place before the eighth year, nor after the sixteenth year. Are these limits mere conventional limits, or have they any real meaning? Now-a-days it is thought that the limits prescribed are conventional, and that parents may seek and study their own convenience. It is certainly not so, and a little consideration will convince anybody that it can not be so. What has the boy to do at the Upanayana Samskâra? He has to study the Vedas, perform the *Prânâyâma* and the *Gâyatri Japa*. What are the characteristics of the Vedic study? *Svara*, *Varna*, and *Chhandas* constitute the very life of the Vedas. What is *Svara*? The Vedic *Svara* or accent is very complex with the distinctions of *Udâtta*, *Anudâtta*, and *Svarita*. *Varna* is not the mere letter of the alphabet; it has also reference to the occult colour of objects and ideas. *Chhandas* is prosody, which is understood with some difficulty. *Prânâyâma* and *Gâyatri Japa* require a fair degree of mental equipment and of moral discipline. Now, the Upanayana Samskâra is intended to mark the commencement of a boy's Vedic studies, not of his ordinary linguistic studies; and as we have just shown that the Vedic study requires a previous knowledge of *Svara*, *Varna*, and *Chhandas*, it is plain that not even an exceptionally intelligent boy can undergo the Upanayana Samskâra before his eighth year. There are boys of different grades of intelligence, and several boys may not be fit for the Upanayana Samskâra even in their thirteenth year owing to their ignorance of *svara*, *varna*, and *chhandas* and their inability to practice *Yama* and *Niyama*. What we have to do then is to give an ordinary training to the boy till he becomes physically, mentally, and morally fit for the Upanayana Samskâra. Thus we see that the Upanayana Samskâra is a very exacting one, and so a wide margin of eight years is given.

We have to bear in mind another point also. During periods of acute illness and of *asuchi*, the whole of Sandhyâvandana is not performed. What may be the reason of this? I believe the reason is that during periods of acute illness, the *Prânamaya* and *Annamaya Kosas* are out of gear, and they cannot bear the acute and rapid vibrations set up by *Japa*. During periods of *asuchi*, steadiness and equilibrium of mind are unattainable, and so Sandhyâvandana is not recommended. Thus it becomes plain that Sandhyâvandana is a sharp-edged weapon which should be used with care.

Now the question arises whether a woman who undertakes the arduous duties of motherhood should or should not have the Upanayana Samskâra. The Upanayana Samskâra or discipline, to be of any real use, should be diligently repeated thrice every day till one becomes a Sannyâsi. Plain it is that a woman, who has undertaken the arduous and responsible duties of motherhood cannot rigorously adhere to the severe discipline; and it was this important consideration, we may be sure, which led the *Maharishis* to deny to *Grihinis* the privilege of Vedâdhyayana, which includes Sandhyâvandana. Because they have no Vedâdhikâra and no Sandhyâvandana, it does not follow that they have no *Brahmacharya Vrata* and no *Brahmacharyâsrama*. These they have and must have. Just like boys, they also have to be trained physically, mentally, morally, and spiritually. The severe occult discipline of Upanayana is, no doubt, denied to them, as it is not quite consistent with the duties of motherhood; but not a careful and well-planned system of education. Until they attain puberty they also should be celibates both in mind and body. They also should not think of sex, and they also should live upon plain food. We may be sure that girls had this sort of education or training during the Sutra Period.

The counterpart for girls of the Upanayana Samskâra for boys is evidently then a system of thorough education minus the Sandhyâvandana and Vedâdhyayana. The Mahâbhârata, which is called the Fifth

Veda, the Ramâyana, the Purânas, and all the so-called accomplishments are certainly open to them; and under proper training they may and do become learned scholars. We have several instances of lady scholars in history. One Lakshmidevi, who flourished in the 14th Century A.D., wrote a work known as "Vivâdachandra", a Smriti still in use in Mithila. Another Lakshmidevi, styling herself as Bâlambhatta, has written a commentary on Mitakshara, a Smriti known in Southern India also. As she controverts the theories of Nanda Pandita, she must have lived in the 17th Century A.D. Her *nom de plume* sufficiently indicates in what estimation lady scholars were held in the 17th Century A.D. In the period of Metrical Smritis, the education of women was almost entirely neglected. When men themselves had become ignorant, it is no wonder they denied education to women. Pre-pubescent marriages had become necessary to save grown-up girls from non-Aryan violence; and as the marriage ceremony had been unsâstraically divided into two parts—*Vivâha* or betrothal and *Garbhâdhâna* or nuptials, an idea was started that pre-pubescent marriage was a sort of *Samskâra* for girls. As a matter of fact, there can be nothing common between *Upanayana* and *Vivâha*, as they mark the commencement of two different *Asramas*. *Upanayana* and *Vivâha* are both *Samskâras*, no doubt; but they both cannot be *Samskâras* for beings of the same age.

Upanayana is for youngsters, and *Vivâha* is for adults. Youngsters and adults require altogether different *Samskâras*. *Vivâha Mantras* can never inculcate celibacy, which is what is required for pre-pubescent girls. In pre-pubescent marriage, a tender girl of 10 or 11 years is exhorted to diligently cultivate conjugal love, to associate with her husband in thought, word and deed, to beget progeny, to have her husband always in her mind, to submit to his embrace, and to learn and remember the secrets of sexual intercourse, &c. If such thoughts constitute the counterpart of the Upanayana ceremony, we may well exclaim with Shakespeare :—

> "O judgment! thou art fled to brutish beasts,
> And men have lost their reason!"

40. THE FRIVOLOUS CHARACTER OF PRE-PUBESCENT MARRIAGE.

It is also our duty to point out how the practice of pre-pubescent marriages has altered the holy character of the Aryan Marriage Ritual, and imparted to it a character of frivolity and levity. Pre-pubescent marriage, as we have shown, is at best a mock marriage; and *sraddha* and *trikarana suddhi* are impossibilities in it. Pre-pubescent marriage cannot be a real Samskâra, as a Samskâra or discipline has to affect both the *sthula* and *sukshma sariras*. The *Samskâra* for the *Sthula Sarira*, as the Sankalpa and the

Samâvesana Mantras clearly indicate, is the sexual act, properly planned and conducted; and this act is a physical impossibility in a pre-pubescent marriage; and, when attempted, it may be construed into a crime according to the Criminal Codes of all the civilized nations on the face of the globe. It can not be supposed that in those days there were no inquiring minds, and no legal technicalities to be attended to. To satisfy the law and to secure wifehood it became necessary to impart to the farce of pre-pubescent marriage a character of seriousness and solemnity, which did not properly belong to it. The question arose as to how pre-pubescent marriage could be constued to be a *Samskâra*, and a real marriage in the eye of the law. It was a question of finding sufficiently specious grounds to support a foregone conclusion.

The Brahman Pandits, who have ever been famous in the art of *Vâkyârtha* or Sophistry, pressed into their service one sloka, and twisted and distorted its meaning to support and justify the practice of pre-pubescent marriage. The sloka was this:—"An idea in the mind, a silent communing, a recurrent pleasurable emotion, a significant gaze, a clever innuendo, a fixed resolve, a well-directed endeavour, the physical consummation—these eight, say the wise constitute Maithuna or sexual intercourse.* In the

---

* స్మరణం కీర్తనం కేళిః ప్రేక్షణం గుహ్యభాషణం ।
సంకల్పోఽధ్యవసాయశ్చ క్రియానిర్వృత్తిరేవచ ॥

A COMPARISON AND CONTRAST.

No.	Constituents of Maithuna.	A girl of 8 years.	A girl of 12 years.	A Pubescent girl.
1	An idea in the mind.	Very faint.	Faint & blurred.	Clear and well defined.
2	A silent communing.	None.	Rare & weak.	Frequent & strong.
3	A recurrent pleasurable emotion.	do.	Weak.	do.
4	A significant gaze ...	None.	None.	Unmistakeable.
5	A clever innuendo ...	do.	do.	Meaningful.
6	A fixed resolve ...	do.	do.	Strong.
7	A well-directed endeavour.	do.	do.	Well-directed.
8	The physical consummation.	do.	do.	Eager.

ఏతన్మైథున మష్టాంగం ప్రవదంతి మనీషిణః ॥

स्मरणंकीर्तनंकेळिः प्रेक्षणं गुह्यभाषणम् ।

संकल्पोध्यवसायश्च क्रियानिर्वृतिरेवच ॥

ऐतन्मैथुनमष्टांगं प्रवदंति मनीषिणः ॥

consideration of the question of marriage, this sloka has probably exercised an influence which no other single sloka has ever done. Even now there are several "learned pandits" who deliberately assert that pre-pubescent marriage is a *sâstraic* marriage, a real *Samskâra,* inasmuch as no less than seven constituents out of the eight are present. Let us examine their statement with some care. A tabular form of statement is desirable, and so we shall adopt it. (See page, 143). We shall take the eight constituents of *Maithuna* or sexual intercourse, and see how far they can be present in the case of (1) a girl of eight years, (2) a girl of twelve years, and (3) a pubescent girl.

In the case of a girl of eight years marriage can not be anything better than a farce, and it is in no sense a *Samskâra.* In the case of a girl of 12 years it may in some cases be the shadow of a *Samskâra* and not the reality. Marriage can be a real *Samskâra* only in the case of a *Rajasvala* or pubescent maiden.

Maithuna or sexual intercourse is an affair of the physical body in which the mind is the directing agent. In the case of a eunuch, for instance, sexual intercourse is not possible. It is usual with many of our pandits to misinterpret *Ashtânga Maithuna* as meaning *Ashtavidha Maithuna.* In this, we are sure, they are not right. They fancy that the eight constituents are so many kinds of *Maithuna.* They assert that *Smarana* or memory is present as the bridegroom knows and remembers his wife, and *vice versa*; that *Kirtana* is present as the wife is made to pronounce the name of the husband, and the husband the name of the wife; that *Keli* or Sport is present as the bridegroom and the bride play with each other with flower-balls and *Hittina Gubbi*, that *Prekshana* or seeing is present as the couple often sit facing each other; that *Guhya Bhâshana* or innuendo is present as clever and witty sayings are interchanged by the boy and the girl in what is called *Urutane*; that *Sankalpa* or resolve is present as Sankalpas for the several *Homas* are stated; that *Adhyavasâya* or endeavour is present as endeavours are made to get through the ceremonies, and lastly that *Kriyâ Nirvriti* or the physical act is also present in a sense as the boy throws his arm round the shoulder of the girl in the course of the ceremonies. This mode of interpretation is altogether wrong, and can only be intended to delude fools. *Ashtânga Maithuna* is sexual intercourse whose *Angâs* or constituents are eight. The relation between the constituents is one of *Ekôttara Vriddhi*, that is, each succeeding constituent adds to its own characteristics those of its predecessor. Thus *Smarana* is not an idea of the girl-wife, but the idea of the sexual act; *Kirtana* is not ordinary talk but the communing of the lower Manas about the sexual act; *Keli* is not the play with flower-balls or the hitting with *Gubbi*, but the recurrent pleasurable emotion which prompts the parties to think of the act and its concomitants again and again; *Prekshana* is not an aimless gaze, but the gaze of a lover that speaks a whole volume at a single glance; *Guhya-bhâshana* is not a mere witty stanza but an innuendo which seeks to ascertain whether the other party favours the idea of intercourse; *Sankalpa* is not the *Sankalpa* of a *Homa* but the fixed resolve to have sexual intercourse; *Adhyavasâya* or endeavour is paving the way for the sexual act; and *Kriyâ Nirvriti* is the consummation of the physical act of sexual intercourse. The eight *Angas* are in reality the eight stages in the development; the *Smarana* or the idea appears first in the mind or the Manômaya Kosa; by mental communing it acquires strength and affects the Prânamaya Kosa; the mind fondly recurs to it on account of the pleasure it yields; *Prekshana* and *Guhya Bhâshana* are advanced stages in which the *Annamaya Kosa* also is involved, and these stages lead to the fixed resolve. After the fixed resolve, appropriate endeavours are made, and the sexual act is the consummation in which both the *Sariras—Sthula* and *Sukshma*—enthusiastically co-operate.

Is our interpretation correct? Where is the test? Take a case of adultery. Adultery is a crime and deserves condign punishment. How are we to decide whether there has been adultery or not? The Sloka which describes the several constituents of sexual intercourse comes to our aid. According to the Penal Code now in force, adultery is complete and becomes punishable severely when there has been effective penetration of the genital organ, that is, *Kriyâ Nirvriti.* There may have been the first seven constituents, *Smarana*, *Kirtana* &c., but if there is no *Kriya* or the actual sexual intercourse, there is no crime of adultery, and so no punishment meant for adultery. Our *Sâstras* dictate the same criterion. Divorce is possible only when the woman has bodily *Vaikalya* or change of appearance in the body. What is this change of appearance? It has reference to the great change of bodily and facial expression which a successful sexual act brings about. The first seven constituents, when not followed by the eighth, do not constitute a crime according to the moral standards of several nations. The ball of the Western nations is a good instance.

41. PRE-PUBESCENT MARRIAGE AND THE DECLINE OF THE HINDU NATION.

There is another important aspect of pre-pubescent marriage to which we have to invite the thoughtful attention of the leaders of the Hindu community. As we have shewn, the decline of the Hindu Nation commenced during the Sutra Period, but the rate of the decline was slow at the commencement. Since the time of the establishment of the Mahomedan Power in India, however, it has been phenomenally rapid. The unsâstraic accretions or interpolations to be found in the several Metrical Smritis furnish an indubitable proof of our statement. It is now our duty to point out what share the extensive practice of pre-pubescent marriage has had in bringing about this rapid decline.

"Unite ye *Lingas* that are covered with hair" is the Vedic injunction; and every Aryan, if he has any respect for the Vedas, is bound to be guided by it. The question now arises—when do the *Lingas* become covered with hair? Is the *Linga* covered with hair when a girl of 12 or 13 years menstruates? It is not in these days of pre-pubescent marriage. What may be the reason?

Gargya and other Rishis state that normally the indications of womanhood and youth show themselves in women in the sixteenth year.* Our *Sâstras* declare that the appearance of the menstrual flow in females before the 16th year of age should be considered an abnormal occurrence. What are the causes of this abnormity? The work, known as Kâla Nirnaya Pradipika states that the abnormal occurrence of the

---

* ఋతుకాలమితిప్రోక్తం గార్గ్యాది మునిసత్తమైః ।
స్త్రీచిహ్నం యౌవనంప్రాప్య షోడశేవత్సరేసదా ॥

ऋतुकालमितिप्रोक्तं गार्ग्यादि मुनिसत्तमैः ।
स्त्रीचिह्नं यौवनंप्राप्य षोडशेवत्सरेसदा ॥

menstrual flow in girls in their 11th, 12th, 13th, 14th and 15th years is traceable to one or more of the three causes—artificial pressure, the use of drugs or medicines, and indulgence in lascivious thoughts or studies. "In the eleventh or twelfth year of age, the menstrual flow may make its appearance in girls owing to the use of artificial pressure (*Kritrima*) or of drugs or medicines. Free indulgence in lascivious thoughts may bring about the menstrual flow in the twelfth, thirteenth, fourteenth or fifteenth year of age.* To these three causes our Medical Science adds a fourth—the preponderance of *Vâta* or *Pitta* in the system. "*Vâta*, *Pitta*, and *Dâruna* are the three things that bring about the menstrual flow. When *Vâta* is the cause, the menstrual flow appears in the twelfth year; when *Pitta* is the cause, menstruation appears in the 14th year; when *Dâruna* or animal heat is the cause, the appearance is in the sixteenth year—this is

* కృత్రిమాద్దశమాదూర్ధ్వం ఔషధస్య నిషేవణాత్ ।
ఏకాదశే ద్వాదశే వా ఋతుకాలంవదంతి హి ॥
అనురాగాద్ద్వాదశాబ్దే త్రయోదశ్యాంతు కేచన ।
చతుర్దశే పంచదశే స్త్రీచిహ్నంతు భవిష్యతి ॥
(కాల నిర్ణయ ప్రదీపిక).

कृत्रिमाद्दशमादूर्ध्वं औषधस्य निषेवणात् ।
एकादशे द्वादशे वा ऋतुकालंवदंति हि ॥
अनुरागाद्द्वादशाब्दे त्रयोदश्यांतु केचन ।
चतुर्दशे पंचदशे स्त्रीचिह्नंतु भविष्यति ॥ कालनिर्णय प्रदीपिका।

certain."* Thus we see that the exuberance of animal heat due to the development of the body is the normal cause of the menstrual flow in the sixteenth year, and that the appearance of it earlier than the sixteenth year is due to an abnormal state of things. It may be taken as an established truth that the foods supplied to the mind and the body exercise an enormous influence in hastening or retarding the commencement of menstruation. Bringing about an early menstrual flow by means of constipating food and lascivious thoughts is highly detrimental to future growth and health. Susruta, our great medical authority, states : "When a youth, less than twenty-five years old, has sexual intercourse with a girl, less than 16 years old, there will probably be no conception ; if there be a conception, there will probably be an abortion ; if there be no abortion, the child born will most probably die early ; if it die not early, weak will it be in all its organs. Do not allow sexual intercourse, then, when the husband and the wife are still

---

* వాతజాపిత్తజాచేతి దారుణీ త్రివిధాస్మృతా ।
వాతజాద్వాదశేవర్షే పిత్తజాచ చతుర్దశే ।
దారుణీ షోడశేవర్షే శోణితంపతతిధ్రువం ॥ (సుశ్రుత).

वातजापित्तजाचेति दारुणी त्रिविधास्मृता ।
वातजाद्वादशेवर्षे पित्तजाच चतुर्दशे ।
दारुणी षोडशेवर्षे शोणितं पततिध्रुवम् ॥

tender in years." * Modern Science also condemns early nuptials. Says John Cowan in his Science of a New Life :—" The great error in fixing the present age for marriage arises from taking the arrival of puberty as the proper time, it being popularly supposed that, when this is present, the woman is capable of reproduction and is ready for marriage. This is a fallacy, for marriage should be consummated only between a physiologically perfect man and woman. Physical perfection implies ripeness, indicated by the full growth of every organ in the human organization. Now, when puberty first shows itself, the osseous part of the system is not fully grown, which implies—seeing that the osseous frame is the structure which supports the muscular, nervous, arterial, digestive and other parts of the body—that the reproductive element is not full grown. Its appearance only indicates its continuance to perfect growth in harmony with all the other organized parts of the body." (Chapter II).

* ఊనషోడశవర్షాయా మప్రాప్తః పంచవింశతిం ।
యద్యాధత్తే పుమాన్ గర్భం కుక్షిస్థ స్సవిపద్యతే ॥
జాతోవానచిరంజీవే జ్జీవేద్వాదుర్బలేంద్రియః ।
తస్మాదత్యంతబాలాయాం గర్భాధానం న కారయేత్ ॥
ऊनषोडशवर्षायाम प्राप्तः पंचविंशतिम् ।
यद्याधत्तेपुमान् गर्भकुक्षिस्थ स्सविपद्यते ॥
जातोवानचिरंजीवेत् जीवेद्वादुर्बलेन्द्रियः ।
तस्मादत्यंतबालायां गर्भाधानं न कारयेत् ॥

Taking the Hindu Society as it now is, all the four causes which bring about early menstruation are found to be at work. *Kritrima* or artificial pressure is believed to be practised in Malabar and some other parts. The use of poisonous drugs and metallic poisons, especially in the Western system of medicine, tends to bring about early menstruation. The free use of condiments, sweets, and fried cakes as well as the daily use of coffee and tea in copious quantities tends to the increase of *Vâta* or *Pitta* as determined by constitutional tendencies, and to bring about early menstruation. Mothers, instead of feeling sorry when early menstruation occurs, gloat over the occurrence, and parade it as if it is an uncommonly good thing. Such is the state of things at present. But what part does pre-pubescent marriage play in bringing about early menstruation? The mischief played by pre-pubescent marriage is greater and more serious than that played by all the other three causes put together. In the first place, the mental attitude of the girl is permanently changed. The girl has become a "wife", and she is taught a number of songs and stories, which all treat of love matters in a more or less vulgar way. In the second place, betel-leaves and nuts, flowers, and scents are freely used; and these, coupled with the constipating food that is usually given, excite the passion of love. In the third place, she thinks constantly of her husband, and whenever she meets *him* sly glances and innuendos pass between the boy-husband and the girl-wife, and sometimes hugging and kissing also take place.* When the boy son-in-law resides in the house of his father-in-law, clandestine meetings take place, which make matters much worse. Without *Brahmacharya Vrata* for a sufficiently long period of time there can be no healthy development of the organs of the body; and infant marriage, especially in the case of girls, abolishes altogether the *Brahmacharya Vrata*, and makes them the poor beings they now are. As has already been said, "pre-mature age, weakness, disease, race-decay, spring from student-marriage against the Ancient Law. (Sanâtana Dharma)."

The non-observance of strict *Brahmacharya* by the boy and the girl produces very serious results in the long run. The bad results produced during the past 500 or 600 years are serious enough in all truth. The Hindu Nation has been steadily declining physically,

---

* Says Dr. Lewis :—"Every sexual excitement is exhausting in proportion to its intensity and continuance. If a man sits by the side of a woman, fondles and kisses her three or four times, and allows his imagination to run riot with sexual visions, he will be five times as much exhausted as he will be by the act culminating in emission. It is the sexual excitement more than the emission which exhausts. Thoughts of sexual intimacies, long continued, lead to the worst effects." (Quoted in Vivaha Nisheka Dharma Pradipika, p. 251.)

mentally, morally, and spiritually. The existing nation is hardly worthy of its spiritual-minded ancestors. What have been the causes at work? The main cause has been the practical neglect of the two important *Samskâras* of *Upanayana* and *Vivâha*. The absence of the *Brahmacharya Vrata* has spoiled the quality of the "seed" and the fertility of the "soil"; and pre-pubescent marriage *has* hastened the decline of the nation. For the uplifting of the Hindu nation, a return to the Vedic Ideal of Marriage is absolutely necessary. Without proper *Samskâras* no nation can prosper. This has been well taught by the Rishis of old, whose descendants we profess to be.

We may now close the consideration of the question of pre-pubescent marriage, and proceed to the elucidation of certain other important points connected with Aryan Marriage. The first of these is Consanguinity.

42. CONSANGUINITY IN MARRIAGE.

The problem of Consanguinity in Marriage is an intricate one in spite of its apparent simplicity. The results arrived at by European and American investigators are, no doubt, valuable, but they are in some cases apparently inoperative. The Report of the Commissioners of the Kentucky Institution for the Education and Training of Imbeciles or Feeble-minded Children says:—"We deem it our duty to the interests of humanity as well as to the pecuniary interest of the State, to bear our testimony in addition to the abundant Statistics heretofore collected and published by Physicians and Philanthropists, and to the observations of every close observer as well as to general considerations of propriety, that a large percentage of deaf-mutes and of the blind, a limited percentage of lunatics, and, no doubt, a much larger one than either, of feeble-minded and idiotic children, are the offspring of the marriage of first cousins." The law, indicated here, does not seem to operate in the same degree or to an equal extent in the case of the several Races of mankind as distinguished by us. Uterine brothers and sisters are much more consanguineous than first cousins are; and if the results of the marriage of first cousins be disastrous as indicated in the report referred to above, much more disastrous should the results be in the case of the marriages of uterine brothers and sisters. Have the actual results been so in the cases of the Karens of Tennaserim * and of the Malagasy nobility,† whose practice for long ages has been, and still is, to marry uterine brothers and sisters? These communities are still more or less virile. Consider also another case. The Mahomedan community is a very large one, and there are in it hundreds of millions of human beings. Marriages have long been, and still are, freely cele-

* Evolution of Marriage. p. 66. † Ibid. p. 309.

brated between families of uterine brothers, and yet we cannot say that they have become a race of idiots or lunatics. The effects of consanguinity are bad, but they have not been equally so in the cases of the inferior races of mankind. How are we to account for this fact?

The division of mankind into Root Races differing in organisation and susceptibility, and the delineation of their characteristics as given by us in previous pages may be expected to throw some light on the rather obscure problem of consanguinity in marriage. Let us see what light it does throw.

As stated by us in the early part of this study, the First and Second Root Races had no bones, and were not differentiated into sexes. "The early Third Race was born under Sukra, Venus, and under this influence, the hermaphrodites were evolved; the later sub-races (of the Third) separated into sexes under Lohitânga, Mars, who is the embodiment of *Kâma*, the passion-nature." The Third Race men, who had only the first three senses—Hearing, Touch, and Sight—had little or no intelligence, and so cohabited indiscriminately and almost promiscuously. It is said that men cohabited even with brute-animals, and that the unions were fruitful. The remnants of the Third Race, found in Australia, Africa and Tasmania, still celebrate grossly consanguenous marriages. "The Chippeways frequently take to wife their sisters, daughters, and even mothers."[1] The social unit during the Third Race was the clan, and not the family. The First, Second, and Third Sub-races of the Fourth Root Race mostly disappeared with the sinking of Atlantis. The Fourth (Turanian), the Fifth (Semetic), the Sixth (Akkadian), and the Seventh (Mongolian) sub-races of the Fourth Race had families, but maternal filiation prevailed. The idea was that "the womb dyed the child." The grosser forms of consanguineous unions—such as the father cohabiting with the daughter, the mother with the son &c.—tended to disappear during the Fourth Race. With the appearance of the Fifth or Aryan Race, paternal filiation came into prominence. The Vedas say:—"Retôham, Retôbhrit Tvam—Retus I am, the bearer of the Retus thou art." In the Third Race body *Kâma* was strong, and there was no *Buddhi* to curb it; in the Fourth Race body, gross materiality and intense *Ahamkâra* were prominent, and sexual morality was lax and confused; in the Fifth Race body, it is that we have high intelligence, order, and balance accompanied by a highly complex nervous organisation; and naturally consanguineous unions produce disastrous results. Thus, instead of stating in vague and general terms that consanguineous marriages produce evil results, it is better to modify the statement and say

---

[1] Evolution of Marriage p. 293.

that the higher the bodily organisation is, the more harmful are the results of consanguineous unions. We have to remember that the degradation of the higher is always much worse than that of the lower.

As Manu states, the husband and wife should form one whole; that is, the husband and wife should be, not counterparts, but complementary halves of each other. Consanguinity prevents or obstructs the amalgamation into one harmonious whole or entity, and hence its increasingly bad effects. Says S. R. Wells:—"In temperament, as in everything else, what we should seek is not likeness, but a harmonious difference. The husband and wife are not counterparts of each other, but complements—halves, which, joined together, form a rounded symmetrical whole. In music, contiguous notes are discordant, but when we sound together a first and a third, or a third and a fifth, we produce a chord. The same principle pervades all nature. Two persons may be too much alike to agree. While, therefore, we do not wholly agree with those who insist upon the union of opposites in the matter of temperament, we believe that a close resemblance in the constitution of the body between the parties should be avoided, as not only inimical to their harmony and happiness, but detrimental to their off-spring. If the mental temperament (in which the brain and nervous system exert the controlling power), for instance, be strongly indicated in both, their union, instead of having sedative and healthful influence, will tend to intensify the already too great mental activity of each and perhaps in the end produce nervous prostration; and their children, if unfortunately any should result from the union, will be likely to inherit in still greater excess the constitutional tendencies of the parents. (Vivaha Nisheka Dharma p. 120.)

The Hindu Aryans being the first sub-race of the great Fifth Race, naturally took the lead in the consideration of the question of consanguinity in marriage, and the conclusions arrived at by them are the best in the world. The other nations of the earth are, as Manu states, learning from the Hindu sacred books according to their varying mental and spiritual capacity.

"To one who is not of the same *Gôtra*, who is not of the same *Pinda*, whose *Pravara* does not contain a common element, do thou marry thy unmarried daughter,"* is the injunction given in the Hindu sacred books, and the injunction is comprehensive enough. *Gôtra*, *Pinda*, and *Pravara* are not translateable into English, and therefore require some explanation.

Gôtra has reference to the Rishis who gave their

---

* అసగోత్రా మసపిండా మసమానప్రవరాం కన్యాం వరయేత్॥

असगोत्रामसपिंडां असमानप्रवरांकन्यां वरयेत ॥

archetypal causal bodies to men of the Fifth Race. The causal body, we have to remember, persists in the several re-incarnations, and into it the *Jiva* builds the results of his experiences during his myriads of re-incarnations. While his mentral, astral, and physical bodies or *Sthula* and *Sukshma Sariras* are renewed at each of his re-incarnations, the causal body persists and develops, and so marriages of persons of the same *Gôtra* are disallowed as not conducive to healthy or normal development—especially as we know that the type and development of the causal body determine the structure of the mental, astral, and physical bodies. Men and women of the same *Gôtra*, are, in a sense, counterparts, not complementary halves, and so altogether unfit for marriage. According to Aryan conception, the man is the seed, which has in it the whole tree in miniature, while the woman is the soil, which, after the implanting of the seed, changes its character, and loses its original individuality. Thus the woman passes into the *Gôtra* of her husband, while the husband always retains his, as the soil cannot permanently alter the character of the seed. Thus marriages between beings of the same *Gôtra* are entirely prohibited. In order that men may not forget their *Gôtra*, they are enjoined to repeat it in the course of the *Sandhyâvandana*—which, from the stand-point of marriage, is a very wholesome practice.

Sapindas are descendants of a common progenitor.* The Hindu Sacred Books prohibit marriages between *Sapindas* or descendants of a common ancestor, up to the seventh generation in the male line, and the fifth in the female line. "The taint of *Pinda* vanishes after the fifth and the seventh generations"† says Gautama. "Take the male-parent as the starting point, and calculate seven generations in the male line; after which the taint of *Sâpindya* disappears, and marriages may be freely celebrated. On the side of the female-parent, five generations alone, calculated in the male line, are enough",‡ Our Sutrakâras and

---

* సమానః ఏకః పిండో దేహావయవో యేషాం తే సపిండాః ।

समानः एकः पिंडोदेहावयवोयेषां तेसपिंडाः ।

† పిండనివృత్తి స్సప్తమే పంచమే వేతి ॥

पिंडनिवृत्ति स्सप्तमे पंचमे वेति ॥

‡ పితృపక్షే కూటస్థమారభ్య తత్పుత్రాది గణనాయాం సప్తమాదూర్ధ్వం వరవధ్వోర్వివాహో న దుష్యతి । మాతృపక్షే కూటస్థమారభ్య తత్పుత్రాది గణనాయాం వరవధ్వో ర్మాతాచేత్పంచమీ భవతి ॥ (వివాహ నిషేకధర్మ. పు. ౨౩.)

पितृपक्षे कूटस्थमारभ्य तत्पुत्रादि गणनायां सप्तमादूर्ध्वं वरवध्वो-र्विवाहोन दुष्यति ।

मातृपक्षे कूटस्थमारभ्य तत्पुत्रादि गणनायांवरवध्वोः माताचेत्पंचमी भवति ॥ (विवाह निषेकधर्म पुट. २३.)

In his Variation of Species, Vol. II. Ch. 17, Mr. Darwin says :—"Thus Lord Orford crossed his famous

Smritikâras prohibit the marriages of *Sapindas* in the most explicit terms. Sâtâtapa says:—"A *dvija* that marries the daughter of his mother's brother, or one that is of his mother's *Gôtra*, or one whose *Pravara* partially coincides with that of his own, should undergo the *Prâyaschitta* (penance) of *Chândrâyana*".* Paithinasa teaches:—"The daughters of the father's sisters, those of the mother's sisters, and those of the mother's brothers are in point of relationship equal to sisters, and therefore they should not be married."† Sumantu affirms that

---

grayhound, which failed in courage, with a bull-dog, which had an excess of ferocity. The consequence was that, at the sixth or seventh generation of descendants, there was not a vestige left of the form of the bull-dog, but his indomitable courage remained."

* మాతులస్య సుతామూఢ్వా మాతృగోత్రాంతథైవచ ।
సమాన ప్రవరాంచైవ ద్విజశ్చాంద్రాయణం చరేత్ ॥

मातुलस्य सुतामूढ्वा मातृगोत्रां तथैवच ।
समान प्रवरांचैव द्विजश्चांद्रायणं चरेत् ॥

Chândrâyana is a religious or expiatory observance regulated by the moon's age, diminishing the daily consumption of food every day by one mouthful for the dark half of the month, and increasing it in like manner during the light half, in atonement for some heinous sin.

† పితృమాతృష్వ స్వదు హితరో మాతులస్య సుతాధమా:తో భగిన్యస్తా వర్జయే దితి విజ్ఞాయతే ॥

"the wives of the father are equal to mothers, their brothers are maternal uncles and their daughters are sisters, who therefore should not be married."* The great Vyâsa prohibits marriages with *Sapindas* on the mother's side.† As a matter of fact, in Northern India *Sapinda* Marriages are not in vogue. In Southern India also, the Brahmans of the Lowlands and Sri Vaishnavas have eschewed *Sapinda* marriages, and one consequence of their custom is that their bodily and mental vitality is still high, while the Badaga Nâdu and some other communities in Southern India are gradually losing their vitality, bodily and mental, through *Sapinda* Marriages. Another evil practice is coming into vogue, which is also strongly condemned. "The *dvija* who marries his son to his sister's daughter should be shunned like a *Chandâla*, and such a one loses his privilege to perform all Sacred rites.‡

पितृमातृष्वसृदु हितरो मातुलस्य सुता धर्मतो भगिन्यस्ता वर्जये-दिति विज्ञायते ॥

* పితృపత్న్యస్సర్వా మాతరస్త ద్భ్రాతరో మాతులాస్తద్దు హితరశ్చ భగిన్యః ॥ (వివాహాని షేకధర్మః. p. 18.)

पितृपन्त्यस्सर्वा मातरस्तद्भ्रातरो मातुलास्तदुहितरश्च भगिन्यः ॥

† మాతృస్సపిండాయత్నేన వర్జనీయాద్ద్విజాతిభిః ।

मातृस्सपिंडायत्नेन वर्जनीयाद्विजातिभिः ।

‡ భగిన్యాః పుత్రికాంస్వస్య పుత్రస్యోపయమేద్యది ।
సతుచండాలవత్త్యాజ్యః సర్వకర్మ బహిష్కృతః ॥

To crown the list of iniquities deliberately practised in these degenerate days, some Brahmans and Kshatriyas have begun to marry their own sister's daughters. It is not out of place to sound a note of warning here to all the communities who are celebrating the prohibited marriages that they are slowly but surely ruining their own families.

The term *Pravara* stands for a line of Rishis who have had a share in manipulating the *Sukshma Sariras* of families of human beings belonging to the Fifth Race. Thus in the *Pravara* of Bhâradvâja there is the group of the three Rishis—Angiras, Brihaspati, and Bhâradvâja. If in the *Pravara* of any other family, one of these three names—Angiras, Bruhaspati or Bhâradvâja —occurs, marriage relations with that family should be avoided.

The problem of consanguinity in marriage has been discussed and settled by the Hindu Aryans on a broad and enduring basis, and it is due mainly to this circumstance that the Brahmans have continued to maintain their social supremacy in India for thousands and thousands of years. As Sir W. W Hunter has somewhere remarked : Nations have came and nations have gone, but the Brahman reigns supreme in India. When the Hindus went and colonized distant countries,

---

भगिन्याः पुत्रिकांस्वस्य पुत्रस्योपयमेद्यदि ।
तद्वंशालयत्याज्यः सर्वकर्म बहिष्कृतः ॥

they took with them the idea of the patriarchate and paternal filiation, and the existing countries on the face of the earth are now slowly learning the truths enunciated by the Aryan Rishis. Some illustrative cases we shall consider as they are also instructive.

(1). **Arabia**. The first sub-race of the Fifth Race in early times went out by a coasting voyage, and settled in Arabia and the adjacent countries, which contained Fourth Race peoples. They lost their caste, but not the Aryan traditions. The Arabians were very rude and barbarous in ancient times. The people of Arabia Felix had commerce with their own mothers before the time of Mahomet.[1] Mahomet did a great deal to civilize Arabia. The Koran prohibits a man from "taking to wife his mother, daughter, sister, his paternal and maternal aunt, his grand-daughter, his mother-in-law, his daughter-in-law, or even his nurse and foster-sister. A man was not to marry two sisters at the same time."[2] The Prophet is admonished in these terms:—"O Prophet, we have allowed thee thy wives unto whom thou hast given their dower, and also the slaves whom thy right hand possesseth of the booty which God hath granted thee, and the daughters of thy uncle, and the daughters of thy aunts, both on thy father's side and on thy mother's side, who have fled with thee

[1] Evolution of marriages. p. 39. [2] Sourate IV. 27.

from Mecca, and any other believing woman, if she give herself unto the Prophet."[1] Marriages are even now common in Arabia between the families of two uterine brothers. These facts make it plain that though paternal filiation exists among the Mahomedans, grossly consanguineous marriages are still celebrated.

(2) **Ancient Greece.** "Tradition relates that at Athens, until the time of Cecrops, children bore the name of the mother. ... ... At Athens and Sparta a man could marry his father's sister, but not his mother's sister."[2] Ancient Greece was inhabited by men of the Fourth Race, before the Aryans went and settled there with Aryan ideas. Patriarchate and paternal filiation were introduced by the Aryan Colonists. Æschylus makes Appollo plead for a patriarchate in these terms:—" It is not the mother who begets what is called her child ; she is only the nurse of the germ poured into her womb ; he who begets is the father. The woman receives the germ merely as guardian, and when it pleases the Gods, she preserves it.[3] The ideas of Æchylus are purely Vedic. Lending wives to friends was common at Athens and Rome.

(3) **Christian Countries.** "According to Strabo the Ancient Irish, like the Mazdeans, married without distinction their mothers and sisters. Irish Marriage,

---

[1] Koran. XXXIII. 47. [2] Evolution of Marriage p. 336. [3] Evolution of Marriage. p. 337.

had in no way the strictness of the Roman Marriage, temporary unions were freely allowed, and customs having the force of law safe-guarded the rights of the wife."[1] Europe is indebted to Christianity for the greater part of her civilization. "Christianity made marriage a Sacrament. All sexual union outside marriage was reputed criminal. Adultery became again a capital offence; marriage was declared indissoluble; second marriages were blameworthy."[2] Though in Catholic countries marriage is considered indissoluble, divorces are freely sanctioned. In Protestant countries divorce can take place any number of times. As marriages of first cousins are allowed, the main principle of cosanguinity in marriage is only partially understood.

(4) **Other Countries**. In many countries, curious notions of marriage are still entertained. In Persia, for instance, "marriages for a term are legally allowed, that is, wives are hired out for a time and for a fixed price."[3] In Japan, houses of prostitution are a national institution; the law regulates the costume of the women who inhabit them, and the duration of their stay. On this point Europe has little to envy Japan. But what is special to Japan is that the *tikakie*, the inmates of these houses, are placed there

---

1 Evolution of Marriage p. 339.
2 Ibid. p. 205. 3 Ibid p. 331.

by the parents themselves, and for a price that is debated beforehand. These inmates of the tea-houses generally enter them from the age of 14 or 15 years, to live there till they are 25 years old. They are taught to dance, to sing, to play the guitar, and to write letters. They are lodged in handsome apartments, where men go to see them openly and without any mystery. They are in no way dishonoured by their trade; many of them marry very well afterwards; it even happens that respectable citizens go to seek an agreeable wife in these houses of pleasure."[1] The system of Levirate, under which, at a man's death, his wife or wives pass to his brother, prevails in some countries. "The old practice of the Levirate still exists in Abyssinia with this curious detail, that it is applied during the life-time of the husband if he has been the victim of an accident of emasculation."[2] "The Afghans also make it a duty of the brother-in-law to marry his sister-in-law on her becoming a widow."[3] In Tibet a sort of polyandrian levirate prevails. "If the principal husband (the eldest brother) dies, then his widow, his property, and his authority pass to the younger brother next in age. In the case of the brother not being one of the co-husbands, he cannot inherit the property without the wife, nor the wife without the property.[4] In Malabar polyandry

[1] Evolution of Marriage. p. 158. [2] Ibid. p. 265.
[3] Ibid. p. 263. [4] Ibid p. 79.

co-exists with a system of maternal filiation. "The Nair husbands are reduced to the modest rôle of progenitors; and it is to the wife (woman) that the fortune of the family belongs. It is not, however, the mother who governs the family, but her brother. To this brother belongs the duty of bringing up his nephews, of protecting them, and of mourning for them, if they happen to die; in reality he is an avuncular father, and when he dies, his nephews inherit his personal property."[1]

We have rapidly reviewed some of the numerous forms of sexual union, which prevail in the several countries of the globe. If we compare these loose marital unions with the strict forms prescribed in the Hindu Sâstras, the excellence of the Aryan Ideal becomes patent. Life-long conjugal fidelity is everywhere enjoined in the Hindu Sacred Books, and the purity of every *Kosa* is strongly insisted on.

43. VIVAHA KUTAS OR MARITAL AFFINITIES.

We have now to consider the *Vivâha Kutas* or marital affinities. Aryan Astrology affirms the possibility of determining the *Kutas* or affinities between two individuals by an examination of their horoscopes. The great point to be ascertained is the exact time of birth; and if that can be done, the existing treatises on Astrology enable the student to determine all the *Kutas*

[1]. Evolution of Marriage. p. 311.

with a fair amount of accuracy, which on subsequent verification prove true in the majority of cases.

The furious attacks of the Materialists of the Nineteenth Century have not done any real harm to the Science of Astrology, founded as it is upon an irrefutable basis. Surya Siddhânta says:—"The Sun is formed of the Agni Tattva, and the Moon of the Apas Tattva. Angâraka (Mars) and the other planets—Budha (Mercury), Brihaspati (Jupiter), Sukra (Venus), and Sani (Saturn) are respectively born of Tejus (Agni), Prithivi, Akâs, Apas, and Vâyu (Tattva). The celestial Bodies, known as the Twelve Signs of the Zodiac, the twenty-seven Nakshatras (asterisms), the whole Universe, moving and unmoving, are similarly formed."* This makes it plain that, go where you will, there are only the five elements or *Tattvas* in the whole Universe as its material cause. Now, as it is stated

* అగ్నిరాపో భానుచంద్రౌ తతశ్చాంగారకాదయః ।
తేజో భూఖాంబువాతేభ్యః క్రమశః పంచజజ్ఞిరే ॥
పునర్ద్వాదశధాత్మానం విభిదే రాశిసంజ్ఞితం ।
నక్షత్రరూపిణం భూయః సప్తవింశాత్మకం వశీ ।
తతశ్చరాచరం విశ్వం నిర్మమే దేవపూర్వకం ॥

(గోళాధ్యాయం).

अग्निरापोभानुचंद्रौ ततश्चांगारकादय: । तेजो भूखाम्बुवातेभ्य: क्रमश: पंचजज्ञिरे ॥ पुनर्द्वां दशधात्मानं विभिदेराशि संज्ञितम् । नक्षत्ररूपिणं भूय: सप्तविंशात्मकं वशी ॥ ततश्चराचरांविश्वं निर्मिमेदेव-पूर्वकम् ॥

that Vâyu is born of Akâs, and Agni of Vâyu, and Apas of Agni, and Prithivi of Apas, plain it is that the whole Universe and everything in it is born ultimately of Akâs.* Thus one substance, Akâs, pervades the Universe, and however distant celestial bodies may be, they are all inter-related and inter-connected. Spectrum Analysis has re-affirmed the old truth taught in our Sacred Books. The phenomena of the Tides, the regular recurrence of the Seasons and the events that accompany them, the stated times when agricultural operations should begin, and a thousand other things make it plain that the heavenly bodies do exercise an enormous influence upon the Earth. Everything happens in Nature according to definite laws. The predictions of Astrology prove true too often to be ignored. Such being the case, the educated public will do well to reverently receive the aid that Astrology offers in determining the marital affinities.

The *Vivâha Kutas* are twelve in number;† and out

---

* ఆకాశాద్వాయుః । వాయోరగ్నిః । అగ్నేరాపః । అద్భ్యః పృథివీ ॥

आकाशाद्वायुः । वायोरग्निः । अग्नेरापः । अद्भ्यः पृथिवी ।

† దినం గణంచ మాహేంద్రం స్త్రీదీర్ఘం యోనిరేవచ ।
రాశిరాశ్యధిపోవశ్య రజ్జూ వేధాః తథాదశా ॥
పునశ్చవర్ణ కూటంచ నాడీకూటం ప్రకీర్తితం ॥

दिनंगणं च माहेन्द्रं स्त्रीदीर्घंयोनिरेवच । राशिराश्यधिपोवश्य रज्जू-वेधास्तथादशा ॥ पुनश्चवर्णकूटंच नाडीकूटं प्रकीर्तितम् ॥

of these we shall select some important ones, and try to explain in general terms their practical bearing upon the institution of Aryan Marriage. The actual calculation and determination of the *Kutas* in individual cases require an expert knowledge of Astrology, which astrologers alone should attempt.

1. **The Yoni kuta.** This *kuta* has reference to the *Annamaya Kôsa*, and it may be termed the cohabitation-aspect of marriage. "Stretch thine arms affectionately; embrace thou her with thy whole mind; O Sarira Atma and O Bride, be lusty both, unite *lingas* together," says the Samâvesana Mantra. For the act of cohabitation to yield the highest pleasure, the sizes of the male and the female *lingas* should be approximately equal, as otherwise there would be dissatisfaction or pain to one or the other of the parties concerned, which circumstance spoils the character of the progeny. Now, the Aryan books divide women into the four classes of Padmini, Chitrini, Sankhini and Hastini, which we may designate by the small letters of the alphabet a, b, c, and d respectively; and men into the four classes of Sasa, Mriga, Vrisha and Asva, which may be designated by the capital letters A, B, C, and D respectively.* The lengths of the male *lingas* of the four classes are taken

---

* పద్మినీ చిత్రిణీచైవ శంఖినీ హస్తినీ తథా ।
శశో మృగో వృషోశ్వశ్చ స్త్రీపుంసోర్జాతిలక్షణం ॥

to be 6, 8, 10, and 12 inches respectively, which figures, taken in their order, also apply to the depths of the *lingas* of the four classes of women.* If we take one capital letter and one small letter, and go on coupling them together, we get sixteen combinations, which we may classify as follows :—

Combinations	*Results.*
Aa, Bb, Cc, and Dd † ...	Mutual satisfaction and harmony.

पद्मिनीचित्रिणीचैव शंखिनी हस्तिनी तथा ।
शशोमृगो वृषोश्वश्च स्त्रीपुंसोर्जाति लक्षणम् ।

* స్త్రీజితో గాయకశ్చైవ నారీసత్య వరస్సుఖీ ।
షడంగుళశరీరశ్చ సశ్శ్రీమాన్ శశకోమతః ॥

శ్రేష్ఠస్తు ధార్మికశ్శ్రీమాన్ సత్యవాదీ ప్రియంవదః ।
అష్టాంగుళశరీరశ్చ రూపయుక్తో మృగోమతః ॥

ఉపకార పరోనిత్యం స్త్రీజితః శ్లేష్మణాస్సుఖీ ।
దశాంగుళ శరీరశ్చ మనస్వీ వృషభోమతః ॥

కాష్ఠతుల్య వపుర్ధృష్టో మిథ్యావాక్యశ్చ నిర్భయః ।
ద్వాదశాంగుళ లింగశ్చ దరిద్రశ్చ హయోమతః ॥

स्त्रीजितोगायकश्चैव नारीसत्यवरस्सुखी । षडंगुळशरीरश्च स श्रीमान शशकोमतः ॥ श्रेष्ठस्तु धार्मिकः श्रीमान् सत्यवादी प्रियंवदः । अष्टांगुळशरीरश्च रूपयुक्तो मृगोमतः ॥ उपकारपरोनित्यं स्त्रीजितःश्लेष्मणास्सुखी । दशांगुळशरीरश्च मनस्विवृषभोमतः ॥ काष्टतुल्यवपुर्दृष्टो मिथ्यावाक्यश्च-निर्भयः । द्वादशांगुल लिंगश्च दरिद्रश्च हयोमतः ॥

† శశకే పద్మినీ తుష్టా చిత్రిణీ రమతే మృగం ।
వృషభే శంఖినీ తుష్టా హస్తినీ రమతే హయం ॥

Combinations		*Results.*
Ba, Cb, and Dc	...	Disagreeableness to the woman.
Ca, and Db	... ...	Pain to the woman.
Da	... ...	Intolerable pain to the woman.
Ab, Bc, and Cd	...	Dissatisfaction to the woman.
Ac and Bd	... ...	Great dissatisfaction to the woman.
Ad	... ...	Extreme dissatisfaction to the woman.

Now, lasciviousness and animal propensities are in proportion to the sizes of the generative organs.* Consider the extreme cases of Da and Ad. In Da, the act

---

शशकेपद्मिनीतुष्टा चित्रिणीरमतेमृगम् ।
वृषभेशंखिनीतुष्टा हस्तिनीरमतेहयम् ॥

* హారిణీ శశయోర్యోగే బడబా వృషయోస్తథా ।
హస్తినీ హయయోశ్చైవ మతం సమరతత్రయం ॥

మృగీ వృషంచ బడబాహాయ ముచ్చరతద్వయం ।
ఏవంద్వయంచ బడబాశశకం వృషహస్తినీ ॥
అత్యుచ్చ మతినీచంచ మృగ్యశ్వం హస్తినీశశం ।
ఇతిప్రమాణ భేదేన నవధారత మూచిరే ॥
ఉత్తమాని సమాన్యాహు ర్మధ్యముచ్చర తద్వయం ।
నీచద్వయం తథా త్యుచ్చమతి నీచం మహాధమం ॥
కండూతేర ప్రతీకారా దంతర్లింగా విమర్దనాత్ ।
నద్రవంతి నతృప్యంతి యోషితో నీచమోహనే ॥

of cohabitation is extremely painful to the woman, and she detests it. The consequence is often the early death of the woman ; and there is abundant reason for mutual infidelity. Children born of distress and pain must be wretched. In the case of Ad, the woman has supreme contempt for the man, and the consequence is often an elopement. Under the circumstances no conception can take place unless there is recourse to the syringe.

As *Yôni-Kuta* is taken into consideration by the Hindus, the numbers of divorces and elopements are comparatively small in India.

Says Dr. Trall in his Sexual Physiology :—" Its length in the adult is usually eight or nine inches." He says further :—Whatever may be the object of

---

ఉచ్చైతు మృదుగుహ్యాం తస్సంపీడాత్సంవ్యథేహృది।
నద్రవంతి నరంజంతి మనస్తంత్రోహి మన్మథః ॥

(వివాహ నిషేకధర్మ. పు. 109-110).

हरिणीशशयोर्योगं वडवावृषयोस्तथा । हस्तिनीहययोश्चैव मतंसमरतत्रयम् ॥ मृगीवृषंचवडवाह यमुत्तरतद्वयम् । एवंद्वयंच वडवाशशकं वृषहस्तिनी ॥ अत्युत्तमातिनीचंच मृग्यश्वं हस्तिनीशशम् । इति प्रमाणभेदेन नवधारतमूचिरे ॥ उत्तमानि समान्याहुः मध्यमुत्तर तद्वयम् । नीचद्वयं तथात्युत्तमतिनीचं महाधमम् ॥ कंडूतेर प्रतीकारादन्तर्लिंगा विमर्दनात् । नद्रवंति नतृप्यंति योषितोनीचमोहने ॥ उच्चैतु मृदुगुह्यान्तस्संपीडात्संव्यथेहृदि । नद्रवंति नरंजंति मनस्तंत्रोहिमन्मथः ॥

(विवाहनिषेकधर्म. पु. 109, 110.)

sexual intercourse, whether intended as a love embrace merely, or as a generative act, it is very clear that it should be as pleasurable as possible to both parties. Indeed, when it is otherwise to either party, unless generation is intended, it is a cruelty. Nor can the offspring be perfect as it should be, unless the act is both desired and enjoyed by both parties. This rule or law, for it is a law of nature, at once suggests the conditions that are necessary to insure this result. (Vivaha Nisheka Dharma p. 110). Fowler paints the opposite picture in these terms:—"But nothing will sting him (or her) so severely with disappointment, despair, and hatred, as unsatisfied desire. The reason is this: as already seen, Amativeness, the cerebral organ of this passion, bears the most intimate relation to the whole body and the entire mentality as the means of propagation of both. Hence its gratification abates that burning fever consequent on its unsatisfied cravings, and calms down that irritability of the animal propensities, which always necessarily accompanies its revised and painful action. (Vivaha Nisheka Dharma p. 111).

2. **The Nadi Kuta.** This *Kuta* has reference to the *Prânamaya Kôsa*, and it may be turned the Health—aspect of conjugal union. As already described, there are five *Kôsas* in man—*Annamaya, Prânamaya, Manômaya, Vignânamaya,* and *Anandàmaya.* In all these *Kôsas,* there are the same five

elements, which make up the Stars and the Planets. The differences are all in the proportions of the five elements or *tattvas*. The *Annamaya Kôsa* is *Jada* (inert), and so incapable of taking any initiative, and it is distinguished by its three principles—*Vâta*, *Pitta*, and *Sleshma*—which are governed and regulated by the ten *Prânic* currents * which incessantly circulate among the *Nâdis* of the *Prânamaya Kôsa*.† Every

* ప్రాణో౽పానస్సమానశ్చో దానవ్యానౌ తతః పరం ।
నాగశ్చ కూర్మః కృకరో దేవదత్తో ధనంజయః ॥
అపానస్తు గుదేలింగే కటిజంఘాంతరేశుభే ।
నాభికందే వృషణయో రూరుజానౌ చతిష్ఠతి ॥
అస్యమూత్ర పురీషాది విసర్గః పరికీర్తితః ।
సమానో నాభి దేశేతు స్థిత్వా జాఠర సంయుతః ॥
ద్విసప్తతి సహస్రేషు నాడీరంధ్రేషు తిష్ఠతి ।
భుక్తపీతరసాన్ సమ్యగాయతో దేహపుష్టికృత్ ॥

(వివాహ నిషేకధర్మ. పు, 115).

प्राणोपानस्समानश्चो दानव्यानौ ततःपरम् । नागश्च कूर्मः कृकरो-देवदत्तो धनंजयः ॥ अपानस्तुगुदेलिंगे कटिजंघान्तरेशुभे । नाभिकंदेवृषणयो रूरुजानौच तिष्ठति ॥ अस्यमूत्रपुरीषादि विसर्गः परिकीर्तितः । समानोनाभिदेशेतु स्थित्वाजाठरसंयुतः ॥ द्विसप्ततिसहस्रेषु नाडीरंध्रेषुतिष्ठति । भुक्तपीतरसान् सम्यगायतो देहपुष्टिकृत् ॥

(विवाहनिषेकधर्म पु. 115.)

† ఇడాచ పింగళాచైవ సుషుమ్నాచ సరస్వతీ ।
గాంధారీ హస్తి జిహ్వాచ కుహూః పూషా యశస్వినీ ॥

individual is born under the influence of some asterism; and at the moment of his birth the *Grahas* are disposed in a particular manner. From the disposition of the Heavenly Bodies at the time of birth, the predominant note in the bodily constitution of the individual is determined, which is termed *Nâdi*, and which fixes the *Prakriti* or temperament of the individual—*Vâta*, *Pitta*, or *Sleshma*. The Sruties declare:—

So Astrology attaches particular importance to the *Nâdi Kuta*. If both the husband and wife be of the same *Nâdi—Eka Nâdi* as it is called—sexual inter course engenders disease, and the health of the couple is sure to be ruined, and also there can be no hope of healthy progeny. So when the *Nâdis* of the intended couple are the same, no marriage should take place. Husband and wife should be of *Bhinna* or different *Nâdis*, in which case their sexual intercourse would

---

వారణాళంబుసావిశ్వ శంఖినీ చపయస్వినీ ।
ఏతాః ప్రాణవహానాడ్యో జీవకోశే ప్రతిష్ఠితాః ॥
తత్ర ప్రధానా నాడ్యస్తు దశ వాయు ప్రవాహికాః

(వివాహ నిషేకధర్మః. పు 113).

इळाचपिंगळाचैव सुषुम्ना च सरस्वती । गांधारी हस्तिजिह्वाच कुहुः पूषायशस्विनी ॥ चारणाळंबुसा विश्वाशंखिनीच पयस्विनी । एताः प्राणवहानाड्यः जीवकोशे प्रतिष्ठिताः । तत्रप्रधाना नाड्यस्तु दशवायु प्रवाहिकाः ॥

exercise a sedative and healthful influence, and also make it possible for healthy children to be born.

American investigators have also arrived at similar conclusions by a round-about process. S. R. Wells in his "Wedlock or the Right Relations of the Sexes" says:—"Prominent among the conditions affecting the happiness of married couples is temperament; and this is one of the first things to be considered by those contemplating matrimony. To enable the reader to fully understand our teachings on this point, we here give a brief description of the three primary temperaments. Temperament is a particular state of the constitution, depending on the relative proportion of its different masses or systems of organs. We are accustomed to consider those constitutional conditions (with which men are born) as primarily three in number, called respectively the Motive Temperament, the Vital Temperament, and the Mental Temperament. The first is marked by a superior development of the osseous and muscular systems, forming the locomotive apparatus; in the second, the vital organs, the principal seat of which is in the trunk, give the tone to the organization; while, in the third, the brain and nervous system exert the controlling power.

"If the mental temperament, for instance, be strongly indicated in both, their union, instead of having sedative and healthful influence, will tend to intensify the already too great mental activity of each, and perhaps in the end produce nervous prostration; and their children, if unfortunately any should result from the union, will be likely to inherit in still greater excess the constitutional tendencies of the parents.

" A preponderance of the vital element in one of the parties would tend not only to a greater degree of harmony and a more healthful influence, but to a more desirable and symmetrical development and complete blending of desirable qualities in their off spring.

" A preponderance of the vital or of the motive temperament in both parties, though perhaps less disastrous in its results, favours in the same way connubial discord and a lack of balance in offspring." (Vivaha Nisheka Dharma. pp. 119 and 121.)

(3). **The Gana Kuta.** This has reference to the *Manomaya Kôsa*, and it may be termed the character-aspect. When Sri Krishna speaks of Divine and Asuric qualities, he classes as Divine those which promote union, and as Asuric those which promote separateness. " Fearlessness, cleanness of life, steadfastness in the Yoga of wisdom, alms-giving, self-restraint and sacrifice and the study of the Sâstras, austerity and straightforwardness, harmlessness, truthfulness, absence of wrath, renunciation, peacefulness, absence of crookedness, compassion to living beings, uncovetousness, mildness, modesty, absence of fickleness, vigour, forgiveness, fortitude, purity, absence of envy and pride—all these are Deva qualities. Hypocrisy, arrogance and conceit, wrath, harshness, and unwisdom are Asuric qualities.* Ahankâra or egoism and selfishness is the characteristic of Asuras, while altruism and benevolence characterize Devas.

Astrology divides men into three classes—*Deva*, *Mânushu*, and *Râkshasa*. Fortitude, stead-fastness and wisdom are the characteristics of the Devas. *Ahankâra*, disregard for the feelings of others and unwisdom characterize the Râkshasas. *Mânavas*

---

* అభయంసత్వ సంశుద్ధిః జ్ఞానయోగవ్యవస్థితిః ।
దానందమశ్చయజ్ఞశ్చ స్వాధ్యాయ స్తప ఆర్జవం ॥
అహింసాసత్యమక్రోధస్త్యాగశ్శాంతిరపైశునం ।
దయాభూతేష్వలోలత్వం మార్దవంహ్రీరచాపలం ।
తేజః క్షమాధృతిశ్శౌచ మద్రోహోనాతి మానితా ।
భవంతి సంపదం దైవీ మభిజాతస్య భారత ॥
దంభోదర్పోభిమానశ్చ క్రోధః పారుష్యమేవచ ।
అజ్ఞానంచాభిజాతస్య పార్థసంపదమాసురీం ॥
దైవీసంపద్విమోక్షాయ నిబంధాయాసురీమతా ।
మాశుచస్సంపదం దైవీ మభిజాతోసిపాండవ ॥ (భగవద్గీత).

अभयंसत्वसंशुद्धिः ज्ञानयोगव्यवस्थितिः।दानंदमश्चयज्ञश्च स्वाध्यायस्तप आर्जवम् ॥ अहिंसासत्यमक्रोधस्त्यागश्शांतिरपैशुनं । दयाभूतेष्वलोलत्वं मार्दवंह्रीरचापलम् ॥ तेजः क्षमाधृतिश्शौच मद्रोहोनाति मानिता । भवंतिसंपदंदैवी मभिजातस्य भारत॥दंभोदर्पोभिमानश्चक्रोधः पारुष्यमेवच। अज्ञानंचाभिजातस्य पार्थसंपदमासुरीम् ॥ दैवीसंपद्विमोक्षाय निबंधायासुरीमता । माशुचस्संपदंदैवी मभिजातोसिपांडव ॥ (भगवद्गीता).

occupy the middle position, and are marked by the characteristics of fear and a spirit of compromise. Astrology easily determines the *Ganas* of individuals, and the rule laid down for marital union is as follows :"—Sameness of *Gana* in both bridegroom and bride is the best (under the circumstances); the union of *Deva Gana* with *Mânusha* stands second; bad is the union of *Râkshasa* and *Deva Ganas*; fatal that of the *Mânusha* and *Râkshasa*. Marry not a bride of the *Râkshasa Gana* to a bridegroom of *Mânusha Gana*; if it is the bridegroom that is of the *Râkshasa Gana*, it is not so fatally objectionable, (as the man can re-marry)."* From the stand point of *Gana kuta*, marriages may be classified as follows :—

Quality.		*Bridegroom.*		*Bride.*
First best	...	Deva	...	Deva
Second best	...	Deva	...	Mânusha
Third best	...	Mânusha	...	Mânusha
Bad ...	...	Râkshasa	...	Râkshasa
Very bad	...	Râkshasa	...	Deva
Fatal ..	...	Mânusha	...	Râkshasa.

* స్వగణంచోత్తమంవింద్యా న్మధ్యమం దైవమానుషం ।
అధమం రాక్షసం దైవం మృత్యుర్మానవరాక్షసం ॥
స్త్రీరాక్షసంనకర్తవ్యం కర్తవ్యంనరరాక్షసం ॥
(వివాహానిషేకధర్మః. పు. 123.

स्वगणंचोत्तमंविन्द्या न्मध्यमंदैवमानुषम् । अधमंराक्षसंदैवंमृत्युर्मानुष-राक्षसम् । स्त्रीराक्षसंनकर्तव्यं कर्तव्यं नरराक्षसम ॥

American investigators have also turned their attention to these points, and S. R. Wells says:—"But while we believe a degree of dissimilarity in character is desirable and promotive of harmony, we are far from wishing to encourage those whose mental organizations are radically and necessarily antagonistic to unite in marriage. A person with a highly developed moral nature, for instance, would be rendered miserable by a union with a partner in whom the animal propensities predominate in development and activity and give the tone to the character and the life. So delicacy, refinement and love of the beautiful cannot associate happily with coarseness, vulgarity, and a hard repulsive insensibility to the finer feelings of the soul.

"If one of the life partners must be superior, it had better be the husband. A woman easily learns to look up, and it is natural for the man to assume a protecting superiority even when there is no real ground for it; but woe betide the couple when the women looks down on him whom she has solemnly promised to love and honour." (Vivaha Nisheka Dharma, p. 125).

(4). **The Varna Kuta** *or the Evolution-Aspect.*

Every thing that exists has its appropriate colour. *Varna Bheda* or difference of colour is not confined to things of the Earth alone. Planets and stars have their own appropriate colours. *Varna Bheda* is recognised in the objects of the four kingdoms—mineral, vegetable, animal, and human. Take the diamond. It is distinguished into the four classes of Brahma, Kshatriya, Vaisya, and Sudra. *Brâhmya Varna* is the most evolved, while the *Sûdra Varna* is the least evolved. Aryan Philosophy recognises evolution in everything that exists—from the tiniest particle of dust up to the largest Solar System.

Passing from the Bhurloka into the Bhuvar and Suvar Lokas, there also we find colour exists, but in a much clearer and more refined form. All feelings, thoughts, and emotions have their appropriate colours. Every time a feeling or desire comes up on the mind a colour flashes out in the astral body or *Sukshma Sarira*. The colour of the act of a cold-blooded murder is black. Red stands for anger. This red changes into a rosy pink in strong affection. In unselfish love it is said to have a still lighter shade of the pink. Yellow is the colour of the intellect, while blue is the colour of devotion. In the *Sukshma Sarira*, the colour is very plain to clairvoyant vision.

We have already stated that the four *varnas* of Sudra, Vaisya, Kshatrya, and Brâhmana mark the four clearly distinguished stages in the evolution of the Jivatma through his millions of earthly births and deaths. The varna or colour of a "Young" or undeveloped Jivatma differs greatly from that of an old or highly evolved Jivatma, and all clairvoyants testifiy to this fact.

Ethel M. Mallet in her " First steps in Theosophy " gives pictures of the astral bodies of young and old Egos, and with reference to them she writes as follows :

" If you Examine the plate on the opposite page (43), you will see a picture of an astral body—in this case the body of a savage or 'Young' Ego.

" You notice two things about this picture, first that the body has several different colours in it ; and secondly that, though roughly the same shape in outline as the physical body, it is all one whole, not divided up into limbs as the physical body is ; and the outline is misty and irregular, not clearly defined as is that of our physical body. You may wonder why this body should have such a different appearance from the one we are accustomed to. If you think for a moment, however, you will see that the astral body has no need for separate limbs such as the physical body has ; for the latter is the body of action ; and in order to act you know that one wants arms, legs, mouth, eyes, ears, &c., through which the Self within can come into touch with the outside physical world. The reason for the cloudy and irregular appearance of the body in the picture, is that it represents the astral body of a man of only slight development ; and in the early stages of evolution the astral body, we are told, is a somewhat shapeless mass, which in the course of many lives becomes more and more definitely formed with ever more clearly defined outlines.

"We have to remember that not only the Ego himself, but the bodies he wears, as well as the worlds he lives in, are all undergoing a process of evolution; and just as at one time, now far back in the past to us, men's physical bodies were not the sharply defined, symmetrical forms we know now, but were shapeless, loosely connected masses, moving cumbrously, and seeming in comparison with the bodies we are now accustomed to, very clumsy and inconvenient vehicles; so at a later stage, when man has developed a well organized vehicle on the physical plane, his desire-body is still a somewhat shapeless, half formed vihicle, which will only in course of time develop into the compact and well ordered body in which he can freely move about on the astral plane. And when he has accomplished that, he will have still higher bodies to work at, in order that they may furnish him with vehicles adapted for his use on yet higher planes of the Universe.

"The other thing we notice in the picture is that there are various colours shown in the astral body. This is a very interesting point, for we learn from those who have clairvoyant sight, that every time a feeling or desire comes up on our mind, a colour flashes out in our astral body. Suppose we are feeling a strong affection towards somebody, a lovely rosy pink appears, (See illustration on page 53); or if we are thinking of some great Teacher, or of God, and feeling a sense of reverence and gratitude towards Him, then a beautiful clear blue will make its appearance; and so on. When evil wishes or desires come into our minds, then ugly colours are seen in our astral bodies—the ugly red of anger, sometimes seen as red flashes darting out towards some one, (See page 18) or the dull brown of selfishness. Just in proportion to the kind of desires which usually dwell in our minds, will be the colouring of our astral bodies. The picture on page 43 shows, as we said, the astral body of a young (savage) Ego, and you see that the colours are not very clear and beautiful. They are mostly tinged with the brown of selfishness which gives a very muddy kind of appearance to this astral body; the outline also is very cloudy, instead of being a clearly marked oval, as it will become later on, and the whole appearance is suggestive of restlessness and variability, with no very definite form.

"As the Ego evolves, and begins to try to purify his feelings and thoughts, the appearance of his astral body changes very much, we are told. If you turn to the plate facing page 47, you will see the astral body of a developed man. Notice how much clearer and purer the colours have become, how much the ugly brown and grey has disappeared, the lurid red being replaced by flashes of lovely rosy pink (unselfish love), whilst around the head is seen the yellow of intellect and the blue of devotion. If we would have our astral bodies flashing only with beautiful colours, we must be careful to allow only loving, pure, and unselfish desires to find a place within our minds." (pp 43—45).

Now in the mantra of the *Saptapadi* ceremony, the husband says :—" We shall live together, and we shall will together; we each shall be an object of love to the other; we each shall be a source of joy unto the other; with mutual good-will shall we live together, sharing equally all foods and powers. Combine I now thy mind, thy actions, thy senses with mine." Since the union is to be complete, and since the object of Aryan marriage, is to beget progeny which excels the parents in character and capacity, the husband and wife should both have reached the same stage of development, as otherwise there would not only be no progression, but there might, perhaps, be even retrogression, owing to unfavourable combinations.

The doctrines of Re-incarnation and Karma are a part of the Sanâtana Dharma. Every Jivatma at the time of his or her re-birth into the physical world, brings a *Sukshma Sarira* which is in consonance with the thoughts and emotions of his or her past or previous life, that is, with a *Sukshma Sarira* in which a particular combination of colours is the characteristic of that Jivatma in that Earth-life. The possession of clairvoyance would make it possible to determine the predominant colour; but in the absence of it we have to depend on Astrology, which lays down the following rule:—

"Beings of the Râsis of Mina, Vrischika, and Kataka are of the *Brahmana Varna*; of those of Simha, Dhanus, and Tula, of *Kshatriya Varna*; of those of Mesha, Mithuna, and Kumbha, of *Vaisya Varna*; and of those of Vrishabha, Makara and Kanya, of *Sudra Varna*."*

Good it is if both the bridegroom and bride be of the same Varna; bad if they are of different Varnas. No marriage should be celebrated if the bride be of a higher Varna than the bridegroom.

The Aryan idea is that the man is "the seed," and the woman "the soil." The seed sown in an inferior soil does not change its characteristics, while a superior soil spoils even an inferior seed, and makes it much worse. We have to remember that the man has the privilege of Vedâdhyayana and Japa, and so can rectify what is wrong, while the woman, not having such a privilege, is at a disadvantage. The explanation of the disastrous effects being produced when a woman of superior Varna is married to a man of inferior Varna lies in the fact that the rates of vibrations of the two bodies differ and jar against each other.

---

* ఝషాళికర్కటా విప్రాః క్షత్రాస్సింహధనుస్తులాః ।
మేషయుగ్మఘటా వైశ్యాశ్శూద్రా వృషమృగాంగనాః ॥

झषालिकर्कटाविप्राः क्षत्रास्सिंहधनुस्तुलाः ।
मेषयुग्मघटावैश्याश्शूद्रावृषमृगांगनाः ।

Representing the *Varnas* of the males of the four classes by the capital letters A, B, C, and D ; and those of the females of the same four classes by the small letters a, b, c, and d respectively, we get the following combinations :—

Aa, Bb, Cc, Dd ... ... First Best.
Ab, Bc, Cd ... ... Second Best.
Ac, Bd ... ... Third Best.
Ba, Cb, Dc ... ... Bad.
Ca, Db ... ... Very bad.
Ad ... ... Extremely bad.
Da ... ... Most destructive.

In the combinations stated above, the word *Varna* is to be understood in its real sense, and not in the sense in which it is understood now-a-days which takes into account only the *Sthula* body, ignoring altogether the Subtle or *Sukshma* bodies. "Statements have been made as to the marks (of conduct) indicative of a man's caste. If those marks are found in another, let him be designated by the caste of his marks (and not of his birth)," says the Vishnu Bhâgavata.* "Not birth, not *Saṁskâras*, nor study of the Vedas, nor ancestry, are the causes of being twice-born. Conduct alone is verily the cause thereof" says the Vanaparva of the

* యస్యయల్లక్షణం ప్రోక్తం పుంసోవర్ణాభివ్యంజకం ।
యదన్యత్రాపి దృశ్యేత తత్తేనైవ వినిర్దిశేత్ ॥

यस्ययल्लक्षणं प्रोक्तं पुंसोवर्णाभिव्यंजकम् ।
यदन्यत्रापिदृश्येततत्तेनैवविनिर्दिशेत् ।

Maha Bharata. The same Vanaparva states:—"Truth, charity, forgiveness, good conduct, gentleness, austerity and mercy,—where these are seen, O King of Serpents, he is called a *Brahmana*. If these marks exist in a *Sudra*, and not in one twice-born, the *Sudra* is not a *Sudra*, nor the *Brahmana* a *Brahmana*. Where this conduct is shown, O Serpent, he is called a *Brahmana*; where this is not, O Serpent, he should be regarded as a *Sudra*."* Hindu Books give different names to the children born of *Varna Sankara* as it is styled, and sub-sections of castes have thus come into existence.†

---

* నయోనిర్నాపి సంస్కారోన శ్రుతం నచసంతతిః ।
కారణానిద్విజత్వస్య వృత్తమేవతు కారణం ॥
సత్యందానంక్షమాశీల మానృశంస్యం తపోఘృణా ।
దృశ్యంతే యత్ర నాగేంద్రస బ్రాహ్మణ ఇతిస్మృతః ॥
శూద్రేతు యద్భవేల్లక్ష్యం ద్విజేతచ్చన విద్యతే ।
నైవ శూద్రోభవేచ్ఛూద్రో బ్రాహ్మణోనచ బ్రాహ్మణః ।
యత్రైతల్లక్ష్యతే సర్పవృత్తంస బ్రాహ్మణః స్మృతః ।
యత్రైతన్నభవేత్సర్పతం శూద్రమితినిర్దిశేత్ ॥

नयोनिर्नापिसंस्कारोनश्रुतंनचसंततिः । कारणानिद्विजत्व स्यवृत्तमेवतुकारणम् ॥ सत्यंदानंक्षमाशील मानृशंस्यंतपोघृणा । दृश्यंतेयत्रनागेन्द्र सब्राह्मणइतिस्मृतः ॥ शूद्रेतुयद्भवेल्लक्ष्यं द्विजेतच्चनविद्यते । नैवशूद्रोभवेत्शूद्रोब्राह्मणोनचब्राह्मणः ॥ यत्रैतल्लक्ष्यतेसर्पवृत्तं सब्राह्मणः स्मृतः । यत्रैतन्नभवेत्सर्पतंशूद्रमितिनिर्दिशेत् ॥

† విప్రాన్మూర్ధావసిక్తోహి క్షత్రియాయాం విశస్త్రియాం ।
అంబష్ఠ శూద్ర్యాం నిషాదోజాతః పారశవోపివా ॥

(5). **Graha-Maitri** *or the Devotedness-aspect.* We have already shown that man owns five Kôsas—*Annamaya, Prânamaya, Manômaya, Vignânamaya,* and *Anandamaya. Yoni Kuta* refers to the *Annamaya Kosa*; *Nadi Kuta* or the Health-aspect to the *Prânamaya Kosa*; *Gana Kuta* or the character-aspect to the *Manômaya Kosa*; the *Varna Kûta* or the Development-aspect to the stage of the development of the *Sukshma Sarira. Graha Maitri* or the Devotedness-aspect has reference to the *Kârana Sarira* or the *Vignânamaya* and *Anandamaya kôsas.*

It is well known that all objects have powers of attraction and repulsion. Milk allows water to unite with it, while oil does not. A load-stone attracts steel-needles, and magnetises them so that needles may be

---

వైశ్యశూద్రోస్తురాజన్యాన్మాహిష్యోగ్రౌసుతౌస్మృతౌ ।
వైశ్యాత్తుకరణశ్శూద్ర్యాం షణ్ణామేష విధిస్మృతః ॥
క్షత్రియాద్విప్రకన్యాయాం సూతోభవతి జాతితః ।
వైశ్యాన్మాగధ వైదేహౌరాజ విప్రాంగనా సుతౌ ॥
శూద్రాదాయోగవః క్షత్తా చండాలశ్చాధమోనృణాం ।
వైశ్యరాజన్య విప్రాసు జాయంతే వర్ణసంకరాః ॥
(వివాహ నిషేకధర్మః. పు. 95-96.)

विप्रान्मूर्धावसिक्तोहि क्षत्रियायांविशास्त्रियाम् । अंबष्ठः शूद्रांनिषादो जातः पारशवोपिवा ॥ वैश्याशूद्रोस्तुराजन्या न्माहिष्योग्रौसुतौस्मृतौ । वैश्यात्तुकरणः शूद्रांषण्णामेषविधिस्मृतः ॥ क्षत्रियाद्विप्रकन्यायां सूतो-भवतिजातितः । वैश्यान्मागधवैदेहौ राजविप्रांगनासुतौ ॥ शूद्रादायोगवः क्षत्ताचंडालश्चाधमोनृणाम् । वैश्यराजन्यविप्रासु जायंतेवर्णसंकराः ॥

tacked on one to another while it exercises no influence on brass or copper. Take frankincense and camphor. They behave in a curious way towards charcoal-fire and flame. All the four—frankincense, camphor, charcoal-fire, and flame—have *Agni tattva* in them; and yet, when you hold a piece of frankincense to a flame, it yields no sweet smell, which it does when it is thrown on a live charcoal. Camphor ignites when held to a flame, while it merely melts when thrown on a red-hot coal. Men also behave in a peculiar manner in the midst of company.

Aryan Science postulates three powers in material objects and men—*Anugraha*, *Parigraha*, and *Nigraha*. By the *Anugraha* power an object transfers its own quality or property to another, while by the *Parigraha* power it receives a quality or property from another object. Flowers transfer their own sweet scent to the sesamum or gingely seed, while the sesamum or gingely seed receives the scent from flowers. Steel needles, for instance, have both the *Saktis*, as they receive magnetism from a magnet, and then magnetise another needle, which is without it. Objects exercise also the *Nigraha Sakti* or the power of repulsion. The same is the case with men and women, who love and are loved, and who repel those whom they do not like. That conjugal union is an ideal one, in which both the husband and wife think the same thoughts and do the same deeds. They must be one in thought, word, and deed; and then only perfect harmony prevails, and beautiful *Sâttvic* children are born. Says Deluze in his animal Magnetism:—"In order that one individual may act upon another, there must exist between them a moral and physical sympathy, as there is between all the members of an animated body. Physical sympathy is established by means which we shall indicate; moral sympathy, by the desire of doing good to one who desires to receive it, or by ideas and wishes which, occupying them both equally, form between them a communication of sentiments." (Vivaha Nisheka Dharma. P. 129.) Perfect conjugal bliss is attainable only when there is *Graha Maitri* or perfect sympathy. Says Fowler:—"Reciprocated affection still more effectually subserves moral purity, while interrupted love is the principal cause of moral pollution in all its forms—a doctrine completely established by the entire constitution of love, its exclusiveness in particular. As long as this spiritual love is reciprocated, so long both parties are perfectly satisfied with each other. Neither wishes to reciprocate one single item of love with any other, but both regard a change of objects as moral treason in its worst aspect, and infidelity as sacrilege; than which absolutely nothing is more abhorrent, because a breach of the most sacred relations of the soul. As long as the affections remain reciprocated, neither has the least occasion to stray abroad,—because completely satisfied at home." (Vivaha Nisheka Dharma. P 137.). Hindu Literature contains several examples of perfect conjugal bliss, such as those of Savitri-Satyavan, and Damayanti-Nala.

There are three classes of feelings—those of Love, those of Indifference, and those of Hate. If we take L to represent Love, I to stand for Indifference, and H for Hate, and if we combine these L, I, and H, taking them two at a time, we get four classes of combinations —(1) LL (love on either side), (2) LI (love on one side and indifference on the other), (3) II (indifference on either side), and (4) LH, IH, HH (in all three of which Hate is actively present). Our Samskrit books represent Reciprocated Love as *Maitri*; Indifference on one side and Love on the other as *Sama Maitri*; Indifference on either side as *Sama* or *Udâsina*; and Hate as *Vaira*. The rule laid down for guidance is :— "Best it is if both husband and wife belong to the *Varga of Maitri* (reciprocated love); tolerably good if they belong to the Varga or class of *Sama Maitri* (love on one side and indifference on the other); bad if they are of the *Sama Varga* (indifference on either side); destructive if they are of the *Vairi Varga* (the class in which one hates the other).* In the first

---

* ఉత్తమో మిత్రవర్గస్స్యాత్సమ మిత్రస్తు మధ్యమః ।
కనిష్ఠస్స మవర్గస్తు వైరివర్గస్తు మారకః ॥
(వి. ని. ధర్మ. 126.)

Varga or class, these is reciprocated love, and the husband and wife are always mutually helpful. In the second class, there is indifference on one side, it is true, but there is love on the other, and so the conjugal union will be more or less happy. In the third *Varga*, there is only indifference on either side, and no love; but as there is no hate, there will be no plotting against each other. In the fourth *Varga*, on the other hand, Hate is present, at least on one side, and the marriage must breed great unhappiness, if nothing worse.

(6). **The other Kutas.** There remain seven other Kutas, known as *Vasya*, *Râsi*, *Rajju*, &c. It is not necessary to inquire into these, if the five Kutas—*Yoni*, *Nâdi*, *Gana*, *Varna*, and *Graha*—which we have described, are inquired into, and carefully ascertained. Anyhow, in the Elementary Treatise which we are attempting to write, it is unnecessary to deal with them, as our object is to show that the *Vivâha Kutas* are worthy of serious consideration.

(7). **A General rule.** In the case of Sudras in whom animal propensities preponderate, *Yôni Kuta* is of very great importance. They have hardy physical bodies and their physical cravings, are imperious and uncontrolled. The Vaisyas are a commercial people, and *Varna Kuta*,

---

उत्तमोमित्रवर्गस्स्या त्समामित्रस्तुमध्यमः ।
कनिष्ठः समवर्गस्तुवैरिवर्गस्तुमारकः ॥

in their case, should be insisted upon. To the Kshatriyas in whom courage is a desideratum, *Gana Kuta*, is of supreme importance. The Brahmans, who are advanced Egos, are the natural leaders of Society, and as the occult training prescribed for them is intended to develop the higher powers, and as there should be no impediment to their spiritual development, *Graha Maitri* is of especial importance to them.*

As the Aryan Marriage alone pays attention to the harmonious development of all the five Kôsas of man, we need have no hesitation in saying that it is the best in the world.

44. THE ARYAN DAMPATYA OR WEDDED LIFE.

The acquisition of *Dharma*, and the begetting of *Sâttvic Praja* are the great objects of married life. Both the husband and wife should lead a life of purity and spirituality. They have to eschew everything that makes their *Kôsas* impure. Flesh foods, alcoholic drinks, and stimulants of all kinds should be scrupulously avoided. The *Ahnikas* or the daily religious rites and the *Pancha Maha Yagna* or the five daily

---

* గ్రహమైత్రంద్విజాతీనాం క్షత్రియాణాం గణ స్తథా ।
వైశ్యానాం వర్ణకూటంతు శూద్రాణాం యోనిరేవచ ॥
(వివాహ నిషేకధర్మ. పు. 129.)

ग्रहमैत्रंद्विजातीनांक्षत्रियाणांगणस्तथा ॥
वैश्यानांवर्णकूटंतु शूद्राणां योनिरेवच ॥

sacrifices should be diligently performed. The Vedic injunction to married couples, as seen in the Samâvesana mantras, is:—"Sacrifice ye to the Devas, conserve your powers, and grow."

It is outside our province to go in detail into the question of *Dharma* in general; and so we shall content ourselves with the consideration of the chief conditions upon the fulfilment of which the begetting of sâttvic progeny depends.

(1). **The seed.** The character of the progeny depends mainly on the quality of the "seed". The Hindu Sâstras declare that the *Jivâtma*, who returns from the *Svargaloka* to re-incarnate on the Earth, first descends into the *Parjanya* or the cloud region, thence to the Earth, thence into the Vegetable Kingdom, and thence into the body of a male. In the body or *garbha* of the male, the *Jivâtma* dwells for three months as *Rethus* or semen, drawing upon the *tejas* or vitality of his several organs.* This period of three months, then, is important, and the husband has to

---

* పురుషేహవా అయమాదితోగర్భో భవతి యద్రేతస్తదే తత్సర్వేభ్యోఽఙ్గేభ్యస్తేజస్సంభృతమాత్మన్యేవాత్మానంబిభర్తితద్యదా స్త్రియాం సిఞ్చత్యథైతజ్జనయతితదస్య ప్రథమంజన్మ.
(వివాహ నిషేకధర్మ. పు. 215).

पुरुषेहवा अयमादितोगर्भो भवति यदेतस्तदेतस्सर्वेभ्योङ्गेभ्यस्ते अस्संभृतमात्मन्ये वात्मत्यस्मानं बिभर्तितयदास्त्रियां सिंचत्यथै तज्जनयति तदस्य प्रथमंजन्म । (विवाह निषेकधर्म पु. २१५).

live a life of purity, bodily and mental, if he is desirous of having *Sâttvic* progeny. Thus sexual intercourse for the sake of progeny is no irresponsible act. Says Dr. Lewis :—" No man should ever beget a child without weeks, or perhaps months, of preparation for this important office."

(2). **The Soil.** " The woman is the soil, while the man is the seed," * is the view propounded in our Sastras. The soil requires preparation no less than the seed. Menstruation, in normal circumstances, first appears in woman in her sixteenth year, and it recurs every lunar month until old age, when she is not pregnant, and not nursing her child. It cleanses the womb; and after the flow has ceased, the " soil " becomes fit for " sowing." During the menstrual period, the woman is enjoined to live a life of rigid purity, bodily and mental. The flow lasts under normal conditions for three days, during which period she has to think holy and pure thoughts, sleep on grass mats and wear no ornaments. She is not to think of sexual intercourse, nor view her husband with lascivious thoughts. She has to eat her food without condiments and stimulants. All elaborate toilet is entirely prohibited. After the cessation of the flow, on the fourth day, she has to take a full bath, wear white dress, and decorate herself with flowers. She should wish to give birth to

* స్త్రీక్షేత్రం బీజినోనరాః । स्त्रीक्षेत्रं बीजिनोनराः ।

a child resembling her husband in appearance. Important it is that she shoul d have her husband in her mind, and that she should not intently gaze at any one other than her husband, as such an act would give to the offspring the features of the person gazed at.*

(3). **The sowing season**. Aryan Science prescribes auspicious days for the several agricultural operations. For instance, the asterisms of Rohini, Mula, Uttara, Uttarâshâdha, Uttarâ bhâdra, Rêvati, Punarvasu, Pushya, and Hasta in the month of Mêsha are prescribed for the commencement of ploughing. Different

---

* తతః పుష్పేక్షణాదేవ కల్యాణధ్యాయనీత్ర్యహం ।
మృజాలంకారరహితా దర్భసంస్తరశాయినీ ॥
క్షీరేయంయావకంస్తోకం కోష్ఠశోధనకర్షణం ।
పర్ణేశరావేహస్తేవా భుంజీతబ్రహ్మచారిణీ ॥
వివాహ నిషేకధర్మ. పు. (201).

చతుర్థేఽహ్ని తతస్స్నాత్వా శుక్లమాల్యాంబరాశుచిః ।
ఇచ్ఛంతీభర్తృసదృశంపుత్రం పశ్యేత్పురః పతిం ॥
పూర్వంపశ్యేదృతుస్నాతా యాదృశంనరమంగనా ।
తాదృశంజనయేత్పుత్రం భర్తారందర్శయేదతః ॥
(వివాహ నిషేకధర్మ. పు. 205).

ततः पुष्पेक्षणादेव कल्याणध्यायनीत्र्यहम् । मृजालं काररहिता दर्भसंस्तरशायीनी ॥ क्षीरेयं यावकंस्तोकं कोष्ठशोधन कर्षणम् । पर्णेशरा वे ह स्ते वा भुं जी त ब्रह्मचारिणी ॥ (विवाह निषेकधर्म पु. २०१).

चतुर्थेह्नितततस्स्नात्वा शुक्लमाल्यांबराशुचिः । इच्छन्ती भर्तृसदृशं पुत्रं पश्येत्पुरः पतिम् ॥ पूर्वंपश्येदृतुस्नाता यादृशं नरमंगना । तादृशं जनयेत्पुत्रं भर्तारं दर्शयेदतः ॥ (विवाह निषेकधर्म. पु. २०५).

asterisms favour the growth of different grains and cereals—such as the nine asterisms following Svâti for wheat, Bengal gram, and so on. Aryan Science affirms that the heavenly bodies—the planets and stars—are made of different *tattvas*, and the sowing should take place only when the Earth is under the influence of those heavenly bodies, in which the *Apas Tattva* is predominant. If the sowing be done when the Earth is under the influence of the heavenly bodies in which the *Agni Tattva* is predominant, there will be either no germination, or the growth of the plant will be very poor. When the sowing of grains and cereals requires so much of forethought and care, surely the sowing of the human seed requires a great deal more of them.

"The sixteen nights, commencing from the time of the appearance of the menstrual flow, constitute the Ritu Period or the period of sexual intercourse. The first four nights, the five *Parva* days, the sixth day of the *Paksha*, the *Vyatipâta* day, the *Srâddha* days as well as those otherwise prohibited, should be avoided; on the remaining days, have thou sexual intercourse with thy wedded wife." * Thus Aryan Science allows

* రజోదర్శనప్రభృతి షోడశ రాత్రయః స్త్రీణామృతుః ।
తస్యాద్యాశ్చతస్రః పర్వాణి పంచషష్ఠీం వ్యతీపాతం ।
శ్రాద్ధాదిదినంచ పరిత్యజ్య స్వదారాన్ ఋతావుపేయాత్ ।
అన్తరాళేపి ప్రతిషిద్ధదినవర్జం ॥

(వివాహ నిషేకధర్మః. పు. 204).

the generative act only on the auspicious days of the Ritu Period, as only *Sâttvic* progeny is to be secured. The results of the act of procreation during the Sixteen nights of the Ritu Period are thus indicated :—

Time of Intercourse.	*Result.*
The First Night	... The early death of the man.
The 2nd ,,	... The early death of the woman.
The 3rd ,,	... The death of the womb.
The 4th ,,	... A poor short-lived son.
The 5th ,,	... A poor short-lived daughter.
The 6th ,,	... A boy of low worth.
The 7th ,,	... A daughter of low worth.
The 8th ,,	... A boy of some real worth.
The 9th ,,	... A chaste daughter.
The 10th ,,	... A superior son.
The 11th ,,	... A wicked daughter.
The 12th ,,	... A son of superior abilities.
The 13th ,,	... A highly lascivious daughter.
The 14th ,,	... A son of princely worth.
The 15th ,,	... A chaste daughter of rare gifts, fit to be a Queen.
The 16th ,,	... A son of rare, mental, moral, and spiritual attainments.*

रजोदर्शन प्रभृतिषोडशरात्रय: स्त्रीणामृतु: । तस्याश्चाद्यतस्त्र: पर्वाणि पञ्चषष्ठी व्यतीपातंश्राद्धादि दिवसंच परित्यज्य स्वदारान् कताउपेयात् । अंतरालेपि प्रतिषिद्धदिनवर्जम् ॥ विवाह निषेकधर्म. पु. २०४.)

* ప్రథమేహ్ని ఋతౌ ప్రాప్తే నిషేకం యః కరిష్యతి ।
ప్రుంసమృత్యుమాప్నోతి ద్వితీయే స్త్రీమరిష్యతి ॥

The principle upon which these *Slokas* are based is that the woman acquires each day a *kala* from the commencement of her menstruation day, and that the

---

తృతీయేహ్ని నిషిక్తస్య గర్భస్య మరణంభవేత్ ।
రాత్రౌ చతుర్థ్యాంపుత్ర స్స్యాదల్పాయుర్ధనవర్జితః ॥
పంచమ్యాంపుత్రిణీనారీ షష్ఠ్యాంపుత్రస్తుమధ్యమః ।
సప్తమ్యామ ప్రజాయోషిదష్టమ్యా మీశ్వరస్సుతః ॥
నవమ్యాం సుభగాదారా దశమ్యాంచ వరఃపుమాన్ ।
ఏకాదశ్యామధర్మ్యాస్త్రీద్వాదశ్యాం పురుషోత్తమః ॥
త్రయోదశ్యాంసుతా లోకవర్ణ సంకరకారిణీ ।
ధర్మవిచ్చకృతజ్ఞస్స్యా దాత్మవేదీ దృఢవ్రతః ॥
ప్రజాయతే చతుర్దశ్యాంగుణౌఘైః జగతీపతిః ।
రాజపత్నీ మహాభోగా రాజవంశగతాధవా ॥
జాయతేపంచదశ్యాంతు బహుపుత్రా ప్రతివ్రతా ।
విద్యాలక్షణసంపన్న స్సత్యవాదీ జితేంద్రియః ॥
ఆశ్రయస్సర్వభూతానాం జాయతేషోడశేపుమాన్ ॥

(వివాహ నిషేకధర్మ పు, 205).

प्रथमेह्नि ऋतौप्राप्ते निषेकंयः करिष्यति । शीघ्रंसमृत्युमाप्नोति द्वितीये स्त्रीमरिष्यति ॥ तृतीयेह्नि निषिक्तस्य गर्भस्यमरणंभवेत् । रात्रौचतुर्थ्यां पुत्रस्यादल्पायु र्धनवर्जितः ॥ पंचम्यांपुत्रिणीनारी षष्ठ्यांपुत्रस्तु मध्यमः । सप्तम्यामप्रजायोषि दष्टम्यामीश्वरस्सुतः । नवम्यांसुभगादारा दशम्यांच-वरः पुमान् । एकादश्यामधर्म्या स्त्रीद्वादश्यां पुरुषोत्तमः । त्रयोदश्यांसुतालोकवर्ण संकरकारिणी ॥ धर्मविच्चकृतज्ञस्या दात्मवेदी धृढव्रतः । प्रजायतेचतुर्दश्यां गुणौघैर्जगतीपतिः । राजपत्नी महाभोगा राजवंश गताधवा । जायतेपंचदश्यांतु बहुपुत्रा पतिव्रता ॥ विद्यालक्षणसंपन्न-सत्यवादीजितेन्द्रियः आश्रयस्सर्वभूतनां जायतेषोडशेपुमान् ॥ (विवाह निषेकधर्म. पु. २०५).

kalas go on increasing till the sixteenth day. The effects are calculated only according to the *kalas* irrespective of other circumstances.

As sexual intercourse should take place only during the Ritu period, and as certain days of this period,—the first seven, the eleventh and the thirteenth days—are probibited, there remain only seven days fit for sexual embrace. European and American investigators have also arrived at the same conclusion. Dr. Lewis says :—"There remain therefore eight days in the month from the fourth to the twelfth, after the cessation of the flow, during which the sexual relations are liable to be fruitful."

Our own Sâstras as well as the independent investigations of European and American Scholars prohibit sexual intercourse during the first seven days from the commencement of the menstrual flow; and so the oft quoted sloka which accuses a man of great sin if he does not cohabit on the fourth day after the commencement of the flow, is one of the later additions of the age of the second made-easy series, and it deserves only to be treated with contempt. The fourth day is not the one from the commencement of the flow, but the one from the cessation of the flow.

(4). **The auspicious days**. Out of the sixteen days of the Ritu Period, the first seven days, and the eleventh and thirteenth days, that is, nine days in all are prohibited. There remain, thus, only seven days in the month; and out of these seven, the following should be avoided :—

(*a*). The *Parva* Days.

(*b*). The asterisms of *Makha* and *Mula*.

(*c*). The days of Solar and Lunar Eclipses.

(*d*). *Srâddha* and *Vyatipâta* Days.

To understand fully why these days are prohibited, long and intricate explanations are necessary, which we cannot attempt here. We shall state only the broad principles upon which the prohibitions are based.

The first principle to be grasped and remembered is that as evolution advances, the organization of the bodies or *Sariras* becomes higher and more intricate and fresh powers are acquired. Compare the intellectual and spiritual capacity of the third Race man—say, a negro—with that of the advanced Fifth Race man. What a difference do we find! The Fifth Race man has by the force of his intellect made electricity his servant. By discovering the Rontgen rays he has practically abolished the opacity of wood and some other substances. The Fifth Race man is able by the nicity of his organization and the subtlety of his reasoning to describe the course of a Solar eclipse, when he is locked up in a closed dark room. This feat was performed by one talented gentleman, named

Hosa Pandit Bhima Rao of Mysore. This he did by the examination of his own pulse. He was able to appreciate the differences in his pulse, caused by the course of the Solar eclipse. That eclipses of the Sun and the Moon do affect the condition of man is a sober truth. On eclipse days man's energy is appreciably less, and so he is advised not to undertake the responsible work of procreation.

Let us consider the case of the other *Parva* days. Take an *Amâvâsya*. On this day the Moon has no rays to shed on the earth. How does this matter? It does matter as the Moon is *Sasyâdhipati* or the Lord of Growth. Conception takes place when the seminal and germinal fluids combine; and from the moment they combine, growth commences. As on the *Amâvâsya* day, the Moon or the Lord of Growth is powerless, sexual intercourse, which is intended wholly for begetting *Sâttvic* progeny, is prohibited.

But, what has a man to do with the Moon?—it may be asked. He has much to do with the Moon is the reply, as the bodies of both are built of the same *Pancha Bhutas* or five elements, and as there is the same *Akâs* pervading and connecting both. According to Aryan conception, man is a microcosm or an epitome of the whole Universe; and as such, he has much to do not only with the Moon but also with all the other bodies of the Solar system. This is a fundamental tenet of the Aryan Philosophy, and its distinguishing feature as well. Man, according to Aryan Philosophy, is not a mere flesh-pot of Egypt, but a developing god. He has rare powers lying latent in him, which only need a careful drawing out by means of *Samskâras*. By *Yoga* and *tapas* he can acquire marvellous powers. Consider the case of Visvamitra, and his marvellous creations. "By means of my Srauta and *Smârta Karmas* do I place seeds in the Vegetable Kingdom. I, forming, as I do, a part of Paramâtma, dwell in all the Lokas. Being thus that that I am, do I beget for the *Pirti Devas*," says one of the *Samâvesana* mantras.

Man being a microcosm, everything that affects the Heavenly bodies or Higher Intelligences, affects him also. Man depends for supplies of energy upon the Cosmic Stores, and when they are poor, his own energies must be poor, and hence the prohibition. *Srâddha* days are consecrated to the *Pitris*, and hence the prohibition of sexual intercourse on those days.

The auspicious days for sexual intercourse are as follows :—

First Best	...	The asterisms of Sravana Rohini, Hasta, Anûradha, Svâti, Rêvati & Satabhishak.
Second Best	...	Dhanishta, Punarvasu, and Mrigasira.

Valueless ... The remaining ones.*

The following *Lagnas* are considered the best:— Vrishabba, Mithuna, Karki, Simha, Kanya, Tula, Ghata, Châpa and Jhasha.

(5). **Sexual Intercourse.** As we know, ideation takes place in the *Manômaya Kosa*, and the impulses therein generated work themselves out in the *Prâna-maya* and *Annamaya Kosas*. Important it is what thoughts the couple entertain before sexual inter-course. The sexual act should be performed in a secret place, away from the gaze of others, for it is essential that there should be nothing to disturb or distract the attention of the couple. Both the husband and wife should, as it were, visualize the sort of progeny they wish to have, its type of beauty and its character, and everything connected with its life and career. All their ideas should take definite forms and have clear cut outlines. Appropriate thoughts they should entertain, and pleasantly they should talk to

---

* సాయణీయే :—విష్ణుప్రవేశ రవిమిత్ర సమీరపౌష్ణమూలోత్త రావరుషభాని నిషేక కార్యేపూజ్యాని। పుష్యవసుశీతకరాశ్వి చిత్రాది త్యాశ్చమధ్యమఫలా । విఫలాస్యురన్యాః ॥ (వివాహనిషేకధమ. పు. 213).

सायणीये :—विष्णुप्रवेश रविमित्र समीरपौष्णमूलोत्तरावरुषभाणि निषेककार्येपूज्यानि । पुष्यवसु शीतकराश्वि चित्रादित्याश्च मध्यमफला । विफलास्युरन्याः ॥ (विवाह निषेकधर्म. पु. २१३.)

each other. The mind should be quite unruffled, and both should be happy, and all in all to each other. The *Prânic* currents should all flow in their normal courses. Thus equipped they should commence the sexual act.*

The following points should be attended to :—

(*a*). *Bodily Posture.* " *Yuvati* thou art ; lie thou below, and with me above, enjoy thou me ; and be thou born in thy son, desirous as thou art of a son, " says the Vedic Mantra. The proper position for the woman is to lie below. If this be not heeded, the *Prânic* currents will be deviated from their normal courses, and evil consequences are sure to accrue. " When the husband lies below, and the wife works above, the male progeny that may be born will have feminine characteristics and qualities, and may become even impotent ; the female progeny will have virile

---

* సంతోప్యాహురపత్యార్థం దంపత్యోస్సంగతింరహః ।
ఇచ్ఛేతాంయాదృశంపుత్రం తద్రూపచరితాంశ్చతౌ ॥
చింతయేతాం జనపదాం తదాచారపరిచ్ఛదౌ ।
సాంతయిత్వాతతోన్యోన్యం సంవిశేతాంముదాన్వితౌ ॥
ఉత్తానాతన్మనా యోషిత్తిష్ఠేదంగైస్సుసంస్థితైః ॥
(వివాహ విషేకధర్మ పు. 231).

संतोप्याहुरपत्यार्थं दंपत्योस्संगतिरहः । इच्छेतांयादृशंपुत्रं तद्रूपचरितांश्चतौ ॥ चिंतयेतां जनपदां तदाचारपरिच्छदौ । सान्तयित्वाततोन्योन्यं संविशेतांमुदान्वितौ ॥ उत्तानातन्मनायोषित्तिष्ठेदंगैस्सुसंस्थितैः ॥
(विवाह निषेकधर्म. पु. २३१).

qualities, and may become a virago."* Thus physical contortions for curiosity's sake are altogether out of place in the generative act.

(*b*) *The Time.* To beget healthy and vigourous progeny, the powers of both the husband and wife should be at their highest; and American authorities say that the best time for sexual intercourse is some hour after midnight—after the husband and wife have both slept soundly and well, as both will then be feeling fresh and vigourous. "Cohabit not before midnight" is the injunction of Baudhayana.†" "Intercourse after midnight is productive of good," ‡ is the verdict of Astrology. Sexual intercourse during the day is strongly condemned by all authorities. "Sexual intercourse in the mornings and evenings will make the offspring cruel and heartless; indulgence in it in

---

* యోభార్యాయామృతౌ మోహాదంగనేవప్రవర్తతే ।
తతః స్త్రీచేష్టితాకారో జాయతేషండసంజ్ఞితః ॥
ఋతౌ పురుషవద్వాపి ప్రవర్తేతాంగనాయది ।
తత్రకన్యాయదిభవేత్ సాభవేన్నరచేష్టితా ॥
(వివాహ నిషేకధర్మ. పు. 232).

योभार्यायामृतौ मोहादंगनेवप्रवर्तते। ततस्त्रीचेष्टिताकारो जायतेषण्ड-संज्ञितः ॥ ऋतौपुरुषवद्वापि प्रवर्तेतांगनायदि । तत्रकन्यायदिभवेत्सा भवेन्नरचेष्टिता ॥ (विवाह निषेकधर्म. पु. २३२).

† పూర్వరాత్రేన సంవేశయేత్ । पूर्वरात्रेन संवेशयेत् ।

‡ అపరరాత్రే సంవేశనం శుభం । अपररात्रे संवेशनं शुभं ।

the day time is subversive of all merit; hell is the award if indulged in on prohibited days; avoid then all these."*

(c) *Frequency.* Important it is to remember that the generative act is a most exhausting one. The loss of semen is loss of vitality. The genital secretion, as already stated, is "the essential oil of animal liquors, the rectified spirit, the most subtle and spirituous part of the animal frame, which contributes to the support of the nerves;" and frequency in sexual intercourse should therefore be avoided. Nachiketu is represented in the Kathopanishat as going to Yama to solve the mystery of Death. Says Yama:—"These splendid chariots, these divine musical appliances, these *Apsara* Damsels, renowned for beauty and accomplishments,—all these which are most ardently and assiduously desired by men, do I give unto thee. Take thou them, and enjoy them. Question me not on the mystery of Death."† The reply of Nachiketu is charac-

---

* సంధ్యయోః క్రూరగర్భః । దివాపుణ్యనాశః । ప్రతిషిద్ధేషు నరకః। తతస్తాన్ పరివర్జయేత్ ॥ (శాండిల్యసూత్రం.)

सन्ध्ययोः क्रूरगर्भः । दिवापुण्यनाशः । प्रतिषिद्धेषुनरकः । ततस्तान् परिवर्जयेत् ॥ (शाण्डिल्यसूत्रम्).

† ఇమారమాస్సరథాస్సతూర్యానహీదృశాలంభనీయామనుష్యైః। ఆభిర్మత్ప్రత్తాభిః పరిచారయస్వనచికేతో మరణం మానుప్రాక్షీః ॥

इमारमास्सरथास्सतूर्या नहीदृशालम्भनीयामनुष्यैः । आभिर्मत्प्रत्ताभिः परिचारयस्व नचिकेतो मरणंमानुप्राक्षीः ॥

teristic enough. Says he :—" These which are prized so much by mortals yield pleasure only in the beginning; they do in the end draw away all vitality from all the *Indriyas* or senses." * " Conserve your powers," says the Vedic Mantra, and so it is the height of unwisdom to indulge much in sensual pleasures. " In the course of a night mayest thou cohabit with woman but once, never twice or thrice " † All authorities endorse this statement.

(*d*) *Bathing.* A tepid bath is always invigourating, and after the exhausting sexual act, it is very necessary for the restoration of vigour. All authorities insist on a wash, if not on a bath. " After the sexual act, cleanse without loss of time; and sleep not together on the same bed," are the injunctions given in the Grihya Sutras. ‡

(*e*) *Effects of over-indulgence.* Excess of all sorts should be avoided. Married men are enjoined

---

* శ్వోభావమర్త్యస్య యదంతకైతత్ సర్వేంద్రియాణాం జరయంతి తేజః । श्वोभावमर्त्यस्य यदन्तकैतत् सर्वेन्द्रियाणां जरयन्तितेजः ।

† ఏకస్యాంరాత్రౌ ఏకదైవ స్త్రియంగచ్ఛేన్నద్విస్త్రిర్వా ॥
एकस्यांरात्रौ एकदैवस्त्रियंगच्छेन्नद्विस्त्रिर्वा ॥

మిథునీభూయతయా సహనశయీత ॥

मिथुनीभूयतयासह नशयीत ।

‡ మిథునీభూయశౌచం ప్రతినవిళంబేత ।

मिथुनीभूयशौचं प्रतिनविलंबेत ।

to lead a life of continence, and the *Tri Ratra Brahmacharya* is the first lesson in it. If a man leads a life of real continence, long he will live, pre-mature old age he shall not have, a healthy glow shall pervade his body; hardy, strong, and muscular he will be. * If, on the other hand, he leads a life of sensuality, all manner of diseases will ruthlessly attack him, and make him miserable. Healthy and vigourous offspring he cannot have. " Over-indulgence in sexual intercourse breeds diseases of all kinds—Fevers, Rheumatism and Colic, Cough and Catarrh, Diseases of the lungs, Emaciation and Anemia, Jaundice, Dyspepsia and Diarrhœa, Consumption, Convulsions, and so on."† The effects on the mind are not included in the above list. Sensuality lowers vitality, and such diseases as are induced by the con-

---

* ఆయుష్మంతో మందజరావపుర్వర్ణబలాన్వితాః ।
స్థిరోపచితమాంసాశ్చ భవంతి స్త్రీషుసంయుతాః ॥
(వివాహ నిషేకధర్మ. పు. 228).

आयुष्मंतो मन्दजरावपुर्वर्णबलान्विताः। स्थिरोपचितमांसाश्च भवन्ति-स्त्रीषुसंयुताः ॥ (विवाह निषेकधर्म. पु. २२८.)

† శూలకాసజ్వరశ్వాసకార్శ్య పాండ్వామయక్షయాః ।
అతివ్యవాయాజ్జాయంతే రోగాక్షేపకాదయః ॥
(వివాహ నిషేకధర్మ. పు 227).

शूलकासज्वरश्वासकार्श्य पांड्वामयक्षयाः। अतिव्यवायाज्जायंते रोगाक्षेपकादयः ॥ (विवाह निषेकधर्म. पु. २२७).

stitutional peculiarity of the individual will make their appearance.

(6). **Pregnancy.** A lady, after becoming pregnant should give up sexual intercourse altogether till she has completed the nursing of her child. Sexual intercourse during pregnancy is a great disturbing factor, and it interferes much with the healthy growth of the child in the womb, owing to the nervous excitement of the sexual act, and the consequent increase of heat in the body. All doctors prohibit it. A pregnant woman has to nourish two bodies—her own and that of the child in her womb, and so a plain and wholesome diet is absolutely essential. She must beware of constipation. She should not do very hard work, nor should she be idle. She should lead a hygienic life. She ought to have plenty of sleep but not during the day-time. She ought to preserve equanimity of mind.* Paroxysms of rage she should avoid, as they give great shocks to the body. Extreme fear and intense grief greatly lower vitality, and seriously interfere with the healthy growth of the child in the womb.

* Anger and worry have a decidedly harmful and dissipating effect upon the rhythmic motion of our physical ether. The magnetic field encircling our bodies is then thrown into violent and distorted undulations, as ungoverned mind impulses impinge upon it, and to clairvoyance the appearance is a series of miniature flashes and explosions. (The Sixth Sense. p. 85.)

The shedding of blood she should not witness.* The idea is that all that affects the mind of the pregnant woman leaves and must leave its impress on the kôsas of the child, as no force in the world is lost.† Her physical cravings should not be left unheeded. When she hankers after any particular thing, it ought to be supplied to her, as a persistent refusal of it

---

* అతివ్యవాయమాయాసంభారంప్రావరణంగురు ।
అకాలజాగరస్వప్న కఠినోత్కటీకాసనం ॥
శోకక్రోధభయోద్వేగ వేగశ్రద్ధావిధారణం ।
ఉపవాసాధ్వతీక్ష్ణోష్ణ గురువిష్టంభిభోజనం ॥
రక్తంవివసనంశ్వభ్రకూపేక్షాం మద్యమామిషం ।
ఉత్తానశయనంయచ్చ స్త్రియోనేచ్ఛంతి తత్త్యజేత్ ॥
(వివాహ నిషేకధర్మ. పు. 307).

अतिव्यवायमायासं भारं प्रावरणंगुरु । अकालजागरस्वप्न कठिणो-त्कटकासनम् ॥ शोकक्रोधभयोद्वेग वेगश्रद्धाविधारणम् । उपवासाध्वती-क्ष्णोष्ण गुरुविष्टंभिभोजनम् ॥ रक्तंविवसनंश्वभ्रकूपेक्षां मद्यमामिषम् । उत्तानशयनंयच्च स्त्रीयेनेच्छंति तत्यजेत् ॥ (विवाह निषेकधर्म. पु. ३०७).

† "During gestation the astral consciousness of the atom expands the etheric design upon which the physical molecules become arranged, the sense organs slowly form, all working from the centre to the periphery. Now more than ever can thought be an important factor; fear, shock, and discord oft times producing lamentable results, while reversely the harmonious astral influences greatly assist nature in the unfolding of the embryo." (The Sixth Sense. pp. 91-92).

affects her mind, and makes her feel miserable, which greatly interferes with the growth of the embryo. * She must preserve her balance of mind and her health; and she will do well to listen to stories of Heroes and Saints, and ponder over their virtues and heroic behaviour, for it should be the ambition of every woman to become the mother of Heroes and Saints. Frederic Fletcher, the author of the Sixth Sense says:—"Especially in embryology is it necessary to remember that harmony and hygiene are important factors while the fœtus is developing, and if many parents realised the power of mind over matter, and how thoughts act almost indelibly upon the delicate etheric matter of the unborn infant, much might be achieved towards the production of a healthier childhood and race." (The Sixth Sense. pp. 37-38).

---

* ఇంద్రియార్థాంస్తు యాన్ యాన్ సాభోక్తుమిచ్ఛతిగర్భిణీ । గర్భబాధాభయాత్తాంస్తాన్ భిషగాహృత్యదాపయేత్ ॥ సాప్రాప్తదౌహృదాపుత్రం జనయేతగుణాన్వితం । అలబ్ధదౌహృదాగర్భే లభేతాత్మనివాభయం ॥ యేషుయేష్వింద్రియార్థేషు దౌహృదేవైవిమాననా । ప్రజాయేతసుతస్తాదృక్ తస్మింస్తస్మింస్తథేంద్రియే ॥

(వివాహ నిషేకధర్మ. పు. 310).

इंद्रियार्थांस्तु यान् यान् साभोक्तुमिच्छति गर्भिणी । गर्भबाधा-भयात्तांस्तान् भिषगाहृत्यदापयेत् । साप्राप्तदौहृदापुत्रं जनयेतगुणान्वितम् । अलब्धदौहृदागर्भे लभेतात्मनि वा भयम् ॥ येषुयेष्विन्द्रियार्थेषु दौहृदेवैविमानना । प्रजायेतसुतस्तादृक् तस्मिंस्तस्मिं स्तथेन्द्रिये ॥

(विवाह निषेकधर्म. पु. ३१०).

(7). **The number of children.** The Vivâha Mantras inculcate a life of continence,* "Conserve your powers, and grow," says one of the *Samâvesana Mantras.* Another Mantra says :—" Be thou born in thy son, thou that art desirous of a son." According to Aryan conception, the father lives in the son in spirit, and the son carries on and completes the work left unfinished by the father. The accumulation of spiritual wealth (*Tapôdhana*) is the chief object of marriage, and the begetting of progeny is undertaken to discharge the debt due to the Pitris. "I, forming, as I do, a part of Paramâtma, dwell in all the lokas. Being thus that I am, do I beget for the *Pitri Devas,*" says one of the *Samâvesana Mantras.* The life of continence, enjoined on all *Grihasthas*, prohibits the begetting of a large number of children.

* "A valuable adjunct to greater mentality and sensory development is a knowledge of the assistance afforded by the spinal column to the brain. Near the base of the spinal cord is an important nerve cluster termed the sacral plexus, and within it is latent the 'Kundilini' force. If conserved by continence and mentally drawn up to the brain, additional mind force is obtained, a reinforcement arrives, and the transmuted reproductive energy can then be used for mental expression. By this method, controlled sex-energy becomes mind power, and the brain thereby gains additional strength." (The Sixth Sense. p. 113).

(*a*) *The Vedic Period.* During this period, the Brahmans led spiritual lives, and their *Sariras* were vigorous and pure. *Sâttvic* children only were begotten, and there were no premature or early deaths. Under these exceptional circumstances, the idea was that the debt due to the Pitris was discharged when a son or a daughter had been brought forth. There was then the same sort of training both for men and women. Woman was the equal of man, and she had the regular *Upanayana Samskâra*, studied the Vedas, performed the *Sandhya*, offered sacrifices, and competed with man in the spiritual field. The practice then was to bring forth a child, soon after marriage, to discharge the debt to the Pitris, and then to devote the remaining portion of the life to the development of the higher yogic powers.* It was considered carnal or non-spiritual to beget two or more children. The

* There is also a nerve connection between the sacral plexus near the base of the spinal column and the Pituitary Body, which becomes reflected in the motor centres of the sympathetic system controlling respiration. Hence one of the Eastern Yoga practices consists of deep breathing, combining an endeavour to draw upwards the reproductive energy, gaining thereby greater mental and psychic powers. This is quite a rational proceeding, for the conservation of generative energy increases our physical magnetism, while the beneficial effects resulting from complete respiration are too familiar to need dilation here." (The Sixth Sense. p. 48).

second, third and other children were all looked down upon as born of lust and not of *Dharma*, and so the first-born received a larger share of inheritance and more honour. This state of things, however, did not last long.

(*b*) *The Sutra Period.* In the course of time, a higher development of the emotional side than of the intellectual asserted itself in women, and the Maharshis prohibited them from studying the Vedas and the higher Vedic Mantras. The object of married couples now was to beget a son, who could continue the spiritual work of the father, and the old idea of giving up sexual intercourse after the birth of the first child had to be given up, except when that child was a male. Men and women had no longer the same *Samskâras*, and there was no certainty of male progeny. Hence, as we see in the *Garbâdhâna Mantras*, devout prayers were offered for male progeny. When male progeny was secured, the husband and wife devoted themselves to spiritual matters, giving up all carnal desires. The first male child was considered to be born of *Dharma*, and all succeeding children to be born of lust. This is the basic idea of the law of primogeniture which obtains in several countries of the globe. In European countries the eldest son inherits titles while the younger ones do not; in India he occupies the position of honour, though he inherits equal shares with his brothers.

(c) *The Metrical Smriti Period.* This period is marked by a great decline of Aryan intellect and spirituality. Men neglected their Vedic studies, and women became ignorant. Neither men or women, except in rare cases, practised Yoga. Even the first requisite of Yoga, self-control was conspicuous by its absence. Man became, as H. P. B. says "the wealthiest heir on the globe to constitutional and hereditary diseases, the most consciously and intelligently bestial of all animals." Infant mortality was high. The same parents often gave birth to children, good, bad, and indifferent; and so in these circumstances, prayers were offered for numerous progeny, so that some at least might turn out good and dutiful. One of the mantras of the *Pradhâna Homa* says :—"O Indra, that bringest rains (prosperity)! do thou give this bride good progeny and good wealth. Ten children do thou place in her, making me her husband, the eleventh. Be thou propitious!" According to this Mantra, ten is the largest number of good children that a woman can bear; and the reason why she cannot bear more is plain. She has to nurse her child for about a year and a half; one year at the least is required by her to recuperate her energies, and ten months more for the child to grow in her womb. Thus the interval between the birth of the first child and that of the second is at the least three years and a quarter; and if she begins to bear in the seventeenth year of her age, she requires about thirty years to bring forth nine more children, when she will be about forty-seven or forty-eight years old, which is about the time of the cessation of the menstrual flow. It is not meant, however, that she should bring forth ten children, as the best part of her life will have been spent in begetting and rearing children. In the Metrical Smritis there are now found slokas which accuse a husband of great sin if he fails to cohabit with his wife during the Ritu Period; but we fearlessly say that they betray ignorance in as much as the practice of sexual intercourse during every Ritu Period abolishes altogether the period of rest which is required by the woman to recuperate her energies after the exhausting duty of nursing. The teaching of the Metrical Smritis is also opposed to that of the *Vivâha Mantras*, which enjoin a life of continence. In the interests of the human race, every married couple is bound to bring forth two children to replace them; and as a life of continence is enjoined, they should not usher into the world more than three or four children. To educate four children takes a long enough period of time, and parents will do well to practise total abstinence from sexual pleasures after they have passed the meridian of life. "When the householder sees wrinkles (on his skin), and whiteness (in his hair) and the progeny of his progeny, then let him retire to the forest,"* says Manu; and Manu's

* గృహస్థస్తుయదాపశ్యే ద్వలీపలితమాత్మనః ।

advice is certainly good to follow. Best it is to beget only two or three sâttvic children instead of a dozen or more of tâmasic ones.

45. Re-marriage.

Re-marriage is the vexed question of the day. We, however, mean to deal with it here only in a cursory manner. We shall only point out what light the marriage-mantras throw on the subject.

Before we proceed to the consideration of the Mantras themselves, it will be well to have clear ideas on certain important points. The Aryan Marriage, in its entirety, is intended only for the *Dvijas* of the First Sub-race of the great Aryan Race: it is not intended for the others. What may be the reason of it? The reason is that Aryan Marriage requires a certain type of *Sukshma Sarira*, in which are found high intelligence, order, and balance. The Aryan *Dâmpatya*, as we have pointed out, is a severe discipline; and to stand its strain, a definite type of *Sukshma Sarira* is needed. Self-control is its key-note, and those races which cannot practise *Yama* and *Niyama* are not fitted for the Aryan Marriage. The Aryan

---

అపత్యస్య తథాపత్యం తదారణ్యం సమాశ్రయేత్ ॥

(మనుస్మృ)తి. అ. ౬. శ్లో. ౨.

गृहस्थस्तुयदापस्येद्वलीपलितमात्मनः । अपत्यस्य तथापत्यं तदारण्यं समाश्रयेत् ॥ (मनुस्मृति. अ. ६, श्लो. २,)

Marriage takes for granted the *Upanayana Samskâra*, and the severe discipline which it implies. The remnants of the Third Race—such as the aborigines of Australia and the Negroes—have hardly any intelligence, and so the Aryan Marriage is not intended for them. In the Fourth Race Peoples the *Asuric* qualities are predominant, and they cannot subjugate their passion-nature or *Kâma*; and so the Aryan Marriage cannot do them much good, as they cannot live the life indicated by the *Mantras*. Similarly the Second, Third, Fourth and Fifth Sub-races of the great Aryan Race are not quite fit for the Aryan Marriage, as they have not the *Samskâras* which precede the *Vivâha Samskâra*. Thus the Aryan Marriage is specially intended for the *Dvijas* of the First Sub-race of the Fifth Race. In the second place, the Aryan Marriage presupposes that the *Vivâha Kutas* have been carefully considered, and that real affinities exist between the husband and wife. In the third place, the Aryan Marriage takes for granted the existence of the Seven *Lôkas* and the Five *Kôsas*; and recognises the doctrines of Re-incarnation and Karma. In the fourth place the Aryan Marriage is intended for the development of spirituality and the higher Yogic powers, and not for sensual pleasures. Thus in the consideration of the question of Re-marriage all these points will have to be borne in mind, and the decision arrived at should be in consonance with them.

The next point for consideration is the distinction of sex. There was a time when there was no sex distinction, that is, when men were hermaphrodites; and there is to be again a time when men will be hermaphrodites. At the very beginning of Creative work, when humanity was to be produced, the Creator divided himself into two halves, one half male and the other half female. "This division of the Divine into two, marks, as it were," says Mrs. Besant, "the very basis of our theory. Both sexes are equally divine, each is one half of God; both sexes have their part to play in human evolution, and in the evolution of the world as a whole. The sex distinction is not simply found in humanity; it goes through all the kingdoms of nature, even though the name of sex is not universally applied. The two great sides of the manifested God in Nature are found in the sexes; on one side show the different attributes and functions which in humanity are found in the male, and on the other side the attributes and functions which in humanity are found in the female. So also we know that in the whole theory of the *Devas*, you do not find a *Deva* without a *Devi*. These two are inseparable, indivisible: the dual manifestation of one life, of one Being.

"The difference of the qualities evolved renders it impossible to develop both sets simultaneously in the same physical form; hence two series of forms, in which the predominant physical characteristics differ;

in one of these series the intellectual qualities find their best expression, in the other the emotional. These forms are the male and the female, and their value to evolution lies in their difference. As evolution nears its ending, the differences become less marked, until the two are united, the halves of one body as at first." (Ancient Ideals in Modern Life. pp. 109-110). According to Aryan conception, husband and wife are not to be thought of as two, but as one. "Husband and wife are not thought of as separate, they are thought as united. Husband and wife are not thought of as capable of division, they are but two halves constituting an entire, single whole. Just as in the *Deva* and *Devi* one Divine life is manifested, so in the husband and wife the perfect type of humanity is shown forth. There is no idea of possible antagonism. There is no idea of possible rivalry. Man and woman, husband and wife, are two halves of the complete man, of the complete human life—that perfect Union, that true Unity, gave the Hindu Ideal of Marriage." (Ancient Ideals. p. 112).

"That thou art" say the Srutis. Man is a developing God, and can by *Yoga* and *Tapas* acquire marvellous powers. Man, when he acquires the higher occult powers, can create beings in a number of ways. In Aryan Books, the Creative Modes are described as five—*Anu Paksha, Paramânu Paksha, Sambhu Paksha, Vibhu Paksha* and *Prakriti Paksha.*

In each of these Modes, two distinctions are made the Higher or *Pakva* and the Lower, or *Apakva*. In the Lower Mode of the *Anu Paksha* (అణుపక్ష), some substance, such as a *pâyasam* or a fruit, is given by a Rishi to a human couple, and this removes some obstacle, and the woman conceives by her husband and brings forth a child in due time; in the Higher Mode of the same *Anu Paksha*, an intensive gaze and a touch with the hand are enough to bring about the result. In the Lower Mode of the *Paramânu Paksha* (పరమాణుపక్ష), the Rishi touches a woman, and blesses her, and she brings forth a child in due time; in the Higher Mode of the same *Paksha* a purposeful gaze makes the woman conceive. In the Lower Mode of the *Sambhu Paksha* (శంభుపక్ష) the Rishi has but to pronounce a benediction to make the woman conceive, and she brings forth a child in due time; in the Higher Mode, the *Sankalpa* of the Rishi makes the woman bring forth a child in a *muhurta* (about an hour and a half). In the Lower Mode of the *Vibhu Paksha*, a Rishi can convert any object,—such as a blade of grass into a human being; in its Higher Mode, with physical objects as a basis, any number of human beings can be brought forth and made to perform many wonderful things. In the Lower Mode of the *Prakriti Paksha*, beings can be created even without the basis of solid objects by the bare *Sankalpa* of the Rishi, while in the Higher Mode of the same *Paksha*, new forces or agencies can be brought into existence, as did Visvâmitra. Such are the dizzy heights which, according to Aryan conception, human beings can hope to scale in the course of the myriads of lives of the Jivâtma. The Aryan idea is that life on the physical plane of the Universe is a discipline for the Jivâtma, and that he should do his utmost to further his evolution while he remains there, instead of frittering away his time in sensual pleasures. (Vivaha Nisheka Dharma. page 267).

We shall now proceed to the consideration of some of the mantras. On the occasion of the *Sapta Padi* ceremony, the bridegroom, in the presence of beings of three planes, says to the bride:—" Become thou now my partner, as thou hast paced all the seven steps. Ay! Partners we have become, as we have together paced all the seven steps. Thy partnership have I gained; apart from thee now I cannot live; apart from me do thou not live. We shall live together, and we shall will together; we each shall be an object of love to the other; we each shall be a source of joy unto the other; with mutual good-will shall we live together, sharing equally all foods and powers. Combine I now thy mind, thy actions, thy senses with mine." How long the two live together and will together is an important question, and the following *mantra* indicates the length of time:—" From the *Varuna Pâsa* with which the well-knowing Sûrya has tied thee (to the wheel of births and deaths in the three Lokas of *Bhuh*, *Bhuvah*, and *Suvah*), I shall liberate thee; in *Brahma Loka*, that Loka of Good Deeds, a place by my side shall I make thee have. ......I shall make thee live with thy husband always." This 'communication makes it very plain that the marital link is to last up to the Brahma Loka, the highest of the Seven Lokas. We know that man has dealings with the three lokas of *Bhuh*, *Bhuvah*, and *Suvah* during his life on the physical plane. In his Srâddhas he deals with the beings of the *Bhuvarloka*, and in the sacrificial rites which he performs he deals with the *Devas*. As our Sacred Writings say, the Lokas interpenetrate one another, and so *Bhuvarloka* and *Suvarloka* are here now; and to get information of them, we have but to focus our consciousness in the required way, as taught in the Sacred Books. There are two parts in *Bhuvarloka*, which are also called Lokas, namely, *Pretaloka* and *Pitriloka*. A man has usually to stay for many years in *Bhuvarloka*, and so the dweller therein is only physically dead, not astrally dead. The explorers of the *Bhuvarloka* assure us, and our own Sacred Writings confirm the assertion, that the *Bhuvarloka* is almost a fac-simile of the *Bhurloka* with the *Apas Tattva* as its predominating element. The man in the *Bhuvarloka* knows what is taking place here on the earth as his *Manômaya Kôsa* is not destroyed, but he has no physical organs of his own to make his desires known. *Pretâs*, both male and female' come and obsess human beings, and by means of suitable mantras, we get them exorcised. With facts like these staring us in the face, it is impossible to affirm that the connection between husband and wife ceases after what is called "death," and that the woman ceases to be one half of her husband. As a matter of fact, life becomes fuller after "death," as the shackles of the physical body have been shaken off. When the *Preta* purifies his *Manômaya Kôsa* and passes on to the *Pitriloka*, he still has connection with the *Bhurloka*, and we invoke the *Pitris* at the *Srâddha* ceremonies, and they come and accept our offerings. Thus Aryan Philosophy does not favour Remarriage, as it cuts asunder the intimate relations solemnly established between two Jivas in their *Manômaya kôsas*.

Since the Aryan Marriage establishes a complete union between a man and a woman, and since the husband says,—"Combine I now thy mind, thy actions, thy senses with mine," the wife, from the theoretical stand point, should be with her husband wherever he may be, whether in the *Bhurloka* or the *Bhuvarloka*. According to Aryan conception, husband and wife are inseparable; one cannot live well without the other. Suppose, now, the husband dies, that is, leaves the physical plane, and passes on to the astral plane or the *Bhuvarloka*. The wife is expected to keep company with him. During the Vedic Period, woman practised *Prânâyâma* and *Yoga*, and could function on the astral plane. It was open to her to remain here on the earth to look after her children, if young, and enjoy the company of her husband at night, functioning on the astral plane. When she did not care to do so, she controlled the *Prânic* currents in her body to obstruct the electric currents therein, and burnt herself to death to join her husband on the astral plane in her stral body. This practice was styled *Sati Dharma** or

* Mrs. Besant says :—" In the perfect realisation of the Ideal of marriage, the lives of husband and wife became so intertwined that any separation of them was impossible, as the ivy twining round the oak becomes one with it, and when the oak falls the ivy falls with it, so was it with the two lives made one. When, therefore, the husband died, the wife died also, not by outer compulsion but by inner will-power; a self-generated fire, result of stainless chastity and perfect love, broke out within the body of the wife who willed to tread the path of Death with her beloved, and thus the body was consumed. Strange, truly, to modern ears, and yet those who know that the body is full of electric currents, and that electric currents, obstructed, generate heat of glowing red and of white intensity, may have an inkling that there is nothing impossible in the theory. Hindu students may remember how Damayanti, threatened with outrage, sent forth from her pure body a flame that consumed the hunter. There are hidden forces in nature whereof men know but little, and at the mention of which they jeer, although the many strange discoveries of modern science should, by this

Wife's Duty. As the emotional development in woman outstripped the intellectual, she was prohibited from studying the Vedas, and she ceased to develop Yogic powers. It was no longer possible for her to burn her physical body to death by means of obstructed electric currents, and then the practice of immolating herself on the funeral pyre of her husband came into vogue. This practice led to several abuses, and it has now been rightly prohibited by the Government. The widow now-a-days is expected to lead a life of renunciation, and cherish the memory of her husband, and duly perform his *Srâddhas*.

As the *Vivâha Mantrâs* are all intended for pubescent maidens, and as *Vivâha* is a *Samskâra*, there is no room in the Hindu Sâstras for virgin or child widows. According to the Sâstraic Marriage Ritual,

---

time, have taught caution to those who base their scepticism merely on ignorance of the secrets yet hidden in Nature's bosom. A few such instances of devoted wives in Ancient India, who died by self-generated fire—rare as such instances were and must be—gave rise to the feeling that a perfectly devoted wife would not survive her husband; and then some, who were true lovers but who wielded not the power to awaken the hidden fire within themselves, died voluntarily beside their husband's corpses in the ordinary flame; and then, by slow degrees, such death came to be regarded as not only admirable but of binding obligation on a truly devoted wife; and then, enforced, became a crime." (Hindu Ideals. Pages 97—98).

sexual intercourse should take place after what has been called "the *Tri Râtra Bramacharya.*"

Four considerations settle the question of the marriage of widows from the *Sâstraic* standpoint. The first is the question of the performance of the *Srâddha* of the husband. If a widow re-marries, she merges herself in her new husband, and so she loses the *Adhikâra* of performing her first husband's *Srâddha*. When a *Dvija* woman ceases to perform the *Srâddha* ceremony, she loses her caste altogether, and she becomes a *Patite.* The second consideration is that a woman can give herself away but once. The story of Sâvitri shows clearly what a wife's duty is. According to Aryan ideas, "re-marriage" is no better than *adultery*, as the husband dead on the physical plane is fully alive on the astral. The third consideration is the fact that the object of the Aryan marriage is to beget *Sâttvic* progeny, and a woman that deliberately snaps her connection with her first husband is not, and cannot be, a *Sâdhvi.* There is also the circumstance of the first sexual intercourse leaving a permanent taint in her constitution. The fourth consideration is the absence of *Mantras* for Re-marriage, and the impossibility of drawing up new ones, which will not violate the principles of the Sanâtana Dharma.

The case of a *Dvija* man is different. He too will do well to become a *Sanyâsi* after the death of his wife.

But if he has no children, he is allowed to re-marry on the ground of his not having discharged the debt due to the *Pitris*. He is the seed; and as he has *Vedâdhikâra* and can perform *Sandhyâvandana* and *Japa*, he is believed to be able to keep his seed pure. We have, however, to remember that Aryan Philosophy tolerates re-marriage of men only as a necessary evil in the case of those who are unable to subjugate their *Kâma* and who are consequently unfit to become *Sanyâsis*.

The Aryan Ideal of Marriage is the highest and noblest that has yet been conceived by the mind of man. As Manu states, it is the Mission of India to teach all the nations of the World. In the matter of Marriage, the other nations of the world are far behind the Hindu Ideal, and it is necessary that in India at least this noble ideal should continue to exist. The Aryan Ideal reveals the best and surest mode of producing *Sâttvic* children; and as *Sâttvic* children in large numbers are needed for the uplifting of India and of the World, it is the duty of every true-born Aryan to endeavour to restore the old Ideal instead of ignorantly trying to pull it down. Even the re-marriage of men should be discouraged as far as circumstances allow, as the children which even the so-called Vaidikas bring forth now are mostly *Tâmasic*. We must go back to the grand old Ideals. We have to remember that we as guardians, owe a duty to the younger generation.

"Unless you can win it (the younger generation) to the old Ideals," says Mrs. Besant in her Ancient Ideals, (p. 137) "and penetrate it with the spirit of the Ancient Faith, there is no hope for the future of India."

AFTERWORD.

We shall close our study here. We have traversed, indeed, a long way, but we hope our ramble has not been profitless. We believe we have shewn that prepubescent marriage is unvedic. We have endeavoured to shed light on some points which are very obscure to ordinary readers—the Law of Racial development, the characteristics of the Root Races of Mankind, the superior Organization of the Aryan Race, the great Mission of India in the world, the spread of Aryan Colonization throughout the world, the Hindu Caste System and its necessity, and the Supreme Importance of *Samskâras* in general and of the *Vivâha Samskâra* in particular. We have sketched the outlines of the Hindu Degeneracy during the *Sûtra* and the *Metrical Smriti Periods.* We have also pointed out some noteworthy instances of Interpolations in the *Smritis.* That there have been several interpolations in the *Smritis* is certain. When and how these came into existence require careful scrutiny. It is clearly the duty of our investigators to examine the *Smritis* critically and purify them.

We have to bear in mind that Times have changed. The age of the predominance of the descendants of the Fourth Race of Humanity is, we may be sure, at an end;

and pre-pubescent marriage, the bane of modern India, can no longer be considered as an evil necessitated by external circumstances. Marriage is, and ought to be, a real *Samskâra*, and not a mere mummery which it has been for hundreds of years past. The Fifth or Aryan Race is triumphing everywhere, and the Fourth Race Peoples are also fast improving. Consider the remarkable advance of the Japanese. The world is progressing rapidly in morality, national and international. The East and the West have met for an unrestricted interchange of ideas. Manu's prophecy is nearing fulfilment. India is fast becoming one nation under the comparatively just and benign rule of the British, the youngest of the Aryan sub-races. *Swadeshism*, though yet in its infancy, is vigorously growing, and will in due course commence its Herculean labours. What India wants now is STRENGTH, physical, mental, moral, and spiritual; and this strength *Samskâras* alone can give. To keep abreast in the march of nations we have to study, appreciate, and follow our *Sâstras* a great deal better than we have been doing. Theosophy has made India its home. A spirit of intelligent inquiry is growing in Western Countries. Let us not lag behind. It is the duty of the Hindu Aryans to work strenuously for the good of all beings, for do we not pray every day :—" Happy be all that is born— సర్వేజనాస్సుఖినోభవంతు सर्वेजनास्सुखिनोभवन्तु ? Should we not, then, strive for *Sâttvic* progeny? Strive we must. Nor can we ignore the cause of Woman, as without *her* hearty co-operation *Sâttvic* progeny is impossible. As Lord Tennyson says:—

> The woman's cause is man's; they rise or sink
> Together, dwarfed or god-like, bond or free;
> If she be small, slight-natured, miserable,
> How shall men grow?

Then "ARISE, AWAKE, FIND TEACHERS AND BE TAUGHT" ఉత్తిష్ఠత జాగ్రత ప్రాప్య వరాన్నిబోధత उत्तिष्ठत जाग्रत प्राप्य वारान्निबोधत." "Tell the truth, Act the right సత్యంవద ధర్మం చర सत्यं वद धर्मं चर." "Truth alone triumphs, not Untruth సత్యమేవ జయతే నానృతం सत्य मेवजयते नानृतम्." The Law of Good is a part of SANATANA DHARMA.

> "Hour after hour, like an opening flower,
> Shall truth after truth expand;
> For the Sun may pale, and the Stars may fail,
> But the Law of Good shall stand.
> Its splendour glows and its influence grows
> As nature's slow work appears,
> From the zoophyte small to the Lords of all,
> Through *Kalpâs* and crores of years."

OM! TAT SAT.

APPENDIX.

INTERPOLATIONS.

The question of Interpolations is an important one, and we mean to deal with it here at some length so far as it relates to our subject of study. The student finds in the Metrical Smritis, *Slokas* and passages, here and there, which are altogether inconsistent with the teachings of the Vedas. Many of our *Sâstris* have ceased to study the *Smritis* critically. Anything and everything that is found in them is held to be sacred—a state of things much to be deplored.

Interpolations are apparently very common in Samskrit works. Few seem to be entirely free of them. In Nârâyana Upanishat there are two recensions known as the *Drâvida Pâtha* and the *Andhra Pâtha.* Scholars are of opinion that the *Andhra Pâtha* is corrupt, and contains interpolations. Even the *Brahma Sûtras* are considered to contain a few of them in as much as the number of *Sûtras* is not the same in different manuscripts. We hear of an Allah Upanishat! The Maha-Bharata is believed to contain additions on a large scale. In Karna Parva the *Tri Purôpâ khyâna* is considered to be an evident interpolation. Valmiki's Ramayana also is believed to contain some interpolations. In the Aranya Kânda of the edition commonly used now, some twenty-six slokas following the 56th

Sarga, which relate that Brahma ordered Indra to carry *Pâyasam* to Sita, are stigmatised as interpolations. In the edition, containing the *Tilaka Vyâkhyâna*, these are not found. The 107th Sarga of the Yuddha Kânda, about *Aditya Hridaya*, found in the edition commonly used, is also considered to be an interpolation. It is the opinion of Western Scholars that additions have been freely made to the Bhagavad Gita at different periods. Dharma Sutra Books also are said to contain spurious additions. "In the *First Adhyâya* of the fourth *Prasna*, this book (Baudhâyana's Dharma Sutra) has a few Slokas bearing on our topic (of marriage). Now both Dr. Buhler and Prof. Macdonnell are of opinion that the entire Fourth *Prasna* is a later addition. In this opinion they have the support of the commentator Govindaswamin. Their reasons, which seem to be conclusive, need not be repeated here." (Marriage after Puberty page. 36). "The text of Vâsishta Dharma Sutra is among the most corrupt in Samskrit Literature. It has evidently received accretions at different times. No argument can, therefore, be founded on any single *Sutra*, or on any few connected *Sutras*. In particular, the *Slokas* of other authors, introduced by the words 'they also say in illustration' are open to suspicion." (Marriage after Puberty. Page. 43).

Mrs. Besant says :—" Manu assigns to woman...... 'impure desires, wrath, dishonesty, malice and bad conduct* (Manu Smriti. IX. 17), and yet he says that 'there is no difference between wives who are worthy of worship and illuminate their homes, and the Devi of fortune.'† (Manu Smriti IX. 26). The statements are flatly contradictory. I do not know how the orthodox Hindu explains these passages; for myself I regard some of the passages as interpolations, obviously showing the temper of a later day, when the woman, as the embodiment of sense temptations, was regarded as the great enemy of the ascetic, the creature whose very nature was evil, and who must ever be kept under restraint, lest she should work havoc on helpless man."

But what are interpolations? And how are they to be found out? The Encyclopædia Dictionary defines interpolations as spurious words or phrases introduced or inserted in a book or writing. 'Interpolate' is derived from 'inter'—between or among, and 'polio'

---

* శయ్యాసనమలంకారం కామంక్రోధమనార్జవం ।
ద్రోహభావంకుచర్యాంచ స్త్రీభ్యోమనురకల్పయత్ ॥

शय्यासनमलंकारं कामंक्रोधमनार्जवम् । द्रोहभावं कुचर्यांच स्त्रीभ्यो-मनुरकल्पयत् ॥

† ప్రజనార్థంమహాభాగాః పూజార్హాః గృహదీప్తయః ।
స్త్రియః శ్రియశ్చగేహేషు నవిశేషోస్తికశ్చన ॥

प्रजनार्थंमहाभागाः पूजार्हागृहदीप्तयः । स्त्रियः श्रीयश्चगेहेषु नविशे-षोस्तिकश्चन ॥

—to polish. To interpolate is to alter or corrupt by the introduction or insertion of spurious matter: as, to vitiate or corrupt a book by the interpolation of words or passages spurious or foreign to the subject. The epithet "spurious" enables us to find out whether a suspicious passage is an interpolation or not. An examination of the context or the attendant circumstances is necessary. Obviously in matters relating to marriage, the Vedic mantras which we religiously repeat, and which reveal the sort of life the married couple have to lead from the time of marriage up to the *Vânaprastha* stage, must be our chief authority; and so we have to consider all slokas and passages, which are inconsistent with them, to be spurious. If a passage, attributed to a Rishi, be found to be inconsistent with the teachings of the Vedas or the Vedic mantras, it cannot be considered to be genuine. So also we have to set aside slokas and passages as spurious, when they have no bearing on the context, when they disturb the general import of the whole section or chapter, and when without them a more sensible meaning can be had.

Say, the following sloka from *Yama Smriti* is pointed out to you as one of the authorities for prepubescent marriage, *viz.*, "In her eighth year a girl is a *Gauri*, in her ninth a *Rohini*, in her tenth a *Kanya*, and after that a *Rajasvala*." Suppose you find in that same Smriti in the preceding sloka a girl of twelve being called a *Kanya* instead of a *Rajasvala*, and in the succeeding sloka the peculiar phrase *Kanyâm Rajasvalâm* also used; would you not say that the sloka in question serves no useful purpose? Suppose also that by omitting the sloka you get somewhat better sense. Suppose you turn up *Parâsara*, and find the same sloka defining *Gauri*, *Rohini*, and *Kanya* followed by the same peculiar phrase *Kanyâm Rajasvalâm*; and that by omitting the said sloka you find *Parâsara* a little more sensible;—would you not say that the sloka in question is an interpolation? In *Samvarta* also you find the same sloka which disturbs the context; and when you omit it, you find the *Smritikâra* speak a little more sensibly.

AN EXAMINATION OF SPURIOUS PASSAGES.

We shall examine now the following passages:—

I. *Angira Smriti*. Slokas 126 to 128.

(1). A *Kanya*, attaining puberty in her father's house, is a *Sudra* and her father incurs the sin of embryo-murder.

(2). The father, mother, and elder brother, seeing the *Kanya* in the menstrual course, go to hell.

(3). The Brahman that, greatly daring, marries

her, is the husband of a *Sudra* woman, unfit to converse or dine with.*

II. *Yama Smriti.* Chapter III. Slokas 18 to 22.

1. If a girl, remaining unmarried in her father's house, attains puberty, he incurs the sin of embryo-murder, and she is a *Sudra.*

2. The Brahman that, greatly daring, marries her, is unfit to converse or dine with ; he is the husband of a *Sudra* woman.

3. If a father fails to give away his *Kanya* when she has reached the twelfth year, he drinks the blood of her menstrual flow every month.

---

* అంగీరస్మృతి. శ్లో. 126-128.

(1) పితృవేశ్మనియా కన్యా రజస్తుసముపస్పృశేత్ ।
భ్రూణహత్యా పితుస్తస్యాః సా కన్యావృషలీస్మృతా ॥

(2) మాతాచైవ పితాచైవ జ్యేష్ఠోభ్రాతా తథైవచ ।
త్రయస్తేనరకంయాంతి దృష్ట్వాకన్యాం రజస్వలాం ॥

(3) ఉద్వహేద్యస్తుతాంకన్యాం బ్రాహ్మణోమదమోహితః ॥
అసంభాష్యోహ్యపాంక్తేయః సవిప్రోవృషలీపతిః ॥

अंगीरस्मृति श्लोक. 126-128.

(1) पितृवेश्मनियाकन्या रजस्तुसमुपस्पृशेत् । भ्रूणहत्यापितुस्तस्याः सा कन्यावृषलीस्मृता ॥

(2) माताचैवपिताचैव ज्येष्ठोभ्राता तथैवच। त्रयस्ते नरकं यान्ति दृष्ट्वाकान्यां रजस्वलाम् ॥

(3) उद्वहेद्यस्तुतांकन्यां ब्राह्मणोमदमोहितः । असंभाष्योह्यपाङ्क्तेयः सविप्रोवृषलीपतिः ॥

4. In the eighth year a girl is called a *Gauri*, in her ninth a *Rohini*, in her tenth a *Kanya*, and after that a *Rajasvala*.

5. The father, mother, and elder brother of a *Kanya*, seeing her in the menstrual course, go to hell.*

---

* యమస్మృతి. అధ్యాయ 3. శ్లో. 18-22.

1. పితృగేహేతుయాకన్యా పశ్యత్యసంస్కృతారజః ।
   భ్రూణహత్యాపితుస్తస్యాః కన్యాసావృషలీస్మృతా ॥
2. యస్తాంవివాహయేత్కన్యాం బ్రాహ్మణోమదమోహితః ।
   అసంభాష్యోహ్యపాఙ్క్తేయః సవిప్రోవృషలీపతిః ॥
3. ప్రాప్తే ద్వాదశమేవర్షే కన్యాం యోనప్రయచ్ఛతి ।
   మాసిమాసి రజస్తస్యాః పితాపిబతిశోణితం ॥
4. అష్టవర్షాభవేద్గౌరీ నవవర్షాచ రోహిణీ ।
   దశవర్షా భవేత్కన్యా అతఊర్ధ్వం రజస్వలా ॥
5. మాతాచైవ పితాచైవ జ్యేష్ఠభ్రాతా తథైవచ ।
   త్రయస్తేనరకంయాంతి దృష్ట్వాకన్యాం రజస్వలాం ॥

यमस्मृति.—अध्याय 3. श्लोक 18-22.

1. पितृगेहेतुयाकन्या पश्यत्यसंस्कृतारजः । भ्रूणहत्यापितुस्तस्याः कन्यासावृषलीस्मृता ॥
2. यस्तां विवाहयेत्कन्यां ब्राह्मणोमदमोहितः । असंभाष्योह्यपाङ्क्तेयस्सविप्रो वृषलीपतिः ॥
3. प्राप्तेतु द्वादशे वर्षे कन्यां यो न प्रयच्छति । मासिमासि रजस्तस्याः पितापिबतिशोणितम् ॥
4. अष्टवर्षाभवेद्गौरी नववर्षा तु रोहिणी । दशवर्षाभवेत्कन्या अतऊर्ध्वं रजस्वला ॥
5. माताचैवपिताचैव ज्येष्ठो भ्रातातथैवच । त्रयस्ते नरकं यान्ति दृष्ट्वाकन्यां रजस्वलाम् ॥

III. *Parasara Smriti.* Chapter VII. Slokas 4 to7

(*a*). In the eighth year a girl is a *Gauri*, in the ninth a *Rohini*, in the tenth a *Kanya*, and after that a *Rajasvala*.

(*b*). If a father fails to give away his daughter when she has reached the twelfth year, her ancestors drink the blood of her menstrual flow every month.

(*c*). The father, mother, and elder brother of a *Kanya*, seeing her in the menstrual course, go to hell.

(*d*). The Brahman, who blinded by ignorance, marries her, is unfit to converse or dine with. He is the husband of a *Sudra* woman.*

---

* పరాశరస్మృతి. అ. 7,, శ్లో. 4—7.

(a) అష్టవర్షా భవేద్గౌరీ నవవర్షా చరోహిణీ । దశవర్షా భవేత్కన్యా అత ఊర్ధ్వం రజస్వలా ॥

(b) ప్రాప్తేతు ద్వాదశేవర్షే యః కన్యాం న ప్రయచ్ఛతి । మాసిమాసి రజః తస్యాః పిబంతిపితరోనిశం ॥

(c) మాతాచైవ పితాచైవ జ్యేష్ఠభ్రాతా తథైవచ । త్రయస్తే నరకంయాంతి దృష్ట్వాకన్యాం రజస్వలాం ॥

(d) యస్తాం సముద్వహేత్కన్యాం బ్రాహ్మణోజ్ఞానమోహితః । అసంభాష్యోహ్యపాంక్తేయః సవిప్రోవృషలీపతిః ॥

पराशरस्मृति अ. 7. श्लो. 4-7.

(a) अष्टवर्षा भवेद्गौरी नववर्षातुरोहिणी । दशवर्षा भवेत्कन्या अत ऊर्ध्वं रजस्वला ।

(b) प्राप्तेतु द्वादशेवर्षे यः कन्यां न प्रयच्छति । मासिमासि रजस्तस्याः पिबन्ति पितरोनिशं ॥

IV. *Samvartâ.* Slokas 64 to 67.

(*a*). When hair appears (on the pubes), Soma enjoys a maiden ; the Gandharva enjoys, when she has attained puberty ; and Agni enjoys her, when he sees her breasts.

(*b*). In the eighth year a girl is called a *Gauri*, in the ninth a *Rohini*, in the tenth a *Kanya*, and after that a *Rajasvala*.

(*c*). The father, mother, and elder brother of a *Kanya*, seeing her in the menstrual course, go to hell.

(*d*). Therefore one should marry a *Kanya* before puberty ; the marriage of a *Kanya*, eight years old, is best.*

(c) माताचैव पिताचैव ज्येष्ठभ्राता तथैवच । त्रयस्ते नरकं यान्ति दृष्ट्वा कन्यां रजस्वलाम् ।

(d) यस्तां समुद्वहेत्कन्यां ब्राह्मणोज्ञानमोहितः । असंभाष्योह्यपांङ्तेयः सविप्रो वृषलीपतिः ॥

* సంవర్త. శ్లో. 64-67.

(*a*) రోమకాలేతు సంప్రాప్తే సోమోభుంక్తేథకన్యకాం ।
రజోదృష్ట్వాతు గంధర్వః కుచౌదృష్ట్వాతు పావకః ॥

(*b*) అష్టవర్షాభవేద్గౌరీ నవవర్షాచరోహిణీ । దశవర్షాభవేత్కన్యా అతఊర్ధ్వం రజస్వలా ॥

(*c*) మాతాచైవ పితాచైవ జ్యేష్ఠభ్రాతా తథైవచ । త్రయస్తేనరకంయాంతి దృష్ట్వా కన్యాం రజస్వలాం ॥

(*d*) తస్మాద్వివాహయేత్కన్యాం యావన్నర్తుమతీభవేత్ ।
వివాహోష్టవర్షాయాః కన్యాయాస్తు ప్రశస్యతే ॥

What have we in these four passages? A number of statements which are altogether inconsistent with the Vedic mantras and also inconsistent with one another. Let us begin with the passage marked IV, the slokas of Samvarta. The first sloka betrays confusion of ideas inasmuch as the functions of the Gandharva and Agni are transposed. The use of the word "enjoy" instead of "protect," as we have explained elsewhere, is very objectionable. A *Kanya* is defined to be a girl in the tenth year in the second sloka, and yet in the fourth sloka a "Kanya of eight years" is used. Moreover, how can a *Kanya*, who is defined to be a girl in the tenth year and not yet a *Rajasvala*, be in the menstrual course as the third sloka implies. The word *Kanya* is deliberately restricted to a ten-year-old girl in the second sloka, and yet it is used in the sense of an unmarried post-pubescent woman in the third sloka, and of an unmarried pre-pubescent girl of

---

संवर्त. श्लो. 64-67.

(*a*) रोमकालेतुसंप्राप्ते सोमोभुंङ्तेथ कन्यकाम् । रजोदृष्ट्वातु गन्धर्वः कुचौदृष्ट्वातु पावकः ।

(*b*) अष्टवर्षा भवेद्गौरी नववर्षातुरोहिणी । दशवर्षा भवेत्कन्या अत ऊर्ध्वं रजस्वला ॥

(*c*) माताचैव पिताचैव ज्येष्ठभ्राता तथैवच । त्रयस्ते नरकं यान्ति दृष्ट्वा कन्यां रजस्वलाम् ॥

(*d*) तस्माद्विवाहयेत्कन्यां यावन्नर्तु मतीभवेत् । विवाहोह्यष्टवर्षा-याः कन्यायास्तु प्रशस्यते ॥

eight years in the fourth! Is it of any use to argue with a writer who does not mean what he says, and who says what he does not mean and who also forgets the fundamental idea of *Vivâha* being a *Samskâra*, affecting all the *Kosas*? The doctrine of Karma is an essential part of the Aryan Philosphy. Why should the elder brother of a girl go to Hell, if his pubescent sister is not married? Where is the authority for this statement? Does he also go to Hell, when she refuses to marry and becomes a *Yogini*?

Now, let us go to the passage marked III, attributed to Parâsara. It also contains objectionable matter. There is the mention of the ancestors drinking the blood of the menstural flow! This puts one in mind of a street-brawl between two vulgar *Sûdra* women. Is a *Smriti*, reputed to be written by a *Rishi*, a place for such vulgar ideas? We reserve this passage from Parâsara for a minute examination at a later stage.

In the passage marked II, and attributed to Yama, nearly the same sentiments are expressed, and many of the words used are the same. *Bhrûna-hatya* or embryo-murder is spoken of. There was a time when men were hermaphrodites and developed embryos without sexual intercourse. But can there be in the present stage of the evolution of the world any embryo or fœtus, when an unmarried woman menstruates? If so, marriage itself is unnecessary. *Bhrûna-hatya*, in the real sense of the term, is an impossibility in the case of an unmarried woman.

Our Pandits themselves are aware of the impossibility, and they endeavour, in their desparation, to put a forced interpretation upon the word *Bhrûna-hatya.* Their reasoning is briefly this :—"The father has prevented sexual intercourse by not marrying the maiden; the maiden could have become pregnant if there had been sexual intercourse ; the prevention of a possible conception may be taken to amount to and therefore may be construed to be embryo-murder." The speciousness of the reasoning is obvious to an educated mind, as a possibility is only a possibility and not an actuality. There must be an embryo before there can be an embryo-murder ; and as in the absence of marriage there is no embryo, it does not stand to reason to say that the father is guilty of embryo-murder. The thing upon which he is to act is itself non-existent, and so the crime itself is non-existent. Consider another aspect of the question. The Vedic injunction is—"Unite ye *Lingas* that are covered with hair," and as the *Linga* of a girl who is only twelve or thirteen years of age, is not covered with hair, to allow sexual intercourse is a great sin, as very serious consequences follow. So the sloka has no philosophy to support it, and can only be intended to mislead the unwary.

We call upon those who make the wild statement that the ancestors of an unmarried pubescent maiden have to drink the blood of her menstrual flow, to support their proposition by quoting *Sâstraic* authorities. The Vedic mantras are fit only for post-pubescent marriage, and we wish to know why the supporters of pre-pubescent marriage religiously repeat post-pubescent marriage *Mantras*, and become conspicuous examples of a glaring inconsistency. If they want to stick to pre-pubescent marriage, they have to give up the use of the recognised Vedic mantras, as *Sradda* and *Trikarana Suddhi* are necessary. This they have not done, and cannot do without ceasing to be Brahmans. The next sloka says that the father, mother, and elder brother go to Hell if a *Rajasvala* girl remains unmarried. The very mantras which they voice forth in the marriage ceremony are against them. Are Vedic mantras less in authority than a baseless sloka of a Metrical Smriti? We ask them to prove and substantiate their statement. Then they want to excommunicate the man who marries a pubescent maiden. Where is the authority for this excommunication? Is a man to be excommunicated for doing what the Vedic Mantras of the Marriage Ritual require him to do? Shall we banish from society all persons who have *Sraddha* and *Trikarana Suddhi*, and have in the community a set of truthless innovators, who do not recognise *Vivâha* to be a real *Samskâra*? Logically these are the consequences of accepting the slokas in question as genuine. Is a

Smriti a Smriti when it inculcates practices which repudiate the Vedic mantras of the *Homas* of the Marriage Ritual?

There is another important point also. Examine the second chapter of Parâsara Smriti. It is in the *Achâra Kânda.* There are only thirteen slokas in it. In none of them does Parâsara mention the desirability of pre-pubescent marriage. There are in fact no slokas in the text, relating to *Upanayana* or *Vivâha.* The commentator it is that has added his ill-digested notions of marriage in page after page of what seems to us a commentary of doubtful value, which forgets the holy character of *Vivâha* as a *Samskâra.* In the text of the second chapter of the *Achâra Kânda*, there is not one word in favour of pre-pubescent marriage, and thus there is no real or satisfactory evidence to believe that Parâsara is in favour of it.

What are we to say then in connection with these passages? We affirm that they were not written by the *Smritikâras* at all, as they are reputed to be *Rishis.** Where is the proof? Here; if you omit the slokas and read the Smritis, you will find the *Smritikâras* to be decent writers and not otherwise.

---

* ఊర్ధ్వరేతా స్తపస్యుగ్రో నియతాశీచ సంయమీ ।
శాపానుగ్రహయోశ్శక్త స్సత్యసంధో భవేదృషిః ॥

ऊर्ध्वरेतास्तपस्युग्रो नियताशीच संयमी । शापानुग्रहयोश्शक्तः सत्यसंधो भवेदृषिः ॥

Try it, if you like, in Parâsara Smriti, and satisfy yourself. How did they find their way into the Smritis then? They were deliberately inserted to gain an important end. What end? Non-molestation at the hands of the lascivious Mussulmans of a dark period of Indian History. The Mahomedan Sacred Books prohibit true believers from laying hands on married females, and prescribe a heavy punishment.* "You are forbidden to take to wife free women who are married, except those women whom your right hand shall possess as slaves: such is the law of God," is what is stated in the Koran, Sourate, IV, 28. The slokas can only be interpolations.

Let us see how the interpolations became necessary. Many Brahmans were officers in the employ of the Mussulman rulers, occupying different grades of service. Physical force they could not use. They also saw that pre-pubescent marriages were in vogue among the non-Aryans. They made themselves indispensable servants by an intelligent discharge of their duties. Their

* Hadis, a Mahomedan Sacred Book says:—

1. "Unchastity bringeth destruction unto the merit of past good deeds as a blazing fire bringeth destruction unto a sapless tree.

(2). "One single act of unchastity doth destroy the accumulated merit of seventy years' virtuous living, and doth, besides, other harm.

Sur-aye-noor, another Sacred Book, says:—

"Adulterer and adulteress—punish ye each with a hundred lashes."

philosophy taught them that nothing is permanent. Their caste they had to preserve. By performing pre-pubescent marriages, they went through all forms of the ceremonies—only prematurely, *i.e.*, before the parties had acquired the *Adhikára.* It was doing violence to the Vedic Ideal, but when violence could not be helped, it was certainly expedient to gain their end in the manner in which they have done it. Says one maxim :—"When the whole is about to be lost, a Pandit willingly foregoes one half."*

Now, let us consider the circumstances. The Mlenchha Kings and Governors, descendants of the Fourth Race, with their partially developed senses of Taste and Smell, cast their sensual eyes on fair-looking girls to fill their harems with all types of beauties. As their Law or Dharma Śâstra probibited them from laying violent hands on married girls, the best and easiest thing to do was to marry girls before their physical development could rouse their feelings

---

"And punish ye, without partiality, the sinners, as ye believe that there is Allah above, and that He adjudges unto you in the higher worlds what ye deserve according to your deeds in this nether world.

"And deal ye out the punishment, due unto the offenders, in an assembly of true believers, to bring shame unto them."

* సర్వనాశే సముత్పన్నే హ్యర్ధం త్యజతి పండితః ॥

सर्वनाशे समुत्पन्ने ह्यर्धंत्यजति पण्डितः ॥

of sensuality. When once a girl was married and was *called a wife*, the Mahomedan Law extended its protection to her.

The interpolations have excellently served the intended purpose, namely, throwing dust into the eyes of alien ignorant rulers to justify their custom, and to save the caste and honour of their own daughters from brutal violence.

Brihaspati says, as stated on a previous page, that the authority of Manu is higher than that of all others. It is worthy of special note that Manu allows marriage to a maiden even three years *after* her attaining puberty.* But now, it is said, that Parâsara is specifically meant for the Kali Yuga.† When did this notion arise and how? After the insertion of the interpolations, it became necessary to exalt one of the *Smritis* into which they had been introduced—*viz*, Angiras, Yama, Parâsara, and Samvarta. Parâsara was chosen as he was reputed to be the father of the great Veda Vyâsa.

There is one very important fact in support of the argument of interpolations, which we have advanced

---

* త్రీణివర్షాణ్యుదీక్షేత కుమార్యృతుమతీసతీ ।
ఊర్ధ్వంతు కాలాదేతస్మాద్విందేత సదృశంపతిం ॥

त्रीणिवर्षाण्युदीक्षेत कुमार्यृतुमतीसती । ऊर्ध्वंतुकालादेतस्माद्विन्देत सदृशं पतिम् ॥

† కలౌ పారాశరస్మృతిః । कलौ पाराशरस्मृतिः ।

It is the singular absence of pre-pubescent marriages in our National Literature. Our Samskrit Literature is a most extensive one; and so far as we are aware, there is no real instance of pre-pubescent marriage in it. What does this show? It shows that it has not the sanction of the *Sâstras*, that it is repugnant to the genius of the nation, and also that it is of recent growth, not finding a place in the ancient literature of the country.

A Verification.

The successive stages of degeneracy which we have described in the body of our book are not idle fancies, but facts which it is possible to verify. As Parâsara Smriti is said to be specifically meant for the Kali Yuga, we shall take up a part of the Seventh Chapter, and throw upon it the searchlight of *Sâstraic* criticism, and see what dark and obscure corners of interpolations will be illumined thereby.

We shall use the edition of Parâsara with the commentary of Màdhava, printed at Madras in Telugu characters in 1871.

The Seventh Chapter treats of penances and other purificatory processes; and for our purposes, it is enough to take the first ten *Slokas*. We shall translate and write them down with the headings given in the book.*

---

* అథాతో ద్రవ్యశుద్ధిస్తు పరాశరవచో యథా ।

अथातो द्रव्यशुद्धिस्तु पराशरवचोयथा ।

"Now the purificatory processes and penances propounded by Parâsara are explained.

The cleansing of sacrificial vessels.

(1). "Washing cleanses wooden vessels immediately; ashes cleanse bronze or bell-metal, and acids copper.

The purification of an unchaste woman.

(1½). "Menstruation purifies a woman, if she has no *vikala*, or change of appearance.

The purification of a river.

(2). "A river by its own current becomes pure, when no impurities are visible.

స్రుక్స్రువాదీనాం శుద్ధిః.

(1) దారవాణాంతుపాత్రాణాం తత్క్షణాచ్ఛుద్ధిరిష్యతే ।
భస్మనాశుధ్యతేకాంస్యం తామ్రమామ్లేన శుధ్యతి ॥

स्रुक्स्रुवादीनां शुद्धिः.

दारवाणांतुपात्राणां तत्क्षणात् शुद्धिरिष्यते ।
भस्मनाशुध्यतेकांस्यं ताम्रमाम्लेन शुध्यति ॥

వ్యభిచార స్త్రీశుద్ధిః.

(1½) రజసా శుధ్యతేనారీ వికలంయా న గచ్ఛతి ।

व्यभिचार स्त्रीशुद्धिः.

रजसाशुध्यते नारी विकलं या न गच्छति ।

నదీ శుద్ధిః.

(2) నదీవేగేన శుధ్యేత లేపోయదినదృశ్యతే ॥

नदीशुद्धिः.

नदीवेगेन शुध्येत लेपोयदि नदृश्यते ।

The purification of ponds, wells, &c.

(3). "Ponds, wells, tanks may be occasionally polluted. The pouring of *Pancha gavya*, following the removal of hundreds of potfuls of water, purifies them.

The purification of Kanyas.

(4). "In her eighth year a girl is a Gauri, in her ninth a Rohini, in her tenth a Kanya, and after that a Rajasvala.

(5). "If a father fails to give away his daughter when she has reached the twelfth year, her ancestors drink the blood of her menstrual flow every month.

వాపీకూపాది శుద్ధిః.

(3) వాపీకూపతటాకేషు దూషితేషు కథంచన ।
ఉధృత్యవైకుంభశతం పంచగవ్యేన శుధ్యతి ॥

वापीकूपादि शुद्धिः.

वापीकूपतटाकेषु दूषितेषु कथंचन । उधृत्य वै कुंभशतं पंचगव्येन शुध्यति ॥

కన్యా శుద్ధిః.

(4) అష్టవర్షా భవేద్గౌరీ నవవర్షాతు రోహిణీ ।
దశవర్షా భవేత్కన్యా అత ఊర్ధ్వం రజస్వలా ॥

कन्या शुद्धिः.

अष्टवर्षा भवेद्गौरी नववर्षातु रोहिणी । दशवर्षा भवेत्कन्या अत ऊर्ध्वं रजस्वला ॥

(5) ప్రాప్తేతు ద్వాదశేవర్షే యః కన్యాంన ప్రయచ్ఛతి ।
మాసిమాసి రజస్తస్యాః పిబంతి పితరోనిశం ॥

(6). "The father, mother, and elder brother of a Kanya, seeing her in the menstrual course, go to Hell.

(7). "The Brahman, who, blinded by ignorance, marries her, is unfit to converse or dine with. He is the husband of a Sûdra woman.

(8). "A Dvija guilty of enjoying a Sûdra woman for a night, is purified by performing Japa every day for three years, living upon the food begged at others' doors.

(9). "How is he purified who, after sunset, is polluted by the contact of a *Chandâla*, a *Patita*, a woman in confinement, or a corpse?

(10). "He is purified if he gazes at a fire, gold, the Moon, or the path of the Moon, and bathes in water with the permission of holy Brahmans."

प्राप्तेतु द्वादशेवर्षेयः कन्यां न प्रयच्छति । मासि मासि रजस्तस्याः पिबन्ति पितरोनिशम् ॥

(6) మాతాచైవ పితాచైవ జ్యేష్ఠభ్రాతా తథైవచ ।
త్రయస్తే నరకంయాంతి దృష్ట్వాకన్యాం రజస్వలాం ।

माताचैव पिताचैव ज्येष्ठभ्रता तथैवच । त्रयस्ते नरकं यान्ति दृष्ट्वा कन्यां रजस्वलाम् ॥

(7) యస్తాం సముద్వహేత్కన్యాం బ్రాహ్మణోమదమోహితః ।
అసంభాష్యోహ్యపాంక్తేయః సవిప్రో వృషలీపతిః ॥

यस्तां समुद्वहेत्कन्यां ब्राह्मणो मदमोहितः । असंभाष्यो ह्यपांक्ते यस्सविप्रो वृषलीपतिः ॥

The passage bears on its very face several marks of corruption.* Let us examine it carefully, bearing in mind that this Smriti is a *Samhita* or compilation.

1. Items of various kinds are jumbled up together without any serious attempt at classification. In the second sloka, the purification of an unchaste woman is coupled with the purification of a river.

2. "The purification of an unchaste woman"

---

(8) యఃకరోత్యేకరాత్రేణ వృషలీసేవనంద్విజః ।
సభైక్షభుగ్జపన్నిత్యం త్రిభిర్వర్షైర్విశుధ్యతి ॥

यःकरोत्येकरात्रेण वृषलीसेवनं द्विजः । सभैक्ष भुग्जपन्नित्यं त्रिभि-र्वर्षैर्विशुध्यति ॥

(9) అస్తంగతే యదాసూర్యే చండాలం పతితం స్త్రియం ।
సూతికాంచ శవంచైవ కథంశుద్ధి ర్విధీయతే ॥

अस्तंगते यदासूर्ये चण्डालं पतितं स्त्रियम् । सुतिकांचशवंचैव कथं-शुद्धिर्विधीयते ॥

(10) జాతవేదస్సువర్ణంచ సోమమార్గం విలోక్యచ ।
బ్రాహ్మణానుగతశ్చైవ స్నానంకృత్వా విశుధ్యతి ॥

जातवेदस्सुवर्णंच सोममार्गं विलोकयच । ब्राह्मणानु गतश्चैव स्नानं-कृत्वा विशुध्यति ॥

* The numbering of the Slokas in the printed book is faulty, and so we have altered it. Is any intelligent man prepared to say that "in her eighth year a girl is a Gauri, in her ninth a Rohini," is the second half of a Sloka whose first half is "the pouring of Pancha Gavya, following the removal of hundreds of potfuls of water, purifies them?"

is the heading, and the first half of the sloka says in effect that there is no purification for her. But does the sloka treat of an unchaste woman at all? The context does not favour the idea. The things previously mentioned are wooden vessels, bronze or bell-metal vessels and copper vessels. The things that follow are rivers, ponds, wells, tanks, etc. There is a whole troop of slokas from the eleventh to the twentieth, or ten in number, devoted to the consideration of the purification of women in different circumstances. The unchastity of woman is no slight matter, and if it had been the object of Parâsara to state any process of purification, is it at all likely that he would have thrown this important subject into the midst of things like wooden vessels, bell-metal vessels, copper vessels, ponds, wells, tanks, etc? It is extremely unlikely as Parâsara is reputed to be a *Rishi*. Now "*Nâri*" means brass or woman, "*Rajasa*" means earth or menstruation, "*Sudhyate*" may be applied to either brass or woman; so is "*vikala*", which may mean a permeating taint of volatile substances or a change of appearance. While there are ten slokas devoted later on to the purification of women in different circumstances, there is no sloka whatever, nor any part of it, devoted to the purification or cleansing of brass vessels, which were extensively used then as they are extensively used now. Taking the context into consideration, the real meaning of the sloka is this, namely,—"Earth or mud cleanses brass,—if not tainted or permeated by volatile substances."

3. Let us pass to the heading of the purification of *Kanyas*. The first sloka marked (4), contains definitions, and no purificatory processes. The second, marked (5), states that certain ancestors drink the blood of the menstrual flow in certain circumstances,—which is not a purificatory process but a disgusting punishment worthy of the age of the second "made-easy" series, *viz.*, the period of the Metrical Smritis. The third, marked (6), sends certain persons to Hell,—which cannot be construed into any purificatory process here on the earth. The fourth, marked (7), makes a particular man a Sudra, which, again, is not a process of purification. The fifth, marked (8), does contain a purificatory process, but it concerns a *Dvija* who has had sexual intercourse with a *Sûdra* woman for a single night, and not a Brahman who marries in the prescribed way a pubescent maiden. Anyhow the fifth sloka relates to a man, and not to a *Kanya*. The last two slokas, (9) and (10), do not relate to *Kanyas* at all. Seven slokas are given under the heading of the Purification of *Kanyas*, and no real purification relating to a *Kanya* is mentioned. How are we to account for this? Is not this heading the relic of a former interpolation? The fifth sloka, marked (8), ought to have a separate heading—"an unchaste Dvija"; but it is either not given

or wilfully suppressed. If it was a deliberate suppression, what was the reason of it?

4. Let us examine the meanings of the word *Kanya* as found in slokas (4) to (7). In (4), the Kanya is a pre-pubescent girl of 10 years; in (5) the Kanya is a pre-pubescent girl of 12 years; in (6) and (7), the Kanya is an unmarried *Rajasvala* or pubescent woman of no specified age. Now no man of average intelligence—much less a *Rishi* knowing the four Vedas,—would be so foolish as to use an important word like *Kanya* in three inconsistent senses in the course of four consecutive couplets; and the only rational inference that can be drawn is that the several slokas were composed and inserted by unscrupulous persons at different periods to serve their own purposes. As there are three different senses of the word *Kanya*, the presumption is that the sloka, marked (4) was inserted at one time; that, marked (5), at another time; and those, marked (6) and (7), at a third time. In what order the additions were made we have to find out.

5. The proper place for the four slokas, (4) to (7), which anathematize post-pubescent marriages, is the *Achâra Kânda*, and not *Prâyaschitta Kânda*. They are singularly inappropriate in their present setting. How is this to be accounted for?

Thus we see that this extract is full of irregularities and blunders of various kinds. If the process of degeneracy, which we have sketched in the course of this study is true, we should be able to show how the passage has come to be what it now is. This work, though difficult it be, we shall attempt.

I. The Passage in its original purity.

Now, in the Vedic period, there were only post-pubescent marriages, as the *Vivâha Mantras* amply testify. So we may be quite sure that the slokas, (4) to (7), which have no Vedic basis, were not in existence. The first half of the sloka, marked (1½), related to brass and not to woman. The passage in its original purity stood thus :—

The cleansing of Sacrificial vessels.

(1). Washing cleanses wooden vessels immediately; ashes cleanse bronze or bell-metal, and acid substances cleanse copper.

(2). Earth or mud cleanses brass ;—if not tainted with volatile substances.

The purification of Rivers.

A river by its own current becomes pure, when no impurities are visible.

The purification of Ponds, Wells, etc.

(3). Ponds, wells and tanks may be occasionally polluted; the pouring of Pancha gavya, following the removal of hundreds of potfuls of water, purifies them.

The purification of a polluted Dvija.

(8). A Dvija, guilty of enjoying a Sûdra woman for a night, is purified by performing Japa every day for three years, living upon the food begged at others' doors.

(9). How is he purified, who, after sunset, is polluted by the contact of a *Chandâla*, a *Patita*, a woman in confinement, or a corpse?

(10). He is purified if he gazes at a fire, gold, the Moon, or the path of the Moon, and bathes in water with the permission of holy Brahmans.

These six slokas, as stated above, contain real information, and there is nothing inconsistent in them. The omission of the slokas, (4) to (7), has vastly improved the passage, which now yields, a sensible meaning. The interpretation of "*Nâri*" as brass is thoroughly appropriate. Note that the proviso—"if not tainted with volatile substances" refers to all the substances previously named, *viz.*, wood, bronze or bell-metal, copper and brass. In case they are tainted with volatile substances,—such as toddy, garlic and so on—a different treatment is necessary,—which is given later on in the same Chapter. We may also note that the proper place for these slokas is the *Prâyaschitta Kânda*, and not the *Achâra Kânda*.

II. The Passage in its first stage of degeneracy.

In the Sûtra Period, as explained previously, post-pubescent marriages were discouraged, and some *Sûtrakâras* prescribed penalties. Some slokas, attributed to Asvalâyana are quoted in *Kâlâmrita*, and their purport is that "if a maiden has come of age before marriage, her father should at the time of giving her away, purify both himself and her by holy ceremonies; that he should give away as many cows as the bride has had Ritus, and that if he be not rich enough for that, he should give away at least one cow." Here we have the idea that the non-performance of a pre-pubescent marriage is a sin, and that it deserves at least a mild penalty, such as the gift of a cow. But how was this practice to be defended? It was defended in this way. Women had been prohibited from learning the Vedas, and so girls could not have the *Upanayana* ceremony with the mantras used in the ceremony for boys. They contended that inasmuch as the *Asramas* were four in number for all *Dvijâs*, the only way in which girls could be made to have a sort of *Samskâra* was to split the marriage ceremony into two parts—*Vivâha* and *Garbhâdhâna*. The *Vivâha* or Betrothal was to be celebrated before puberty, and the *Garbhâdhâna* or the nuptials after puberty. The *Vivâha* or Betrothal ceremony conferred on her *Dvija-hood*, and the Mantra that was, and is, paraded, is :—

"This bride doth praise and entreat Agni for a balanced mind, for Sâttvic progeny, for spiritual wealth, and for physical vigour. For the holy ceremony of Vivâha do I now tie this *maunji* to make her happy."* This mantra mentions a *maunji*, and a *maunji* is also used in the Upanayana ceremony, and so there was room, it was thought, to call it a counterpart or sort of *Upanayana*. They also quoted :—" By mere birth one is but a Sûdra, and Karma it is that confers on one Dvijahood.† Apparently, they did not care to consider critically the applicability of the quotations. It was anyhow good enough to confuse ignorant minds. They also said that the *mantras* affect the inner bodies, and would make the outer body develop well. Whatever the circumstances were, we have the fact that post-pubescent marriages were discouraged, and penalties prescribed. The passage in its first stage of degeneracy probably stood thus :—

The cleansing of sacrificial Vessels.

(1). Washing cleanses wooden vessels immedi-

---

* ఆశాసానా సౌమనసంప్రజాగ్ం సౌభాగ్యంతనూం ।
అగ్నేరనువ్రతాభూత్వా సన్నహ్యే సుకృతాయకం ॥

आशासानासौमनसंप्रजाः सौभाग्यंतनूं । अग्नेरनुव्रताभूत्वा सन्नह्ये सुकृतायकम् ॥

† జన్మనాజాయతే శూద్రః కర్మణా జయతే ద్విజః ॥

जन्मनाजायते शूद्रः। कर्मणा जायते द्विजः।

ately; ashes cleanse bronze or bell-metal, and acid substances cleanse copper.

(2). Earth or mud cleanses brass;—if not tainted with volatile substances.

The purification of Rivers.

A river by its own current becomes pure, when no impurities are visible.

The purification of ponds, wells, etc.

(3). Ponds, wells, tanks may be occasionally polluted; the pouring of Pancha gavya, following the removal of hundreds of potfuls of water, purifies them.

The purification of Kanyas.

If a Kanya has come of age before marriage, her father should at the time of giving her away, purify both himself and her by holy ceremonies. He should give away as many cows as the bride has had Ritus. If he be not rich enough for that, he should give away at least one cow.*

---

* కన్యామృతుమతీంశుద్ధాం కృత్వానిష్కృతి మాత్మనః ।
శుద్ధించకారయిత్వా తాముద్వహేదా నృశంస్యధీః ॥
పితాబుతూన్ స్వపుత్రాస్తు గణయేదాదితస్సుధీః ।
దానావధి గృహేయత్నాత్ పాలయేచ్చరజోవతీం ॥
దద్యాత్తదనుసంఖ్యాగాః శక్తః కన్యా పితాయది ।
దాతవ్యైకాపి నిస్స్వేన దానేతస్యా యథావిధీ ॥

The purification of a polluted Dvija.

(8). A Dvija, guilty of enjoying a Sûdra woman for a night, is purified by performing Japa every day for three years,living upon the food begged at others' doors.

(9) and (10). As before.

This passage can have a place only in the Prâyaschitta Kânda, not in the Achâra Kanda. The heading—the Purification of Kanyas—has a real meaning, and is thoroughly appropriate.

III. The passage in its second stage of degeneracy.

The fear of non-Aryans had increased greatly and with it gross ignorance. Proofs have already been given of the degeneracy of the Metrical Smriti Period. People ceased to possess a balanced mind. It became necessary to appeal to self-interest, and to pronounce heavy anathemas to discourage post-pubescent marriages. The *unsâstraic* slokas—

> "The father, mother, and elder brother of a Kanya, seeing her in the menstrual course, go to hell.
>
> " The Brahman, who, blinded by ignorance, marries her, is unfit to converse or dine with. He is the husband of a Sûdra woman "

कन्यामृतुमतींशुद्धां कृत्वानिष्कृति मात्मनः । शुद्धिचकारयित्वातम्मुद्ध-हेद्दानृशंस्यधीः ॥ पिताऋतून् स्वपुत्यास्तु गणयेदादितस्सुधीः । दानावधि गृहेयत्नात्पालयेच्च रजोवतीम् ॥ दद्यात्तदनुसंख्यार्गाः शक्तः कन्यापितायदि ॥ दातव्यैकापिनिःस्वेनदानेतस्यायथाविधि ॥

were inserted. This act necessitated the removal of the slokas, which prescribed slight penalties—such as the gift of a number of cows or at least of a cow—for the non-performance of pre-pubescent marriages. The question arose whether the heading of the purification of Kanyas should be retained or removed. There was the consideration that *Vivâha* or Betrothal was a sort of *Samskâra* which conferred *Dvijahood* on the girl, and so it was allowed to remain. *Suddhi* or purification implies the existence of impurity; and to establish the existence of impurity, "*Janmanâ jayate Sûdrah*" was affirmed. But what about the heading of the purification of a polluted Dvija? Times had changed, and the practice of concubinage had become extremely common among the higher and the middle classes. The Mussulman rule had given a great impetus to concubinage, which was now a mark of nobility and masculinity. Examine the literature of the period, and you will find how disgustingly full it is of descriptions of indecent and even revolting scenes. Pre-pubescent marriages tend to favour concubinage, and as it was next to impossible to enforce the prescribed penalties, owing to the position of the men committing the sin, the heading was quietly dropped, and the sloka prescribing a three years' *Japa* for purification was allowed to remain as being connected with the slokas newly inserted. The last two slokas which treat of minor pollutions had become a dead letter as the Brahmans had to associate with the Mlenchhas every day of the year. They did not deserve a separate heading. So the passage in its second stage of degeneracy probably stood thus :—

(1), (2), and (3). As given on page 266.

The purification of Kanyas.

(6). The father, mother, and elder brother of a Kanya, seeing her in the menstrual course, go to hell.

(7). The Brahman, who, blinded by ignorance, marries her, is unfit to converse or dine with. He is the husband of a Sûdra woman.

(8). A Dvija, guilty of enjoying a Sûdra woman for a night, is purified by performing *Japa* every day for three years, living upon the food begged at others' doors.

(9) and (10). As before.

The question probably occurred to the interpolators whether the slokas which prohibit post-pubescent marriages should not be transferred to the Achâra Kânda from the Prâyaschitta Kânda. There being only thirteen slokas of a most general character in the Second Chapter, and no slokas at all relating either to Upanayana or to Vivâha in the text of the Smriti, the transference was impracticable; and besides, they probably thought that if through the grace of the Almighty, in whom they had strong faith, the Mlenchhas should be driven out of India, there would

18

be no need of the new slokas. We have to remember that the object of the interpolators was not to spoil the *Sâstras* but simply to throw dust into the eyes of the alien rulers.

There is one point to be noted in connection with the interpolated slokas relating to the damnation of the parents and the elder brother, and to the excommunication of the husband. The slokas refer solely to the Brahmans, and they leave out the Kshatriyas and the Vaisyas. The Brahmans had no power or authority to compel the Kshatriyas to adopt pre-pubescent marriage. The welfare of the Vaisyas, probably, they did not care for. The sloka about the three years' *Japa* refers to all Dvijas, while the interpolated slokas refer solely to Brahmans; and so it was hardly logical to tack on the sloka treating of a polluted Dvija to the previous ones; but these were *Sâstraic* matters which did not trouble the highly elastic conscience of the interpolators and their supporters.

IV. The Passage in its third stage of degeneracy.

People were becoming more and more accustomed to live under the rule of the non-Aryans and Mussulmans, and as the slokas which had been previously inserted, had answered their purpose, there were now no qualms of conscience to introduce additional ones. In Samvarta we find :—" In her eighth year a girl is a Gauri, in her ninth a Nagnika, in her tenth a Kanya; in her twelfth a Sûdra Woman".* Ignorance had increased; and as the Mussulmans had prospered, and as they were carrying off to their harems, girls who were eleven or twelve years of age, the disgusting sloka about the drinking of the menstrual blood was inserted. The passage then stood thus:—

(1), (2) and (3). As before.

The purification of Kanyas.

(5) If a father fails to give away his daughter when she has reached the twelfth year, her ancestors drink the blood of her menstrual flow every month.

(6) The father, mother, and elder brother of a Kanya, seeing her in the menstrual course, go to hell.

(7) The Brahman, who, blinded by ignorance, marries her, is unfit to converse or dine with. He is the husband of a Sûdra woman.

(8) A Dvija, guilty of enjoying a Sûdra woman for a night, is purified by performing *Japa* every day for three years, living upon the food begged at others' doors.

(9) and (10). As before.

---

* అష్టమేతు భవేద్గౌరీ నవమేనగ్నికాభవేత్ ।
దశమేకన్యకా ప్రోక్తాద్వాదశే వృషలీస్మృతా ॥

अष्टमेतु भवेद्गौरी नवमेनग्निका भवेत् ।
दशमेकन्यकाप्रोक्ता द्वादशेवृषलीस्मृता ॥

V. The passage in its fourth stage of degeneracy.

For long years together pre-pubescent marriages had been practised; and there were hardly any in Southern India, with the exception of the Nambûdiri Brahmans, to question about their *unsâstraic* character. An intelligent study and interpretation of the Vedas had become extremely rare, and the Samskrit scholars of those days, like the Samskrit scholars of modern days, were satisfied with the study of Kâvya books and the Purânas. The meanings of the Mantras of the Marriage Ritual were not understood. Pre-pubescent marriage was believed to be the counterpart of Upanayana for boys. Under these circumstances the senseless sloka about the definitions of the terms *Gauri*, *Rohini*, *Kanya*, and *Rajasvala*, was inserted. As this sloka has already been dealt with in a former place, it is unnecessary to say more about it here.

When a commentary was added to Parâsara Smriti in the reign of Veera Bukka,* the King of Vijayanagar, who assumed the proud title of *Veda Mârga Pravartaka*, the first half of the sloka which relates to the cleansing of brass was con-

*There is a great deal of confusion about the time of the death of this King. The most probable date seems to be 1418 A. D. The commentator, Mâdhavâmâtya is probably not the Vedic scholar Mâdhava Vidyâranya, but Mâdhava, the General, who captured Goa.

sidered to refer to an unchaste woman. An elaborate defence of this interpretation is attempted in the commentary. Probably the laxity of the sexual morals of this period required this interpretation. But considering the import of the several mantras of the Marriage ceremony and the principles of Aryan Philosophy, it is hardly possible to believe that there is any *Prâyaschitta* for adultery committed by a Brahman Woman. The *Samskâra* or discipline, prescribed for Brahmans, who are considered to be *Bhûsurâs* or Devas of the physical plane, is an ideal one, and to maintain that high ideal, excommunication and divorce is the only remedy, as women have no *Mantrâdhikâra* and no *Sandhyâvandana*. This rule is still acted upon in spite of the recommendations of the commentator of Parâsara. One sloka, which has been attributed to Atri, we have already examined, and it is needless to discuss this question any further. When the commentator of Parâsara made " రజసా శుధ్యతే నారీ వికలం యానగచ్ఛతి. रजसाशुध्यतेनारीविकलंयानगच्छति " refer to a woman and not to brass, the proviso of the " taint as of volatile substances " ceased to refer to the substances previously named, *viz.*, wood, bronze or bell-metal, and copper. The consequence is that Parâsara's directions have become worthless, and even untrue. Say, you keep strong smelling substances—Jasamine, Champaka, the juice of onions and garlic—in wooden, bronze, or copper vessels for a day or more, and then follow the directions of Parâsara. You may wash and wash with water the wooden vessel, rub and rub the bell-metal vessel with ashes, clean with tamarind or lime juice the copper vessel, and—the smell will *not* go. You have to scrape off layers of wood in the wooden vessel, and heat the metallic vessels red-hot to get rid of the smell. In order to show that Parâsara is a sensible writer, you have to make the proviso of *vikala* or taint applicable to all the substances previously named, as Parâsara did really intend it. This the commentator has failed to do.

There is another aspect of this question. If there is a purificatory process for an unchaste *Dvija Man*, why should there not be a similar process for a *Dvija Woman?* There can be, if she can also perform *Japa* in its real sense, and has *Mantrâdhikâra*. Why should she not have it? She may have it, provided she learns the Vedas, and performs the *Sandhyâvandana* as it ought to be performed, that is, yogically. Can she not do it? She cannot do it, if she undertake the duties of motherhood as the chief function of her life. Why not? For the evident reason that no woman can practice *âsana* and *prânâyama* with a growing child in the womb or at the breast. So woman has now the alternative of becoming a *yogini*, and have *Mantrâdhikara*, and be the equal of man, or of resigning that right, and be a noble mother of splendid *Sâttvic* children for the uplifting of humanity. Even without the regular *Sandhyâvandana*—the mighty weapon of the Dvija in his fight with the Evil Powers—a great deal can be done by householders. *Prânâyâma* and meditation in easy forms are open to women, and with these a great deal may be done. As Brahman men have now almost ceased to perform *Sandhyâvandana* yogically, except in very rare cases, they can hardly claim more privileges than Brahman women. What the ideal is, is very clear. To take away *Mantrâdhikâra* from woman, and then say that there is *Prâyaschitta* for her adultery is hardly admissible from the *Sâstraic* standpoint.

The insertion of the sloka about *Gauri*, *Rohini*, *Kanya*, and *Rajasvala* together with the misinterpretation of the first half of the second sloka treating of brass, and the addition of a separate heading—the purification of an unchaste woman—has brought the passage in its original purity through intermediate stages, as pointed out, to its present worthless condition. It is not necessary to re-write it, and the reader may now sorrowfully refer to pages 259–262 for it.

Thus the passage, which we have examined, has all these several tales to tell when properly and intelligently questioned. The tales they relate are mournful and speak only of degeneracy. All our Smritis should be *critically* examined, and the spurious portions expunged. Our learned Samskrit Pandits may well direct their energies in this direction, and benefit both themselves and the world. We sadly require expurgated editions of the Smritis.

-:0:-